CW00952106

THE BRITISH REGULATORY STATE

The British Regulatory State

High Modernism and Hyper-Innovation

MICHAEL MORAN

OXFORD
UNIVERSITY PRESS

*This book has been printed digitally and produced in a standard specification
in order to ensure its continuing availability*

OXFORD
UNIVERSITY PRESS

Great Clarendon Street, Oxford OX2 6DP

Oxford University Press is a department of the University of Oxford.
It furthers the University's objective of excellence in research, scholarship,
and education by publishing worldwide in

Oxford New York

Auckland Cape Town Dar es Salaam Hong Kong Karachi
Kuala Lumpur Madrid Melbourne Mexico City Nairobi
New Delhi Shanghai Taipei Toronto
With offices in
Argentina Austria Brazil Chile Czech Republic France Greece
Guatemala Hungary Italy Japan South Korea Poland Portugal
Singapore Switzerland Thailand Turkey Ukraine Vietnam

Oxford is a registered trade mark of Oxford University Press
in the UK and in certain other countries

Published in the United States
by Oxford University Press Inc., New York

ISBN 0-19-924757-9

For
Charlie and Tom

ACKNOWLEDGEMENTS

Most of the work for this book was done while I held a Leverhulme Major Research Fellowship, 2000–2. I owe a great debt to the Trustees, both for their financial support and for the 'light touch' regulation accompanying that generous support. I have pestered colleagues, friends, and even family with earlier drafts, and it is a pleasure to thank them by name: Martin Burch, Francesca Gains, Andrew Gray, Steve Harrison, Ian Holliday, Anthony Ogus, Joe Moran, and Tony Prosser. I have often ignored their good advice, so it is doubly important to say that all mistakes, omissions, and stupidities are my responsibility alone.

Michael Moran

University of Manchester
November 2002

CONTENTS

1

Introduction: From Stagnation to Hyper-Innovation

For the first two-thirds of the twentieth century, governing arrangements in Britain were among the most stable and least innovative in the advanced capitalist world. In the decades since then, her governing systems have been in turmoil and she has been a leader in institutional and policy change. Why did the transformation happen? What did it amount to? What were its consequences? This book answers these questions, and this introduction summarizes the argument developed in succeeding chapters.

Consider first the epoch of stability, especially notable in the half-century after the end of the First World War. The extensions of the franchise in 1918 finally established something close to formal democracy. Labour emerged as the Conservative's main rival, ushering in a half-century when partisan argument was organized around two class blocs. With the creation of the Irish Free State 4 years later, the single most contentious issue in British politics—the character of the United Kingdom itself—went underground for half a century. The consolidation of a unified civil service after Warren Fisher's appointment as Head of the Service in 1919 fulfilled the final conditions for the creation of a culturally homogeneous metropolitan mandarin class. The biggest domestic change over the next half-century was, simply, continuing, gradual, miserable economic decline.

This stability or stagnation—depending on taste—was remarkable when viewed comparatively. These decades saw political transformation in the world's greatest capitalist democracy: the rise of the United States of America as the hegemonic international power; the creation of an Imperial Presidency; the construction of a powerful regulatory state through the New Deal. In the other big capitalist countries, the turmoil was even greater. Japan went from militarist, imperial autocracy to industrial superpower via a catastrophic military defeat and foreign occupation. Germany, France, and Italy all went through unstable constitutional government, to dictatorships, to military defeat, emerging to build democratic institutions and revitalized capitalist economies.[1] The most important countries of Western Europe spent the 1950s and 1960s laying the foundations for a new regional superpower—an enterprise in which Britain only sporadically and reluctantly participated, and then usually with the object of its frustration and limitation. Even the single most important domestic innovation in British politics—the creation of a Keynesian welfare state during and immediately after the Second World War—was more limited in scope, and later in arriving, than in most of the rest of the advanced capitalist world. In Esping-Andersen's famous classification of welfare state regimes, Britain emerged as a member of a liberal family of nations: one where state welfare coexisted uneasily with the market, in contrast with the socially inclusive universalism of Scandinavian systems or the deep institutionalization of corporatist regimes.[2]

Now, consider Britain during the 1970s to the 1990s. There have been two major continuing changes in the broader institutional setting of British government: those stimulated by our original entry into, and gradual integration with, the European Union; and those stimulated after 1997 by the Labour Government's constitutional reforms. But it is when we place Britain in the wider world of change that the most startling transformations appear. Since the early 1970s—when there ended the '30 glorious years' of growth in the leading capitalist economies—sustained waves of institutional and policy reform have swept across the advanced capitalist world. Britain, once a byword for stagnation, has been a pioneer. The great renewed burst of globalization in the world economy after 1970 was powered by the liberalization of financial markets; Britain was a pioneer of financial liberalization, in the process securing London's place as one of the three great world financial centres. In the world privatization revolution, Britain was at the forefront among the first world nations. In scale and timing, only the much smaller economy of New Zealand matched her privatization performance. In the regulatory aftermath of privatization, the country's institutional upheaval was also remarkable, compared with the other national privatizers in Western Europe: the scale and complexity of the institutional apparatus designed to regulate privatization was, as we shall discover in Chapter 4, much more elaborate in Britain than in the other leading economies of the European Union.

Through liberalization and privatization, Britain thus led the way in redefining the boundaries between the public and private. In another sphere where there has been widespread upheaval since the 1970s—the organization of government itself—her performance has been similarly pioneering. The changes usually labelled the New Public Management were diverse.[3] But here, once again, the scale and radical character of British reform ambitions stand out. In their comparative survey of public sector reform, Pollitt and colleagues consider change along six dimensions: privatization, marketization, decentralization, output orientation, quality systems, and intensity of implementation. Britain achieves the highest scores for change along all of these.[4] Rhodes catches this distinctiveness more synoptically in his observation that what marked out the British reforms, especially after 1979, was their comprehensive range.[5]

Liberalization, privatization, and the reconstruction of public sector management are three 'headline' areas where the scale of the British revolution is particularly striking. But, as we shall see in the following pages, there are other, less noticed, domains where the changes are if anything even more remarkable. In Chapter 4, I look at one of the most important of these. Had we examined what

I there call the British system of self-regulation in the early 1970s, we would have noticed three things: that systems of self-regulation were central to the government of markets—for labour, services, and goods; that the British system was unique among leading capitalist nations in the extent to which it was run by private institutions beyond the reach of the state or the law; and that it was remarkable also in its stability, displaying cultures and institutional patterns that originated in the nineteenth century. Every one of those observations now has to be radically revised: the uniqueness of British self-regulation has declined dramatically; the private character of the most important parts of the self-regulatory system has been transformed, to be replaced by tighter state controls; and the institutions and cultures bequeathed to us by the Victorians have either disappeared or are embattled.

For about the first two-thirds of the twentieth century, therefore, British government slumbered in the historical equivalent of a long Sunday afternoon—the political parallel of the dreadful, dead British Sunday afternoon that was itself mercifully ended by the measures deregulating retail trading in the 1990s. Since then, we have a history of upheaval and innovation. This book is about the contrast between the two epochs.

The core of my argument is unsurprising: that the two phases—of stagnation and of hyper-innovation—are connected. The connection is forged by crisis, and in particular by the crisis of a governing order. That crisis had two faces. One is well known: it had to do with the content of economic policy, and with the failures of policy. The second is less known: it had to do with the crisis of a system of rule itself. The scale and intensity of the British revolution are traceable to the way the two faces of crisis—the policy and institutional—are enmeshed.

The policy crisis came to a head in the early and mid-1970s and is well documented. At its root lay the end, in the early 1970s, of the great 30-year period of global economic expansion. That buoyant epoch had concealed the weaknesses of the British economy, masking relative economic decline behind full employment and rising real prosperity. The last couple of years of life of the Heath Government destroyed many illusions. The latter half of 1972 saw the abandonment of that Government's brief experiment with economic liberalism and deregulation, and the introduction of a disastrous attempt to run a prices and incomes policy on command lines. The consequences of that latter catastrophe continue to shape our politics 30 years on. The destruction of the Heath experiment in command economics, mostly at the hands of the miners in 1973–4, caused the greatest constitutional crisis since the General Strike. It destroyed Mr Heath's Premiership and Leadership of the Party, and in the longer run destroyed the kind of Conservatism that he stood for. It led directly to the accession of Mrs Thatcher to the party leadership and then the Premiership, to the rise of Thatcherism, and thus to the great economic reforms of the 1980s. But, as the connection with wider problems of the international order showed, this was much more than a crisis of Heathite Conservatism. Economic catastrophe pursued Mr Heath's immediate successors, culminating in the *annus terribilis* of 1976, when a runaway crisis of the currency forced the British government into the humiliating acceptance of policies dictated by the International Monetary Fund. That episode provoked a wider crisis in the British governing elite, comparable in magnitude to the Great War crisis of 1940. The agonies of the 1970s produced revolutionary change. That revolution, still by no means finished, wrought profound institutional and policy transformation in the 1980s and 1990s.

The great policy crisis of the 1970s was itself sufficiently intense to produce revolutionary change. But the peculiar intensity, instability, and often catastrophic character of the British revolution are due to the fact that the eruption of the policy crisis interacted with a deep institutional crisis. In summary, I call this, borrowing language from Marquand, the crisis of club government.[6] Club government ruled Britain during the long twentieth-century stagnation. To anticipate the argument of later chapters: it had three striking features. First, its operations were oligarchic, informal, and secretive. Second, it was highly pervasive. In other words, it was not just practised in the core of the metropolitan governing machine in Whitehall, though it was peculiarly at home in that world. It also shaped government in the overlapping spheres of self-regulation and the vast, labyrinthine world of quasi-government. Third, it was anachronistic, and deliberately so. The institutions and the ideology of the club system were the product of the Victorian era, and of the threats that confronted governing elites in that first industrial nation. But the system survived as a deliberate anachronism, because in the twentieth century it protected elites from more modern forces: from the threats posed by the new world of formal democracy, and from an empowered and often frightening working class. Thus, the persistence of oligarchy and secrecy in governing arrangements, though it looked superficially odd in a state that practised formal democracy, was nothing of the kind: it was the very threats from democratic politics that made the maintenance of club government so imperative.

The great institutional changes that, during the 1970s to the 1990s, have come over the core of the state, the world of quasi-government, and the world of self-regulation, also amount to a sustained crisis of club regulation. One of the purposes of this book is both to describe and to try to account for the collapse of the club system. But, since club rule was plainly an anachronistic enterprise—an attempt to practise oligarchy under conditions of formal democracy—an equally pertinent question asks why it survived so long in the first place. The summary answer is that survival involved large doses of ideological mystification dressed up as constitutional and regulatory theory; the detailed answer is found in the narratives of the decay of the club system in the following chapters.

Why encapsulate these revolutionary changes in the phrase 'regulatory state'? Observing historical exactness would indeed compel us to speak only of a 'new' British regulatory state. As I show, especially in Chapter 3, the creation of the club system in Victorian Britain involved the rise of institutions—both state and private—concerned with the regulation of new areas of social and economic life, principally in response to the problems of the new industrial society.

Understanding what sense to make of the destruction of the club system, and what sense to make of the policy responses produced by the epoch of hyper-innovation, is the nub of the problem. The 'new' British regulatory state can indeed be understood in two almost diametrically opposed ways. One of these largely dominates existing understanding; the alternative, I argue in the following pages, makes better sense, notably of the transformation from stagnation to hyper-innovation. I later examine these issues at greater length, especially in Chapters 1 and 2, but it will help the reader to sketch them here briefly.

Three images dominate accounts of what has happened to governing arrangements in Britain during the 1970s to the 1990s, and they amount also to a particular theory of the new British regulatory state. The first image pictures transformed ambitions, involving a withdrawal by the state from many of the grand interventionist projects that it had accumulated over the preceding century. The change can be seen as part of the wider crisis of what Scott calls high modernism—that commitment to massive, purposive social change which marked both democratic and authoritarian regimes, and which spanned projects as different as waging total war or comprehensively clearing slums.[7] After the crisis, the state's rhetoric—and some of its practice—shifted, becoming 'regulatory' in a more or less exact sense. The most straightforward meaning of regulation is to govern in the sense of balancing a system: the regulator in a mechanical system, like a steam engine or a central heating system, works in exactly this way. That new image of a state steering and balancing social and economic systems is exactly captured in the famous metaphor offered in the most influential public management handbook of the 1990s: the metaphor of a new kind of state that concentrates on 'steering' rather than 'rowing'—on making strategic decisions about the direction of government rather than on delivering services.[8]

A second prevailing image summons up the concrete experience of institutional creation in Britain during the 1970s to the 1990s. These were plainly regulatory decades in an obvious commonsense way: they were years when British government created, or recreated, regulatory agencies, and decades when the profession of regulator in an American sense seriously developed. Three of the best-known instances of this burst of creativity are: the making of a whole new regulatory world for the privatized industries; the reconstruction and expansion of such traditional domains as the regulation of human impact on the physical environment; and the reconstruction and expansion of what Hood and colleagues call 'regulation inside government'.[9]

These dominant images—of withdrawal and of institutional innovation—are inspired by the particular British experience during the 1970s to the 1990s. The third image is more analytical and invokes explicitly the language of a 'regulatory state'. The most important source lies in the work of Majone.[10] In his hands, the regulatory state is both the product of a crisis of an older interventionist order and a harbinger of a new kind of state.

The great crises of British government in the 1970s are on this view part of a wider crisis of the Keynesian welfare state: of a state that practised ambitious comprehensive intervention in forms as various as large-scale public ownership, large-scale direct social welfare provision, and purposive economic management to achieve goals like full employment. The successor to this state is emerging in the linked spheres of the nation and the European Union. It is born of a recognition of the limits to state resources, and is regulatory in two linked senses: it largely confines itself to the creation of frameworks of rules that are then implemented elsewhere; and it practices regulatory policies—addressing the task of remedying market failures rather than the more ambitious interventionism of the Keynesian era. This new regulatory state thus renounces the command modes of the Keynesian era.

These images, then, identify the regulatory state with withdrawal from utopian interventionism, with the construction of regulatory institutions to fit the new tasks of steering, and with the renunciation of command. They offer us a powerful means of making sense of what has been happening to British government during the 1970s to the 1990s. They provide a synthesis that can place the British crisis in the wider crisis of high modernism, make sense of a raft of institutional changes both within and outside the state, and integrate our account of changes within Britain to changes at the level of the European Union. They are images of great analytical and rhetorical power. Unfortunately, they are also inaccurate, or at best only half accurate.

After the great crisis of the 1970s, the state in Britain did indeed scale down many of its central ambitions, but as I show in succeeding chapters it also acquired some startling new ones. It did indeed renounce many responsibilities, notably some that lay at the heart of the Keynesian welfare state, but the turn to a regulatory mode also greatly widened the range of social and economic life that was subject to public power. The regulatory state is a colonizing state with its own utopian projects quite as ambitious as those that characterized Scott's high modernism. And the image of a turn from command is, as we shall see, hard to reconcile with the growth of a vastly expanded apparatus of surveillance and control within the public sector—the subject of much of Chapter 6—and with the transformation of self-regulation described in Chapter 4, where the direction of change has been towards more hierarchy, more formality, and more state control.

These observations can be reconciled with the prevailing images of the regulatory state, but at tremendous intellectual cost. We could, for instance, picture them as arising from the incompleteness of the anti-interventionist revolution, from perversity in the policy-making process, or from the unexpected outcomes of regulatory change. Key features of the new kind of state that has developed in Britain since the 1970s—its persistent interventionism, its drive to ever more systematic surveillance, its colonization of new regulatory spheres—thus have to be viewed as deviations from the teleology of the regulatory state, perversions of its essential purpose.

I propose something simpler: that we recognize these features as part of the essential character of the state that is being created. The matter becomes clearer when we realize that the hyper-innovation in the British system in recent decades is a product, not of one crisis, but of the conjuncture of two: the policy crisis that erupted in the 1970s and the crisis of the system of rule itself, of club government. The crisis of the club system amounts to the exhaustion of a historically ancient project—preserving oligarchic government in the face of democratic institutions and a democratic culture. The new regulatory state is, therefore, not only a matter of coping with the policy crisis of the 1970s, it is also about reconstructing institutions on the ruins of the club system. That involves trying to displace key features of club government. Informality, reliance on the tacit knowledge acquired by insiders by virtue of their insider status, autonomy from public scrutiny and accountability: these are succeeded by standardization and formality, by the provision of systematic information accessible both to insiders and outsiders, and by reporting and control mechanisms that offer the chance of public control. New forms of intervention, shifts to formality and hierarchy in organization, the expansion of audit into ambitious systems of surveillance: these are not, therefore, unexpected consequences of the development of the new regulatory state in Britain. They are central to its existence, because they are the key response to the ruins of club government. Thus, the new state is not a retreat from the utopian ambitions of high modernism. On the contrary, we shall see in subsequent chapters that Scott's key principles of high modernism—'standardization, central control, and synoptic legibility to the centre'—are exactly what are shaping this epoch of hyper-innovation.[11]

Viewing the new British regulatory state in this manner has obvious analytical implications, but it also has important normative ones. Understanding the hyper-innovation of recent decades as an attempt to replace oligarchic, secretive rule with something more open and accountable restores to the teleology of the regulatory state a distinctly modernist cast. Far from being a reaction against utopian projects of large-scale interventionism, it has its own utopian ambitions, and these ambitions are entirely congruent with Enlightenment modernism. In his study of the pursuit of objectivity and quantification in public life, Porter describes the modernist, democratizing roots of the drive to standardize, to quantify, and thus to transform the tacit knowledge of insiders into public knowledge available to all. Quantification and democratization are linked. Porter might have been thinking of the new British regulatory state when he wrote these words: 'the impersonal style of interactions and decisions promoted by heavy reliance on quantification has also provided a partial alternative to a business culture of clubs and informal contacts.'[12]

We can also now throw a fresh normative light on the sources of resistance to the great changes described in these pages. Resistance to features that are now central to the new regulatory state—standardization, quantification, public reporting—came historically from defenders of aristocratic government anxious to prevent popular rule. The most important modern philosophical exposition of that view is in the work of Oakeshott, with his insistence that the act of governing depends on culturally acquired tacit knowledge available only to those who have been fortunate enough to absorb the rules of the governing game.[13]

The modernizing project of recent decades, by contrast, has prompted resistance from elites who might have been thought of as quintessentially modern: professional elites in the welfare state; academic elites in the higher education system created by the twentieth-century interventionist state; and elites within that state apparatus. This apparently surprising inversion of roles becomes understandable when we realize that the club system privileged precisely these elites—and its replacement by something more open and modern threatens their independence from popular control.[14]

This compressed outline of the argument of the book is inevitably not much more than a series of assertions; the ensuing chapters are obviously designed to provide the supporting evidence and argument.

In Chapter 2, I lay out the main contours of the analytical puzzles that have been referred to briefly above. I examine the various meanings we commonly ascribe to regulation, and the various accounts of the rise of regulation, both as a narrative used by policy actors and by those who analyse policy. I then show the links between this regulation narrative and the rise of 'risk' as a policy narrative, examining how far new vocabularies of risk can illuminate the rise of regulation. The final substantive part of the chapter involves moving from the analytical to the concrete: I show the connections between the regulatory state and the British state, and sketch in particular the way in which the great crisis of the 1970s led to the rise of the so-called regulatory state in Britain.

In Chapter 3, I take us back over a century. I show that the institutional constructions of the 1980s and 1990s were not erected on unbroken ground. There was a pre-existing regulatory state in Britain, most of which was a response to earlier crises—in particular to the great crises in Victorian England produced by the tremendous impact of history's first industrial society. Indeed, images of 'ground' and 'foundation' do not accurately convey the connection between the Victorian legacy and what was done in Britain in the 1980s and 1990s, for they suggest a stable Victorian structure on which could be built modern institutions. But, in truth, the Victorian legacy provided no stability. On the contrary, by the 1970s, there was another, deeper crisis to add to the very observable public crisis of the British state: the Victorian regulatory legacy—the institutions it created, the practices it sanctified—was itself spent, unable to survive any longer outside the historical conditions that had given birth to it. Yet, though in crisis, it continued to shape much regulatory thinking, and to supply a peculiarly British ideology of regulation, which, in the manner of ideologies, continued to mystify practice throughout the 1980s and 1990s. The substance of much of this chapter is historical, focusing on two critical periods: those decades of the nineteenth century when what I call a Victorian regulatory state was created; and those early decades of the twentieth century when there took place a consolidation of the institutions and ideologies of that state. I show that this consolidation was needed for a reason that in the end proved the undoing of the Victorian regulatory legacy: the Victorian regulatory state was created in an undemocratic society and in a pre-democratic political system; in the twentieth century it had to find some way of surviving the forces of encroaching democracy.

This last observation also conveys the essential rationale for Chapter 3, for its function is much more than to provide a historical 'frame' or backdrop to the events of the closing decades of the late twentieth century. Understanding the nature of the regulatory state the Victorians created, and then bequeathed to us, lies at the heart of making sense of the puzzles and anomalies that characterized the late twentieth-century upheavals. The crisis of the 1970s was peculiarly deep because it was not just an immediate, serious crisis of performance, as revealed by the chronic failures of economic management, it was also a matter of deep fractures in the inherited institutions and cultures of the state. Much the most important clue to what was going on lies in the realization that while 'new build' was in progress—for instance in the wake of privatization—there was also being attempted a rescue, and reconstruction, of the Victorian regulatory legacy.

That final clue makes Chapter 4 particularly important. Nothing encapsulated the Victorian regulatory legacy quite so perfectly as the British system of self-regulation. Self-regulatory bodies in two domains—the professions and the City of London—were critical in the regulatory response to the new world of the Industrial Revolution. Their critical character lay, in part, in something obvious: the substantive importance of these two groups to the British economy. But the importance also lay in something deeper: these two regulatory domains were where a dominant British ideology of regulation was hammered out, and was then diffused throughout much of the twentieth century to other parts of the British state and economy. Thus, the crisis of self-regulation, when it came, was much deeper than a crisis of particular domains, like the financial markets and professions. A whole way of thinking instinctively about regulation, and a whole way of intellectualizing regulatory activity, was called into question. Behind these great stresses lies one of the most counter-intuitive developments of the last decades of the twentieth century—counter-intuitive, at any rate, if we pictured the regulatory state as a state in retreat: the reconstruction of self-regulatory institutions and practices along lines that made them both more hierarchical and more closely integrated with the state. Many summary formulae have been offered to explain these changes, and many of the formulae are not confined to Britain. But the changes were particularly momentous in Britain precisely because the old British system was, as we shall see, unusual by the standards of many other advanced capitalist democracies—unusual, to put it in summary terms, in the degree to which 'self'-regulation really did stress the autonomy of the self, whether that self was a market, a firm, or a profession.

The fact that new regulatory institutions were being built at a moment of crisis in the wider, historically inherited regulatory system is central to the two chapters that follow our examination of self-regulation. Chapter 5 starts from a point that seems to be uncontestable: that privatization in the United Kingdom was not only an economic, but also a constitutional revolution. It was a constitutional revolution for a very obvious reason. Constitutional understandings perform one major function, which is to help define the boundary between the public and the private, and the most elementary thing accomplished by privatization was to reshape that boundary: simply, a large number of industries that had been in the public domain were shifted to the domain of private ownership. This fact itself need not have entailed any regulatory innovations, and that it in practice did so was highly revealing about both the nature of 'traditional' business regulation in Britain and about the nature of the privatized industries. Establishing specialized independent regulatory agencies for the most important of the newly privatized industries indicated that the traditional system of business regulation was inadequate. In Chapter 5, we will see some obvious ways in which many of the newly privatized utilities had characteristics that distinguished them from other forms of private enterprise, and how these differences compelled special regulation. But this decision, in turn, had immense implications for the character of the constitutional revolution that privatization amounted to, for it meant that, while the public/private boundary was indeed redrawn, it was redrawn in complicated and often unexpected ways. The chapter traces two particularly important contours of the unexpected. The first is the long-term impact of creating a corps of regulators: their impact on the substantive control of their own industries; the impact of this dense network of actors in the public sector; and the impact the very introduction of a discourse of regulation had in that wider public sector. The second long-term impact concerns consequences less internal to the regulatory system and more to do with the relations between that system and the wider business community. We shall see that one unexpected consequence of privatization and its attendant regulation was to destabilize the wider traditional system of business regulation.

This last is also a story about the destabilization of the Victorian legacy. I show that many of the characteristic assumptions about public regulation of business in Britain—notably doctrines about the nature of the corporation—had a peculiarly English cast, and this English cast had a great deal to do with the legal history of the corporation, notably with the doctrines invented to cope with new business forms under the pressures of industrialism in the nineteenth century. Even to put the point in this way is to imply that the system was already fragile by the 1980s—for how could a set of doctrines created in the Victorian world not encounter some problems when applied over a century later? And indeed by the 1980s many of the key assumptions of corporate governance in Britain—assumptions about who were legitimate stakeholders in the firm, about the mechanisms of corporate governance, and about the means of determining the scale of corporate reward—were the subject of increasing quarrels. The effect of the revolution in regulation accompanying privatization was greatly to widen the range of these quarrels. It openly politicized—in the sense of transforming into partisan argument—a whole range of issues about corporate governance and reward, which had, since the Victorian settlement, been viewed as technical issues of business government that were properly the concern of the business community itself. Domains of constitutional silence were, thus, transformed into domains of regulatory contestation.[15] A key argument of Chapter 5, therefore, is that the ramifications of the regulation of privatization went wider than the regulation of privatization itself, important though that was: there were huge implications for both the public world of regulation itself and for the business community.

Chapter 6 takes us right to the heart of the club world and, therefore, to some of its most intense moments of crisis. Club government referred to more than the regulation of the business system, it also referred to what is best described as the regulation of the public sector—the 'regulatory state inside the state' described by Hood and colleagues.[16] This chapter is about the collapse of the heartlands of club government and about their attempted reconstruction. I show how the institutions and ideologies of the club system were vital to protecting elites in three key domains: in the world of inspection created originally by the Victorians; in the world of quasi-government that, for much of the twentieth century, allowed powerful interests like the elite universities to feed off the state while escaping democratic control; and in the world of the metropolitan governing elite itself, which was allowed to run its affairs by informal, confidential understandings. Above all, I show how these bastions of the club system collapsed, and explore the ensuing chaos, and the rage and bitterness of displaced elites.

Chapters 2–6 might summarily be described as accounts of the chronic crises that gave rise to the new regulatory state: chronic in the sense of being inscribed in the very nature of the old world of stagnation. But this old world had a context, and the new world too has its context. Chapter 7 is about old and new contexts. That is why so much of the chapter is taken up with exploring the implications of globalization and Europeanization for the new regulatory state. One important purpose of Chapter 7 is to help us think out one of the great puzzles that lies behind the whole book: why did the club system collapse so spectacularly, and so quickly? The cultures of subjection on which it rested—'deference' in the short-hand term—evaporated in a few years. Earlier attempts to solve this puzzle—like the effort of the great anglophile American political scientist Samuel Beer—traced it to a wider change in the whole character of popular culture in Britain in the 1960s.[17] The account implicitly misquotes Philip Larkin: 'The regulatory state began in nineteen sixty-three / Between the end of the *Chatterley* Ban and the Beatles' first LP.'[18] But what the new worlds of globalization and Europeanization alert us to is that the decay of the cultures of subjection more or less immediately followed the conclusion of another great historical enterprise: imperialism. Empire was connected to the development of much of the state that the club system ran in the first two-thirds of the twentieth century. The most obvious link is the connection of imperialism to social welfare reform, but empire provided much more: images of hierarchy to reinforce the domestic cultures of subjection; a stock of symbolic capital for governing elites; and a public language in which to express the country's providential destiny. All vanished as empire melted away in the two decades after the end of the Second World War. Globalization and Europeanization, not the strange ghost of the Commonwealth, now offered elites in the new regulatory state alternative providential missions.

This sketch of the argument of the book is not much more than an assertion, indeed a provocation. The pages that follow try to substantiate the case.

2

Images of the Regulatory State

GOVERNANCE AND THE REGULATORY STATE

In the closing decades of the twentieth century, fundamental changes took place in the governments of the advanced capitalist democracies. States across Western Europe and much of the Anglo-Saxon world divested themselves of industries that for generations had been publicly owned.[1] Coalitions made up of public agencies and private interests tried systematically to dismantle regulations restricting competition in markets.[2] Inside states, there took place fundamental reorganizations of the core of governing machines with the aim of stripping down the core and reshaping the way governing tasks were defined.[3] In policy fields as diverse as central banking, regulation of the physical environment, regulation of food safety, and regulation of health and safety at work, governments began to set agencies free from partisan political control in an effort to guide policy by technocratic imperatives rather than by the outcomes of partisan, majoritarian politics.[4]

What sense can be made of these changes? Two powerful, linked images have dominated understanding: images of governance and of a new kind of state—the regulatory state. In the early 1990s, Kooiman offered these twin images to encapsulate the new forms of governance in the advanced industrial world.[5] A few years later, Rhodes summarized the shift in similar terms, this time for Britain:

The shift from government to governance in the differentiated polity is my preferred narrative . . . It focuses on interdependence, disaggregation, a segmented executive, policy networks, governance and hollowing out. Interdependence in intergovernmental relations and policy networks contradict the authority of parliamentary sovereignty and a strong executive. Institutional differentiation and disaggregation contradict command and control by bureaucracy. Thriving functional representation contradicts territorial representation through local governments.[6]

The image of the new governance as an exercise in the management of networks lies at the heart of these new understandings, and also creates the link to the image of a new 'regulatory state'. Networks involve links of (mostly institutional) actors; they ignore conventional public/private sector boundaries; they link actors in relations of mutual dependence, a dependence originating in resource dependency, whence it follows that decisions have to be negotiated in this environment of mutual dependence; and as a further consequence they impose a governing style that departs from the hierarchy- and rule-bound characteristics of Weberian style administration. It is the importance of networks that leads to the coinage of 'governance' in place of 'government', a coinage intended to suggest a shift from the hierarchy of authority to 'soft bureaucracy'.[7]

The marketing of these ideas to policy practitioners on both sides of the Atlantic was done with huge success earlier in the 1990s by the public management gurus Osborne and Gaebler, in a book that contained three dazzling rhetorical devices: a title (*Reinventing Government*) that promised a wholesale redesign of failing public institutions; a series of inspirational tales of reinvention, like the parables of renewal and redemption used by evangelical preachers to call sinners to the path of righteousness; and a compelling image that graphically communicated the supposed shift that had come over, and needed to come over, the practice of government: 'entrepreneurial governments have begun to shift to systems that separate policy decisions (steering) from service delivery (rowing).'[8]

This image of a new kind of steering state provides the most direct connection between the language of governance and the language of a 'regulatory state'. 'Regulation' is a notoriously inexact word, but its core meaning is mechanical and immediately invokes the act of steering. A regulator governs equilibrium in a physical system—whether that system is as humble as thermostatically controlled domestic central heating or as elaborate as a large mainframe computer. Regulation in this sense is a form of cybernetic control: the regulator is a governor receiving information about the state of the system and its interaction with its environment. If anything could take us to the kernel of the regulatory state, it would be this cybernetic image.[9]

These paragraphs offer, in effect, a stripped-down theory of the regulatory state: a theory suggesting that it is a new kind of state, which differs from predecessor forms in turning away from hierarchy, command, and large-scale interventionist ambitions. But before we can make any progress with that theory we have to see how far this theoretical image actually matches the image of regulatory behaviour that we can glean from 'real existing' regulatory states. For the regulatory state not only exists as a set of analytical postulates or normative prescriptions, there are actual state formations, which also proffer the image of regulation. Not surprisingly, therefore, there are competing images of the regulatory state, and not all picture it as a turn to 'soft' law and soft bureaucracy. In the following pages, therefore, I examine the most important competing images, and show how they jostle with each other when we try to use them to make sense of the thing called the British regulatory state.

THE REGULATORY STATE AS AN AMERICAN STATE

The modern regulatory state is an American invention. It has to be considered that on four grounds: on historical precedence; on the way its range has widened

:r time; on the evidence of the problems that have afflicted it; and on the idence of its global spread. Each is considered here in turn.

Historically, the United States of America invented the characteristic institution of the regulatory state: the specialized agency designed to manage public control as an alternative to public ownership. The story is easy to summarize briefly because it has been told often.[10] This regulatory state is a product of three great phases of institutional innovation in American government: the Progressive Era, the New Deal, and the era of the new social regulation in the 1960s.

The impact of the Progressive Era was wide in American political life, spreading beyond the particular domain of regulation into the whole organization of government and the relationship between the spoils system and American administration. Progressives, in Vogel's words, 'promoted the values and ideals of professionalism, scientific and technical expertise, administrative competence and neutrality, and efficiency in both business and government.'[11] Socially, Progressivism was an alliance of urban merchants and middle-class professionals; culturally, it was a movement for efficiency and merit as the guiding spirit of public institutions.[12] Institutionally, its legacy was the idea of the specialized administrative agency where the spirit of neutral, scientific administration would prosper, above party strife and sectional interest:

Expert administrators required independence. They were set in executive agencies, apart from the corrosive politics and interest groups of the legislatures. Each agency would preside over a narrowly delineated functional area—railroad rates, food and drugs, banking, public health, commerce.[13]

The characteristic creations of this regulatory state were the Interstate Commerce Commission (1887), the Food and Drug Administration (1906), the Federal Reserve Board (1913), and the Fair Trade Commission (1914).[14] Its ideological legacy lay in its assumption that this kind of state could be, in Hofstadter's phrase, 'a neutral state', sympathetic to business but guided by legal impartiality.[15] This ideology of neutrality in the face of partisan politics is, as we shall see, a recurrent feature of the contemporary regulatory state in Britain. It represented, not an anti-business impulse, but the impulse of the most modern and enlightened section of business:

it is perhaps worth emphasizing that the first important steps toward the modern organization of society were taken by arch-individualists—the tycoons of the Gilded Age—and the primitive beginning of modern statism was largely the work of men who were trying to save what they could of the eminently native Yankee values of individualism and enterprise.[16]

The New Deal, which produced the second burst of regulatory innovation, was also animated by the same impulse to modernize and regulate the free enterprise system. It was the product of the profound crisis of American capitalism that followed the boom of the 1920s, the great crash of 1929, and the wider economic slump, both American and worldwide, that followed the crash. It was the great formative influence on the modern American regulatory state. Within three years of Roosevelt's election to the Presidency, a 'perplexed state' (in Landis's phrase) had created sixty specialized executive agencies within the Federal Government.[17] Among them were a host of esoterically specialized agencies bound to specialized interests, but they also included agencies that were to symbolize the New Deal and establish a place as major players in the bureaucratic politics of the new regulatory state: a good example is the Securities and Exchange Commission, charged with the regulation of securities markets. The New Deal, thus, established a distinctive form of economic intervention by American government, a distinctiveness that can be defined negatively: it rejected public ownership in favour of regulating the competitive behaviour of private actors.[18] The regulatory state created by the New Deal was designed, not to suppress competitive forces, but to create the conditions where competition could take place most efficiently. Thus, an agency like the Securities and Exchange Commission was established, in part, due to a perception that fraud and imprudent trading had marked Wall Street in the boom years of the 1920s. The purpose of establishing the Agency was not to suppress the workings of the markets, but to establish confidence in the probity of firms so as to encourage trading.[19] More generally, the regulatory programme of the New Deal was fairly narrowly economic in focus: it was designed to address cases of market failure, such as the failure of markets independently to regulate entry so as to exclude fraudsters, and the failure of markets to police trading so as to ensure honesty in exchange.[20]

That narrow economic focus altered after the early 1960s in an evolutionary turn that, as we shall see, anticipated the character of regulatory states elsewhere. The United States of America entered the age of the new social regulation. That social turn reshaped the institutions, the mission, and the problems of American regulatory agencies. Whereas the New Deal had produced agencies that specialized in regulating particular sectors, the new social regulation created agencies that regulated conditions widely across the whole economy. The mandates of the Occupational Safety and Health Administration or of the Environmental Protection Agency—to take two characteristic creations of the new age of social regulation—were plainly not restricted to a particular industry or even sector.[21] Sunstein summarizes the wider significance of these institutional changes: 'the United States witnessed a rights revolution—the creation by Congress of legal entitlements to freedom from risks in the workplace and in consumer products, from poverty, from long hours and low wages.'[22]

This new institutional turn was associated with a change in the range of agency mission. We speak of the new agencies as forming a new 'social' regulation because, unlike the classic agencies of the New Deal, they were not primarily concerned to promote competitive conditions but to address the social consequences of market failure, or to promote objectives that were extraneous to the functioning of markets. The three most obvious examples of this were: the defence of the physical environment against the consequences of industrial activity; the protection of the health and safety of workers within enterprises; and the regulation of employment conditions so as to promote equality of treatment between groups of workers, notably those distinguished by gender and race.[23]

From this expanded regulatory mission followed an important feature of the regime of social regulation, one identified by Stewart:

After 1960, Congress created many regulatory programmes—most notably health, safety, environmental, and anti-discrimination programmes—that apply to many or all industries or employers. Faced with the necessity of regulating very large numbers of firms, agencies shifted from case-by-case adjudication (the traditional procedure for making and enforcing regulatory policy) to adoption of highly specific regulations of general applicability. These regulations—almost inevitably overinclusive or otherwise arbitrary in many applications—were a fertile source of controversy. At the same time, the large numbers of firms and industries affected, and the conflicts of interests among them, made negotiated solutions more difficult.[24]

Stewart's remark also introduces a new and troubling feature of the American regulatory state: as economic regulation became institutionalized, and as the range of regulatory activity widened beyond the control of particular markets to the promotion of wide social programmes, the state became afflicted with a twin crisis of legalism and command. The rise of social regulation coincided, therefore, with a rise in the extent to which regulation involved the attempt to enforce the commands of law, and a rise in the extent to which these commands were adversarially contested by the regulated. Thus:

The further legalization of regulation that has occurred in recent decades can be understood as an effort to ameliorate some of the problems and characteristics associated with the new generation of regulatory programmes: the proliferation of regulation; the greater reliance on centralized, uniform and therefore inevitably overinclusive or arbitrary standards; the high social and economic stakes involved in the new environmental health and safety programmes; the serious implementation gaps that attend society-wide efforts at regulatory transformation; the displacement of political decision-making mechanisms by bureaucratic and technocratic ones.[25]

These pathologies of command and legalization were, in part, a product of engrained American conditions. The turn to new regulatory programmes and new regulatory institutions took place in a regulatory culture where the law and lawyers already occupied a central place, and where the courts as adversarial arenas for settling social and economic disputes were already well entrenched.[26] But this pathological turn acquires an added importance because of a final feature of the American regulatory state: its increasingly global reach.

The American regulatory state is special for a host of reasons, but one of the most important from the viewpoint of this book is American structural power.[27] The renewed burst of globalization since the early 1970s has not only spread the reach of American goods and services, and of American firms, but also of American regulatory standards, of American regulatory culture, and of American regulatory institutions. Perhaps the single most important mechanism by which this has been achieved has been through processes of world trade diplomacy, especially diplomacy covering trade rules in the most important industries of the new era of globalization, notably financial services, software, and automobiles.[28]

America can claim copyright to the title 'regulatory state', for it is in the USA that the concept of regulation has been most closely studied, the regulatory agency most deeply institutionalized, and the idea of guiding the state's economic mission by regulation most historically entrenched. Yet, even the simple sketch offered above shows that this real existing regulatory state has in its development and problems been a world away from the images of strategic steering, governance, and management of networks that we find in analytical accounts of the new regulatory state. The American experience is particularly important to the British case. The global penetration of American institutions was especially marked in the UK: we only have to think of the critical case of financial services regulation, which will loom large in Chapter 4. And we shall see that when the British came to create new regulatory domains, the American regulatory state— both its achievements and its perceived diseases—fascinated and repelled British institution builders. But the American experience had another importance: as we shall see, it deeply influenced emergent theories of a European regulatory state.

THE REGULATORY STATE AS A EUROPEAN MADISONIAN STATE

Majone virtually invented the notion of a 'European' regulatory state and his work dominates scholarly research.[29] His analytical starting point considerably clarifies what the term 'regulatory state' means in Europe. Three major functions are ascribed to the modern state: redistribution, stabilization (e.g. in the form associated with Keynesianism), and regulation (meaning promoting efficiency by remedying market failure). The rise of the regulatory state consists of the rise of this third function at the expense of the first two.[30] Within nations, this is due to the exhaustion of Keynesianian and some of the modes of command with which it is associated, notably public ownership. At the level of the EU, conversely, the rise of regulation is due to the very lack of modes of command. The Union has neither the budget-raising capacity nor the bureaucratic muscle to impose policies on either national members or sectional interests. Promulgating regulations potentially solves this problem: 'regulatory policy-making puts a good deal of power in the hands of the Brussels authorities while, at the same time, giving the possibility of avoiding tight budgetary constraints imposed by the members.'[31] Constitutional ideologies such as subsidiarity allow institutions like the Commission to expand ruling domains while pushing the responsibility, and the cost, of regulation down to national and sub-national levels. The characteristic EU institution is thus the regulatory agency. The problem that lies at the nub of Majone's regulatory state is a long way from the pathologies of command that have come to dominate arguments about the American regulatory state: it is how to legitimize these institutions and the regulatory policies they pursue. Majoritarian democracy, according to Majone, is not suited to the task. His argument is, in part, functional (the world of expert regulations is necessarily separate from the world of majoritarian democracy) and, in part, to do with the kind of state the EU amounts to:

> The Union is not, and may never become, a state in the modern sense of the concept. It is, at most, a 'regulatory state' since it exhibits some of the features of statehood only in the important but limited area of economic and social regulation. In this area, however, non-majoritarian institutions are the preferred instruments of governance everywhere.[32]

Thus, the appropriate model of democratic legitimation is non-majoritarian (after Dahl, Madisonian): 'the overriding objective is, to use Madisonian language, to protect minorities against "the tyranny of the majority".'[33]

This account, covering as it does the same period as the creation of the new British regulatory state, in some ways clarifies our understanding of what is going on in Britain, but in some ways deepens the puzzle of what has been happening. Let us look at some areas of enlightenment and at some puzzles.

Majone pictures the rise of the new regulatory state as only, in part, a product of the imperatives of the new world of European Union government. It is also a product of a particular kind of crisis within the government of national economies. What that crisis amounts to is signalled by his distinction between the different functions of state activity—regulation, redistribution, stabilization—summarized above. The Keynesian welfare state was historically associated with a range of aims—with macroeconomic stabilization, with policies of positive redistribution—and was also associated with particular instruments of intervention. Most important, in Majone's account, it was associated with intervention through command, typified by the widespread resort to public ownership—in effect, a 'command' mode of regulation that can be contrasted with the modes of market intervention classically employed by the American regulatory state. The crisis of the Keynesian welfare state discredited a whole way of economic management and control. Above all, it discredited public ownership as the traditional European alternative to the American regulatory state's modes of regulating markets. The sign of this was the wave of privatization, which, at different times, swept over the big European national economies. We know, however, that the big European economies differed both in the extent to which they experienced privatization and in the way they subsequently regulated privatized sectors. Central features of the British regulatory experience—the great economic crisis of the 1970s, the pioneering turn to privatization, and deregulation—can, therefore, be assimilated to this picture of the wider crisis of the Keynesian regulatory state.

Majone's account also illuminates key institutional features of the new regulatory state. The illumination is provided by his case for Madisonian decision procedures. The rise of the regulatory state has also seen the rise of non-majoritarian institutions because they are a functional response to the new tasks and the new governing environment that the regulatory state faces. The account fits neatly the imagery of governance. As the state retreats from the command mode of the Keynesian era, the essence of its task turns into the management of complex networks. The key objective is to mobilize the range of interests scattered through distributed networks, which cannot be compelled by the old modes of command, and to mobilize the necessary technical expertise demanded by the tasks of the regulatory state. In effect, this amounts to a hypothesis that the new kind of governance demanded by the world after command will bring forth a new kind of politics, shrinking the domains of partisan, competitive politics. And indeed, summing up one of the most ambitious studies of the new worlds of regulation across Europe, Thatcher and Stone Sweet conclude:

A transformation in governance has swept across Western Europe. During the past half-century, states, executives, and parliaments have empowered an increasing number of non-majoritarian institutions (NMIs) to make public policy. In the fields of utility regulation, telecommunications, antitrust, and media pluralism, and even in the provision of health and welfare benefits, myriad independent regulatory bodies have been created and become the loci for making new rules, or applying existing ones to new situations, at the national level. At the supranational level, central bankers, insulated from direct political control, set monetary policy. In Brussels, European Commission officials propose legislation and enforce ever wider European Union regulation. In Luxembourg, the Court of Justice controls member state compliance with European law, reviewing the lawfulness of activities of national parliaments, governments and administrators.[34]

These images of the European regulatory state as a turn from command, and a turn to Madisonian democracy, are reinforced by what we know about the emergent style of daily policy making in the Union, and the impact this has on daily policy making at the national level in Britain. One of the most compelling pictures offered in the new governance of networks is precisely the image of the dissolution of cohesive, often hierarchically organized, policy communities into more open, unstable networks of actors. There is mounting evidence that the policy process in the EU is itself a powerful force favouring this process of dissolution. Policy making in Brussels resembles Heclo's famous image of the networks of Washington as 'a government of strangers'[35]: of open and unstable policy networks rather than the more enclosed policy communities of national systems; of networks more easily penetrated by new groups of political actors; but of networks where, precisely because there is not the assured position of privilege offered by integration into stable policy communities, access to influence over the policy process has to be won afresh in each domain, and each policy episode, by constant investment in policy monitoring and the skills of lobbying.[36]

The theory of the European regulatory state is, therefore, a potentially powerful source of illumination and even of exact hypotheses for understanding the new regulatory state in Britain. It can integrate the particular British experience into wider accounts of change; for instance, into an account of the wider crisis of the Keynesian welfare state. It can integrate the rise of the regulatory agency— one of the most characteristic pieces of the recent British experience—into a powerful functional account of the spread of Madisonian rule. And it can even—because the changing character of European regulatory politics impacts on domestic British politics—help explain the recent domestic evolution of the British system. It also emphasizes the extraordinary range of experiences now commonly summarized by the phrase regulatory state: in the United States of America, it is synonymous with a century-long growth of state power and with a crisis of the command mode; in Europe, it is supposed to represent the alternative to a century of growing state power and a turning away from command.

But picturing the new British regulatory state in this European language also raises serious difficulties of understanding: simply, a puzzling amount of recent British experience is hard to reconcile with these images of a world that has renounced command, turned to the management of networks, and embraced Madisonian government. We should not, of course, be surprised by national-level deviations from a wider European pattern. The problem is that the fundamental forces that seem to be driving change within the British system appear to contradict the most important theoretical insights claimed by the theory of the European regulatory state. The fundamental problem arises from the picture of the European regulatory state as a kind of 'post command' system of governance, in which public ambitions more modest than those of the Keynesian welfare state are developed, in which instruments of command are abjured in favour of the management of dispersed networks, and in which the range of majoritarian politics is curbed in favour of a newly emergent Madisonian system. Each of these run directly counter to the recent British experience. The character of that contradicting experience is described at greater length in the following pages, so here I only indicate the difficulties briefly. Three principal sources of contradiction can be identified.

First, there is striking evidence that the regulatory state in Britain is not a state marked by diminished ambitions. It is true that many of the central aims, and many of the key institutional instruments, of the Keynesian era have been renounced, but it is also the case that the epoch in which these ambitions were renounced also saw the entry of the state into new regulatory domains. In particular, the state replicated much of the process of substantive policy expansion and of institutional innovation that had marked the 'social' turn in the United States of America: the regulatory state colonized new areas, developed new agencies, reformed old ones, and increasingly used command law as an instrument of colonization. (Some of the most important examples are discussed in Chapters 4 and 6.)

Second, as we shall see time and again, the institutional hyper-innovation of recent decades is very difficult to fit into an image of retreat from hierarchy in favour of management through dispersed networks crossing the conventional private/public sector divide. On the contrary, the dominant experience in the case of self-regulation involves the disappearance of precisely this kind of dispersed, non-hierarchical world where the private and public overlapped and where boundaries were confused. This world is being replaced by one of increasing institutional formality and hierarchy, where the authority of public institutions has been reinforced both by the explicit command of law and by substantial fresh investment in bureaucratic resources to ensure compliance.

Third, the thesis of the rising importance of non-majoritarianism is hard to reconcile with the British regulatory experience during the 1970s to the 1990s. It is true that this has been a golden age in the creation, and recreation, of regulatory agencies. It is also true that many of these agencies—most notably in the world of privatization regulation and in the autonomy granted to the Bank of England Monetary Policy Committee after 1997—do conform in their ambitions to Madisonian theory. And it is true that the British have—as befits their new role as hyper-innovators—led Europe in the creation of new non-majoritarian bodies. But, as I show in the succeeding pages, ambitions are one thing, reality another; and the reality is that the regulatory agencies have been ineluctably drawn into the majoritarian arena and, just as important, the domains of majoritarianism have expanded, mostly because of the breakdown of old, enclosed regulatory communities. The age of hyper-innovation is also the age of hyper-politicization: the invasion of hitherto 'non-partisan' policy domains by the actors, language, and strategies of adversarial party politics. That is a major theme of Chapters 5 and 6.

These unexpected features of a state, which is supposed to be the product of moderated ambitions and the renunciation of command, could obviously be explained in a number of ways. It may be that the European regulatory state is not at all as Majone imagines; that it has its own interventionist ambitions and utopian projects quite as marked as older interventionist systems. It may be, alternatively, that 'Europe' is irrelevant to the building of key features of the regulatory state in Britain. Or it may be that the unique mix of European forces and the British crisis have concocted some special state-building formula. All three of these possibilities will recur in later chapters.

Whatever particular arguments one might have with the theory of the European regulatory state, it has the inestimable benefit of setting the British crisis in a wider international setting. This is also true of a related body of theory which I call the theory of the smart state, and to which I now turn.

THE REGULATORY STATE AS A SMART STATE

Among the many puzzling features of the changing organization of the state in advanced industrial economies during the 1970s to the 1990s were the changes in the roles of rules, law, and the institutions of regulation. As we saw above, images of state withdrawal and the dissolution of hierarchy hardly fit much of the actual experience of regulation in the Anglo-Saxon world. On the other hand, the history of regulatory law displays intriguing developments, which reach across the boundaries of individual nation states. In summary, the most important of these developments are: the elaboration of a web of regulatory bodies at the international level that rely for authority on sources beyond the usual command modes of nation states; the continuing spread within individual nations of institutions of self-regulation; and the reconstruction of many traditional state institutions of inspection and surveillance in a manner that seems to abandon or modify traditional reliance on command in favour of more cooperative, or at least more indirect, styles of regulation.[37] The image of the regulatory state as a new kind of 'smart state' is obviously highly congruent with the images of governance and steering with which we began. In the hands of some legal scholars, these developments are what characterize the new regulatory state: they are a response to the limits of old modes of command law and the search for new, smart modes of regulation.

On this account, the kind of regulatory law that characterized the modern interventionist state was a particular pathological mode of social control. Teubner describes this regulatory law as follows: 'In its function it is geared to the guidance requirements of the social state, in its legitimation the social results of its controlling and compensating regulations are predominant. In its structure it tends to be particularistic, purpose oriented and dependent on assistance from the social sciences.'[38]

This form of law is now in crisis, trapped in a 'regulatory trilemma' involving the irreconcilable demands of law, politics, and the substantive area of social life to which particular regulations are addressed. Thus, we begin to understand why regulatory failures 'must in fact be the rule rather than the exception and that this is not merely a problem of human inadequacy or social power structures but above all one of inadequate *structural coupling of politics, law and the area of social life.*'[39]

The failures of command law arise in three particular forms: circumvention, perversity, and negative feedback.

Circumvention is a summary characterization of one of the best-known problems of all command systems: where regulation imposes rule by command, rather than through cooperation, it leads to attempts at circumvention by rationally self-interested actors. The shadow of Durkheim lies over most theorists of smart regulation, and circumvention is what prompts his famous remark 'everything in the contract is not contractual'.[40] In business regulation, in particular, the rewards of successful circumvention—either within the law or outside it—can be high. The institutions typically subject to regulation—large firms—have ample resources to devise modes of circumvention. The result is that in critical areas of regulation—the best documented of which are in the linked areas of corporate tax regimes and the regulation of financial markets—a battle of wits is constantly conducted between regulators and regulated intent on evading compliance altogether, or in producing only 'creative' compliance.[41]

It is this battle of wits, which, in turn, produces the second pathology: perversity, the process by which general command rules produce a whole variety of unintended consequences, which, in turn, frustrate the objects of regulation. There is a large literature on implementation failure and the 'limits to administration', which precisely addresses this issue.[42] Perversity is built into one of the limits of command law: the ubiquity of circumvention and, therefore, the existence of a constant process by which rationally self-interested actors reshape and distort the effects of regulation. According to this account, command law is bound to be mired in failure, through a combination of unintended consequences, subversion, circumvention, direct defiance, and the sheer impossibility of fitting general rules into particular circumstances.

Perversity and circumvention, in turn, are connected to the third pathology of command. Negative feedback refers to the process by which failures of command law, due to circumvention and perversity, produce an intensification of command. As rules are circumvented, increasingly elaborate means are adopted to try to counter the circumvention. The process is intensified by the connection between the command mode and the law, for part of the process of negative feedback involves the wholesale juridification of regulatory spheres: the transfer of regulatory debate and bargaining to legal arenas; the increasingly frenetic attempt to write rules in the fine language of the law; and the development of an increasingly elaborate jurisprudence governing both the content and the administration of regulatory systems.

These pathological symptoms are hardly unfamiliar. They virtually sum up the crisis of legalism in American regulation, which we sketched earlier, and they lie behind the rise of deregulatory ideologies in recent decades on both sides of the Atlantic. What distinguishes theories of smart regulation is that they amount to an attempt to transcend this deregulation debate. They have both a normative and a descriptive element, for they simultaneously say that we can build new kinds of regulatory institutions that escape the traps of command law, and that the developments summarized at the start of this section are a sign that these new smart regulatory states are being constructed.

'Transcending the deregulation debate' is indeed the subtitle of one of earliest and most influential statements of the smart regulation thesis, produced by Ayres and Braithwaite.[43] Their argument is unusual in that the starting point is not the supposed problems of one mode of regulation—command, self-regulation, or deregulation—but a recognition of the dilemmas and limits that all regulatory modes face. They then try to reconfigure institutions and cultures so as to escape those dilemmas—hence, the argument that we can transcend much of the argument that obsessed us in the deregulation debates of the 1980s. This transcending is to be done by a mixture of cultural change, institutional innovation, and the strategic selection of enforcement instruments. Cultural change involves mobilizing the support of the regulated for the regulatory process itself. In the end, any effective system of regulation rests on self-regulation, and, indeed, the more regulatory responsibility is pushed down hierarchies, to the lowest level even within firms, the more likely is it to be effective. A regulatory culture has to be created where the regulated take responsibility for the rules.[44] This is obviously very different from the command mode, but it is also very different from most of the established patterns of self-regulation in competitive markets.

The institutional elements in Ayres and Braithwaite's framework are encapsulated in the their model of 'enforced self-regulation'. The model is closely related to those advocated by theorists like Teubner. Heavy reliance is placed on self-regulatory institutions in a framework of partnership or 'coregulation'. But the 'self' in this system of coregulation need not be self-regulatory bodies as traditionally conceived; it could just as easily, for instance, be individual firms.[45]

In turn, enforced self-regulation is backed by a distinctive enforcement strategy represented by their famous image of an enforcement pyramid. At the base of the pyramid rules are entirely self-enforced; as we move up the pyramid we shift increasingly to an assertive role for external regulators, until at the top we reach enforcement by command and the threat and use of sanctions backed by law. The image of the pyramid is designed to convey critical parts of the argument: it is expected that once institutions of coregulation are established, most regulation will indeed take place consensually without the need for either surveillance or sanctions—which are deliberately confined to the tip of the pyramid; and the image of the pyramid is also intended to convey that there is a measured cycle to enforcement in the regulatory process, by which the most extreme resort to command only happens as a last resort after other strategies more compatible with cooperative regulation have been tried and found wanting.[46]

Braithwaite's later work moves beyond the prescription, which dominates this early work, to offer a historically informed account of the rise of a new kind of smart state. The modern regulatory state is pictured as the latest in the historical evolution of the state system: from the Westphalian State inaugurated in 1648, to the Keynesian State, which lasted from the early 1930s to the 1980s, to the Regulatory State, which is now being born.[47] And the distinguishing feature of the Regulatory State is that it is 'decentred': part of a recursive system of regulation where states are embedded with other important regulatory institutions, notably large corporations and globally organized institutions of industry self-regulation and of trade diplomacy.[48]

What is smart about the smart regulatory state? As the image of the pyramid suggests, being smart means intelligently moving between different regulatory modes according to circumstance. The work of Gunningham and colleagues starts to fill out the argument. Gunningham and Rees assemble an impressive body of evidence to argue that modes of industry self-regulation are spreading globally, both within states and at the level of the global system, and that this spread is a reaction to problems of command and regulatory overload.[49]

Gunningham *et al.* identify different regulatory modes, or in their language regulatory instruments, and attempt to specify the contingent conditions of their effective use.[50] In effect, we are offered a hierarchy of regulatory modes, ranging from the most command-like to the most voluntaristic. Thus, command and control 'refers to the prescriptive nature of the regulation (the command) supported by the imposition of some negative sanction (the control)'.[51] Geographically, the home of command and control is the United States of America; analytically, it is commonly used in prescription of standards, typically technology standards, performance standards, or process standards. Economic instruments, by contrast, attempt to shape behaviour by the prospect of financial incentives and/or penalties. They cover broad-based instruments such as the tradeable emission permits common in pollution regulation; supply-side incentives such as subsidies or tax breaks designed to encourage particular kinds of investment or industrial activity; or the threat of legal liability under which firms can be held responsible for acts such as pollution or endangering the safety of employees. Self-regulation, in turn, is an arrangement whereby 'an organized group regulates the behaviour of its members'.[52] Voluntary regulation is a variant, based not on social control by an industry association but 'on the individual firm undertaking to do the right thing unilaterally', often after intervention by government to facilitate voluntary agreement. Finally, information strategies can range from the most permissive education strategies to modes that come close to organized self-regulation, such as product certification.[53]

This kind of typology is tremendously fruitful. It takes us beyond the simplicities in the argument between command regulation, self-regulation, and deregulation; and it starts us thinking about, and investigating, the conditions under which different combinations of instruments work best—in other words, starts us working out the conditions of smart regulation. What these contingent conditions are begins to be revealed in a companion study, Gunningham and Johnstone's comparative examination of workplace safety regulation.[54] They establish precisely how sensitive is the choice of mode (or instrument). Consider, for example, the merits of 'systems-based' approaches to the regulation of work-based safety, a mode that was mandated in the regime for offshore oil industry safety in the UK in the wake of the Piper Alpha rig disaster of 1988.[55] The approach manages problems 'in terms of systems of work rather than concentrating on individual deficiencies. That is, it involves the assessment and control of risks and the creation of an inbuilt system of maintenance and review'.[56] It is a perfect example of a smart mode of coregulation. Now, consider how dependent is the appropriateness of this mode on basic features of employment, work organization, and technology in two industries:

in respect of the control of major hazardous facilities, a systems-based approach is particularly appropriate. As one senior British regulator put it: 'visual inspection is a thing of the past in high hazard, large, complex facilities. You can't walk round a chemical plant and see much. All there is is shiny tanks and pipework.' In consequence, the (Health and Safety Executive) rely very largely upon auditing the management system and on interviewing personnel based on that system. In contrast, the construction industry has many features that make the introduction of a systems-based approach problematic. These include the fact that standard employment is daily hire or for the length of the project, the large number of small employers, the lack of expertise in (occupational health and safety) within the industry, the fact that risk assessment often falls on external consultants so that employers have less involvement and take less responsibility, the fact that construction is project-based, involving differing and multiple teams of subcontractors with no long-term relationship, and the lack of opportunity for employers and employees to develop mutual relationships of trust.[57]

That regulation should be smart we can take as self-evident, and as equally self-evident that different regulatory modes are appropriate to different circumstances. 'Smart regulation' theory, when applied to Britain, offers a template against which to measure the new institutions and practices of regulation. But as an empirical theory of the new British regulatory state it is drastically wanting. The following pages will show that the history of the state is marked by anything but the measured selection of regulatory institutions and instruments. It is marked instead by crisis and chaos. Its recent history is one of hyper-innovation: the frenetic selection of new institutional modes, and their equally frenetic replacement by alternatives. One reason for this frenetic history is that recent decades have also been marked by hyper-politicization. Far from creating stable worlds of coregulation, the new regulatory state in Britain has seen the destruction of old worlds of self-regulation and of old enclosed policy communities. This has exposed the regulatory process to the workings of partisan politics, drawn politicians into the micro-management of regulatory institutions, and turned regulatory issues into symbolic resources for partisan electoral struggles. As we shall see in Chapter 7, the age of the regulatory state has, indeed, also been an age of fiasco.

The British regulatory state, far from being smart, is, therefore, often remarkably stupid. It succeeded a governing system that was even more stupid, and these stupidities arise from a factor neglected by legal theorists of smart regulation: the role of partisan politics in democratic government. One of the attractions of the theories to which we now turn is that they are more sensitive to the consequences of political struggles.

THE REGULATORY STATE AS A RISK STATE

Consider the following:

Modern industrial societies are hence peculiar social entities. The bases of their solidarity and sense of collective identity have been eroded and at the same time the substantially realistic expectations of their citizens to security, well-being and improvement in their circumstances are constantly increased by the success of their economies and by the application of science and technology.[58]

This combination of eroded solidarity, expanded security and heightened expectations produces societies where the overriding purpose of regulation is to act as 'the counter to risk as an essential basis for sustaining trust in a radically individualized, risk-sensitive society'. Regulation is the response to the now instinctive reaction that 'something ought to be done about it'.[59]

These passages from Clarke radically transform our image of the regulatory state, and cast it in an especially troubling light. We have moved from a cybernetic world of strategic steering, where the state is a kind of Platonic pilot making general decisions about societal direction or about the 'smartest' modes of control, to one where regulation is a struggle with deep-seated social and cultural crisis. 'Risk society is a regulatory society': Ericson and Haggerty, thus, summarize an emergent orthodoxy about the forces shaping the regulatory state.[60]

The very rise of risk as an organizing notion in making sense of the regulatory state, however, creates its own problems of understanding. As 'risk' has become a key concept, it has suffered the fate of all such concepts in the social sciences: it has been colonized by different intellectual and ideological schools. Accounts of the rise of risk, and of its central place in the modern state, come from many different directions, and all suggest very different accounts of what links risk and the regulatory state. I illustrate the point by taking three particularly influential accounts: those derived from grand narratives of modernity; those derived from pluralism, accounts that essentially argue that the rise of democratic egalitarianism has crowded out old methods of control; and those derived from elitism, accounts that see the rise of risk regulation as part of a wider remanagerialization of social spheres that hitherto operated as autonomous domains of civil society.

Risk as part of the characteristic grand narrative of modernity has come in two subtly different forms, one popularized by Giddens and the other by Beck: they may crudely be distinguished as the cultural and the technological. Giddens sees the new stress on risk as a consequence primarily of heightened sensitivities and capacities that are associated with late modernity.[61] His arguments might be summarized as a kind of distillation from Durkheim and Schumpeter. The condition of modernity undermines many of the old hierarchical restraints of the past, endows citizens with new sources of knowledge and confidence, and reshapes institutions—like the mass media—so that they focus much more than in the past on the incidence of risk. The regulatory state is forced to concentrate on the regulation of risk, not necessarily because risks are greater than in the past, but because the cultural climate in which risk is experienced and debated has changed radically, simultaneously heightening knowledge of risk, heightening sensitivity to its consequences, and heightening the capacity to mobilize to demand action against those perceived consequences.[62]

The variant on the theme of modernity offered by Beck repeats many of these claims, but adds the argument that the scale of modern social organization, and the character of the most modern technologies, reinforce cultural changes by actually creating new risks and, perhaps, new kinds of risk. In the now famous opening words of *Risk Society*: 'In advanced modernity the social production of *wealth* is systematically accompanied by the social production of *risks*.'[63] Beck's great example of the new kind of risk associated with modernity is the threat to life and health from contamination from nuclear power, and it illustrates to perfection what he claims to be special about risk in the risk society: the potential risk from fallout from a nuclear accident is, as the chilling example of Chernobyl shows, catastrophic; the risks incurred are collective rather than individual, and there is, thus, little that a single individual can do to protect against the risk; and these catastrophic risks are in many cases unknowable or incalculable.[64]

The second—pluralist—account of the rise of the risk narrative is also connected to notions of modernity. It is most heavily influenced by cultural theories of risk that derive, in particular, from the work of the anthropologist Mary Douglas. One starting point—particularly associated with the work done by Douglas and the American political scientist Aaron Wildavsky—is the great disjunction that seems to exist between perceptions of risk and what the systematic evidence tells us about the actual incidence of risk.[65] Simply, some remote risks seem to arouse a high sense of danger; some very high incidence risks seem to be of low salience, or if recognized seem to be treated with indifference. The result is a pattern of regulatory politics highly charged with risk issues—but not in any way connected to the measurable magnitude of risk. Open, pluralist cultures produce, notably through media effects, periodic manias and panics about risks, and these panics are not rationally related to the incidence of risk.[66] How might the existence of these mistaken perceptions be explained? One obvious explanation is that the place of risk on the political agenda, and the perception of risk on that agenda, is not systematically controlled by rational debate but is the product of forces such as popular fears and the way those fears are reported in the media. This is why this account of risk pictures the rise of the risk narrative as the result of the breakdown of the influence of old elites unable, in a more open, unstable, and less deferential world, to control risk debates. This reasoning depends on moving from the grandest 'macro' level of analysis to immediate everyday fears. Cultural modernity is for Douglas an illusion. She writes of her most famous book: 'In *Purity and Danger* the rational behaviour of primitives is vindicated: taboo turns out not to be incomprehensible but an intelligible concern to protect society from behaviour that will wreck it.'[67] Risk sensitivities are not to be explained as part of a grand narrative of modernity. Rather, they arise from some particular things that exactly chime with the language of pluralism: 'the scales of cultural change are tipping toward a more pervasive individualism'; and as they tip we move into a world of 'public backlash against the great corporations' and assertions of egalitarianism.[68] If risk perceptions are culturally shaped, more egalitarian cultures will produce more popular sensitivity to risk. The account fits well the extraordinary growth of the 'risk industry' documented by the Royal Society's landmark report of 1992.[69]

To this account of risk as representing a moment of transition from oligarchy to egalitarianism, we can contrast the third, elitist, account. We might best start this account with a question: if the rising salience of risk is connected with the passing of oligarchy, why does its management so often take the form of developing new modes of hierarchical control? This picture of new hierarchies is what emerges from Power's study of the 'audit society', which, he argues, is also a risk society: one where the response to risk and perception of risk is to elaborate and strengthen modes of surveillance and reporting.[70] This Power sums up as 'the remanagerialization of risk': a process by which risk prompts the creation of new managerial structures devised, not just to produce more full reporting in an auditing sense, but to develop techniques of managerial control.[71] This puts a very different complexion on the risk narrative, for now, far from being a symptom of the decline of elites, as in the work of Douglas and colleagues, it marks a reassertion—a remanagerialization—by controlling elites. As he writes, with specific reference to audit:

The mission of sustaining systemic control must continually be reaffirmed and reconstituted in the face of events which threaten its credibility. This process of reaffirmation reflects anxiety about the mission of regulation . . . . within the politics of failure there is a continual re-intensification of available instruments of regulatory control.[72]

Though Power's is an argument about the broader forces shaping risk and regulation in advanced capitalist economies, most of his empirical material is drawn from Britain, and it is striking how far work on risk is used to analyse both what is changing, and what is distinctive, about the British regulatory case. Some of the most illuminating examples come from sociologists of science and science policy interested in the analysis of risk communities. The case studies that we have of the characteristic 'modernity risks' in Britain—for example, studies of the BSE catastrophe, of the management of risk in modern food processing, the management of risk in the wider world of biotechnology generally—all paint pictures of cohesive, enclosed regulatory communities where tightly knit oligarchies made assessments about risk in a highly cooperative fashion.[73] These features are particularly starkly revealed in studies of risk assessment that involve comparison with the other national culture that in many respects quite closely resembles the United Kingdom, the United States of America. Risk assessment in the United States of America has been very different from Britain, and the comparison points up what is 'exceptionally British' about the process. Van Zwanenberg and Millstone, describing published case studies of risk assessment as well as drawing on their own work on pesticide controls, summarize the comparative evidenced as follows: 'in Britain, by contrast with the United States, there is an informal commitment to the imposition of far harder burdens of proof before regulators will classify chemicals as hazardous; and this difference is due to the greater secrecy, informality and freedom from democratic oversight of the British system.'[74] Risk assessment and management in the United States of America are done in the shadow of the law—indeed, in the shadow of a highly litigious culture, and in the shadow of a culture that encourages a great deal of public, adversarial debate. The upshot is that risk assessments in the United States of America contrast strikingly with those in Britain: they are more systematic; they are more likely to be challenged, which is why they are more systematic; and, as evidence suggests, they are also objectively more robust.

Some views of risk can, therefore, be used to paint a picture of the uniqueness—viewed comparatively—of the British regulatory state. Some views, equally, can be also used to paint a picture of a *changing* regulatory state. Stirling has put this case with particular force. He begins by painting a familiar picture of British elitism, secrecy, and manipulation of popular expectations.[75] But even the UK, he argues, is changing under the pressures of pluralism, though not as markedly as more open societies like that of the United States of America.[76] The challenge of how to manage the discussion of scientific risk under conditions of pluralism also lies at the centre of accounts of the management of debates about environmental risk. Consider Weale's account of the traditional network by which environmental risk assessment was made in the UK: 'Without the conditions of trust among those drawn into policy networks, the idea that standards could be set by appeal to scientific evidence often in an informal way would have lacked credibility. Within the framework of the Westminster system, it proved to be possible for many years.'[77] As this remark suggests, Weale's argument takes us full circle to one of the central arguments of this book: indeed, he explicitly invokes the passing of 'club government' in environmental regulation as an occasion to discuss the problems of democratizing risk assessment and control.

Picturing the regulatory state as a risk state, therefore, offers some powerful illumination in the British case. Risk theorists—whether writing out of grand narratives of modernity, using elitist models, or exploring the links between risk management and pluralist politics—all emphasize themes that also recur in the chapters that follow: themes to do with trust, with secrecy and openness in decision making, and with the impact of long-term historical change on the relations that exist between governing elites and those who are governed.

Yet, using the image of the regulatory state as a risk state also poses some serious difficulties. Part of the problem is analytical, and lies in the fate of 'risk' as an idea. As it has become a key concept in social science narratives of the modern state, it has suffered the fate of other key concepts: lost sharpness of meaning and become itself a site of contestation. Just as a whole industry now exists to elucidate the meaning of 'regulation', a similar industry is growing servicing the concept of risk. And in the process of broadening the range of the concept, some strange mutations have occurred. For instance, much modern usage of 'risk' treats it as a kind of unknowable, incalculable future outcome—more or less precisely the meaning attributed to 'uncertainty' in Knight's original famous distinction between the two.[78] There are some obvious commonsense reasons for this shift in usage, not least that 'uncertainty' has nothing like the rhetorical force of 'risk'. But it is now unclear precisely what we are gaining by applying the language of risk to arenas as different as: 'BSE; the troubles at Lloyds; the Nick Leeson affair; global warming; drinking red wine; declining sperm counts.'[79] When an increasingly disparate range of social problems are reconceived in the vocabulary of risk, we gain in rhetorical power but lose in analytical precision.

To these analytical problems we can add the considerable difficulty created by the most systematic attempt yet made to explore risk regulation regimes in Britain, that produced by Hood and colleagues.[80] Their study of nine risk regimes in Britain ranges across domains as varied as the control of radon in homes, of dangerous dogs, of paedophiles, and of pesticide residues in food and drinking water. The most important findings include: there are striking variations not only between states, but also between different domains in the same state, in terms of salience, mode of decision, and the pattern of groups who dominate the separate regimes; systemic explanations—such as those that invoke modernity, or the general power of particular groups or interests—perform less well than middle-range theories that produce a complex mosaic of explanations differentiated by domains.[81] Thus, 'there is no such thing as *risk* society, only different risk regulation regimes';[82] there is no need to invoke epoch-making changes—such as those central to narratives about modernity—to explain change; and the actual politics of risk management are characterized by extraordinary variety.[83]

The discussion thus far amounts to an attempt to estimate how far some of the more ambitious narratives of the modern regulatory state can help us make sense of the British case. Simply, what do we gain if we try to picture the British regulatory state as an example of some general form: as the result of the diffusion of the institutions and ideologies of the paradigmatic regulatory state, the American; as an emergent 'European' regulatory state; as a novel kind of smart state attuned to the new worlds of governance; or as a risk state? All plainly provide some analytical purchase, but all equally are wanting in key respects. One very obvious source of deficiency arises precisely from their generalizing character, for this cannot take account of British exceptionalism. And since the rise of the British regulatory state during the 1970s to the 1990s has taken place under the influence of particular British conditions, this exceptionalism is important. In the next section I turn to these matters.

THE BRITISH STATE AS A REGULATORY STATE

All states are exceptional, in the obvious sense that all have a special historical trajectory, a unique place in the wider global system, and distinctive ideological patterns. I focus here on British exceptionalism only because Britain is our subject—and because this exceptionalism shaped the regulatory patterns that developed before the era of hyper-innovation, and has continued to shape during the 1970s to the 1990s.

Of these dimensions of exceptionalism—history, global setting, and ideology—the first is the most important because it is the most fundamental, intimately shaping in turn the remaining two. As the extended discussion in Chapter 3 shows, what we conventionally call the Victorian era was critical in shaping both regulation in Britain and the surrounding state system. It was the social and economic consequences of industrialism—the effects on class formation, on interest group formation, on economic structure, and on social problems—that created the pressure for the great Victorian bursts of regulatory institution building: innovation in the state system such as the creation of a network of inspectorates; innovation in the self-regulatory system, such as the creation of modern patterns of self-governing professionalism; and self-government in the critically important financial markets. Historical timing—early industrialization, early regulatory innovation, the early development of a state presence in regulation—proved critical. The great Victorian innovations were made in a political world governed by oligarchy, albeit an oligarchy riven by divisions both on lines of ideology and economic interest. They were made not only before the development of formal democracy in Britain but also in the shadow of Victorian apprehensions about the challenges of democracy and the new, threatening working class that was created by industrialism. They were made in an administrative world where the state's domestic administrative capacity was weak, whether measured either by the resources in people or money available or—at least until after the great Victorian administrative reforms—by the quality of the administrative machine at the state's command.

This was the historical world in which the original system of club regulation was formed. 'The atmosphere of British government was that of a club, whose members trusted each other to observe the spirit of the club rules; the notion that the principles underlying the rules should be clearly defined and publicly proclaimed was profoundly alien.'[84] In writing these words, Marquand was writing of the general constitutional understandings that underpinned the system of government, but we will find time and again that they apply to the narrower sphere of regulatory activity. Nor is that surprising: we would expect the regulatory state to be a subset of the wider state system; and since regulation was a major portion of public activity, we would expect the character of public life to be itself deeply affected by the character of regulatory institutions. But there is another feature of the state system that is only hinted at in this passage from Marquand, but which is critical. It lies behind the innocent use of the adjective 'British'. In Marquand's original account the 'Westminster Model' is used as a synonym for the 'club model', and that is entirely appropriate, especially for the club model as it triumphed after 1918. The Westminster Model assigned supremacy to metropolitan politics. After 1918, there took place a massive centralization of British life: constitutional ideology elevated to supremacy Diceyian notions of the sovereignty of the Westminster Parliament; both major parties became powerful supporters of metropolitan supremacy; and, as a corollary, both the vitality of provincial political culture diminished and the powerful separatist movements within the United Kingdom were either partially amputated (in the case of Ireland) or went underground.[85] Anti-localism—as Sharpe puts it— dominated even the Labour Party that had grown out of provincial roots before 1918.[86] In one of the last great studies (and celebrations) of the club system, Heclo and Wildavsky put it bluntly: 'British political administration is concentrated spatially as well as numerically . . . . Basically, if you are not in (or within easy reach of) London, you are politically nowhere.'[87] Dale's picture of the elite of the civil service at the end of the 1930s—perhaps the apogee of the club era— shows how far, indeed, club government actually overlapped with the social world of the elite institutions in London's own clubland.[88]

This emphasis on the metropolitan world contains an important echo of another key feature of the kind of state that emerged out of the Victorian world, and was consolidated after 1918: the distinction, made in classic form by Bulpitt, between high and low politics.[89] The assignment was critical to the way the regulatory state functioned up to the 1960s—and the breakdown of the assignment is critical to understanding the chaos of the intervening decades. 'Regulation' was low politics, a world of mundane technicalities. Where the central state directly accepted responsibility—as in those fields covered by the great Victorian institutional innovations that created inspectorates—small regulatory communities clustered around these agencies conducting the business of regulation informally and, for the most part, beyond the wider public gaze. A much larger part of the regulatory world was dispersed beyond the formal world of politics: lost in the maze of quasi-government or assigned to explicitly autonomous worlds, as in the domains of City regulation and most professional regulation.

Our image of the British regulatory state—one originally shaped in Victorian England and then consolidated in the face of the rise of formal democracy after 1918—is, thus, necessarily entwined with our broader image of the British state itself. For the era of institutional stagnation—the epoch spanning, in particular, the half-century or so after 1918—the broader character of the governing system could be summarized in the terms used above: oligarchy, metropolitanism, and the assignment of critical policy domains to a world of low politics. The terms also exactly summarize the meaning of the British regulatory state in the era of stagnation; and, correspondingly, the era of hyper-innovation during the 1970s to the 1990s is intimately connected to the wider collapse of this old governing system.

The state's peculiar historical trajectory was also obviously closely connected to the second dimension of exceptionalism identified above: its place in the wider global system. That place was itself dominated by two entwined experiences: imperialism and globalization. The creation of empires was central to the creation of a global economy, and the creation of the greatest nineteenth century empire, the British one, was a key to the founding of the modern global system.[90] The connections with club government are immensely complex, but one way of simplifying is to look, in turn, at external and domestic experiences. Externally, the British regulatory state has been shaped by two of the great historical episodes in the development of globalization: the great burst of globalization that occurred after 1870 and was ended by the outbreak of First World War; and the burst of globalization that began in the early 1970s and is still continuing. One common set of institutions connects these two separated episodes: the City of London. The City was a major agent in that earlier phase of globalization, both as a great world financial centre and as a main conduit by which British economic and imperial power flowed into, and helped make, the global system.[91] But the economic transformations associated with that involvement in globalization also transformed the City domestically, and, in particular, transformed its modes of government. As we shall see in detail in Chapters 3 and 4, this was the period when the 'classic' City mode of regulation was formed—when its institutional structures were created and its legitimizing ideology elaborated. That 'classic' mode, stressing the autonomy of regulation from the state, and developing the City's own distinctive system of club government, exercised a unique importance in the British regulatory state. This importance was due in part to the objective importance of the City in the British economy and in British society over the next century; and in part due to the fact that the City mode became, precisely, a 'classic'—an institutional and an ideological formation that was admired and copied throughout much of the rest of the state system. Thus, the ripples of the great world changes wrought by imperialism and globalization can be traced back into the domestic contours of the club system of regulation.

The second burst of globalization, since 1970, has, as we shall see in Chapter 4, helped destroy that classic: barely a vestige of the City's own club system now remains, and the destruction is traceable in large part to the City's deep participation in this latest era of globalization, notably to London's emergence as one of the three great centres in the new world of globalized financial markets. The significance of this development is once again twofold: it has broken up one of the most important parts of the system of club regulation; and, in so doing, has transformed what was one of the most important originating sources of the wider practice of the club system. What is more, not only has this era destroyed its characteristic institutions and undermined its legitimizing ideology, the very dynamism of the globalizing process has introduced powerful and continuing destabilizing forces into City regulatory arrangements. In short, in the crucial case of the City we can see an important connection between the globalizing process itself and the onset of the epoch of hyper-innovation.

This complex mix of the import and export of economic processes and institutional practices is mirrored by a more domestic face of the British regulatory state. The system of club government could not have originated, or survived, without the support of a wider culture of deference. Deciphering cultural patterns from the past, especially popular cultural patterns, is a notoriously tricky business.[92] But there is convincing accumulated evidence, albeit much of it fragmentary and circumstantial, for the widespread existence of popular deference to the hierarchies of the club system. One of the most convincing pieces of evidence, because it comes in the form of systematic comparative survey evidence gathered in the twilight of club government, is provided by Almond and Verba's study of popular political cultures, in which the British emerged as uniquely trustful of, and respectful to, hierarchical political authority.[93] The origins of this popular deference are themselves complex, but there is one very striking historical coincidence in the rise and fall of popular deference: it was fashioned at the high point of British imperialism; invoked the hierarchies of Empire; and it vanished as a significant force in the popular mind shortly after the British Empire itself vanished.[94] (I return to this argument in Chapter 7.)

Club government was also tied to the third dimension of exceptionalism identified above: the ideological. Here, the weight of comparative work is all in one direction: wherever we look, the ideological assumptions that underlay the theory and practice of regulation in the era of club government marked Britain out among the advanced capitalist democracies. She was distinguished from the great systems of European capitalism in the extent to which law was marginalized, and in the degree to which, conversely, private associations dominated regulation.[95] She was distinguished from American capitalism in the degree to which regulation was as a matter of cooperation between insiders, rather than of open adversarial conflict.[96] The distinctive power of British regulatory ideology shaped both 'practical' and academic accounts. We shall see time and again in the following pages how often ideologies stressing voluntarism and the tacit knowledge of insiders were offered by practitioners as the self-evidently best way to practise regulation. These ideologies needed elaboration and systematization, and the job was done in key areas of British social science. In scholarly work, two brilliant systematizations of the ideology of informal cooperative regulation are both, appropriately, linked to the University of Oxford—appropriately because Oxford was one of citadels of the club world. The Nuffield School of industrial relations, which dominated both theory and practice until well into the 1970s, pictured the regulation of the whole industrial relations system as one where law was the opponent of trust and flexibility.[97] Nuffield theorists exerted an extraordinary influence: they largely educated the first generation of specialist scholars in industrial relations, and they were central to policy making for much of the 1960s and 1970s. They were the key influence on the report of the Royal (Donovan) Commission on trade unions and employers' associations.[98] Indeed, the divisions within that Commission precisely about the role of law in regulating industrial relations were an early sign of the decline of the club system.[99]

A second example is provided in Hawkins's brilliant ethnography of water purity control in Britain.[100] The example is particularly telling because Hawkins's is the most outstanding statement of the distinctive view of regulation that emerged from a generation of socio-legal scholars.[101] But it is also apt for more substantive reasons: pollution control was one area of economic life where— unlike arenas such as the financial markets and industrial relations—the law and public agencies had penetrated as long ago as the nineteenth century. Hawkins documented in wonderfully subtle detail how both regulators and regulated sought to avoid the literal interpretation of the law, and to practise cooperative regulation. He systematized this into a highly influential account of the limited capacity of law generally to govern the complex regulation of economic life, arguing as follows. From the point of view of anyone operating with an expectation that the law would be obeyed in economic regulation, his study reveals a highly unsatisfactory state of affairs. Not only are legally specified standards breached, the breaches are institutionalized: 'non-compliance with standards is thus organizationally sanctioned.'[102] This is not to say the law is unimportant. It is 'a kind of *eminence grise*, a shadowy entity lurking off-stage'.[103] The account, thus, systematizes the cultural assumptions of British regulatory actors into a general theory of the regulatory process:

Regulation may be contemplated by the law as the dispassionate sanctioning of misconduct by the even-handed application of a criminal law unconcerned for the niceties of *mens rea*, but regulation in practice, mediated as it is by a bureaucracy in which people have to exercise their discretion in making judgments about their fellows, is founded upon notions of justice. Pollution control is done in a moral, not a technological world.[104]

What informed this moral world? The answer is a profound ambivalence about the role of law in the enforcement process: 'regulatory enforcement is a symbolic matter, reflecting intimately the conjunction of privately-held (but shared) values with organizational interests in enforcing a secular code of conduct about which there is a high degree of social and political ambivalence.'[105] And whence comes this ambivalence? From a source that will provide one of the main themes of Chapter 3, the nineteenth-century development of regulation in Britain that constructed regulatory offences as of a different order from other criminal offences, even where criminal law was formally involved: 'offences against regulation have not been culturally absorbed and do not invite the same condemnation as breaches of the traditional code.'[106]

This sketch of British exceptionalism is designed to suggest that the British regulatory state is *sui generis*, and that in this special nature lies much of the difficulty in assimilating the British experience to the prevailing theoretical images of the regulatory state. It could be retorted that all states are exceptional, but it happens that our concern here is with Britain. The original entry into regulation was shaped by this exceptionalism: by the experience of pioneering industrialism; by the linked experiences of imperialism and the fashioning of the global system; and by the rise of a distinctive British regulatory ideology. And the transition to a new regulatory state during the 1970s to the 1990s has been shaped by the crises arising from the exhaustion of some of the key sources of this exceptionalism. It is hardly surprising, therefore, that the British regulatory state has gone its own way in the age of governance and strategic steering.

CRISIS, CLUB RULE, AND THE BRITISH REGULATORY STATE

My purpose in this chapter has been simple: to suggest that there is more to the regulatory state than meets the eye.

The dominant scholarly orthodoxy of recent years has linked the regulatory state to images of retreat and dissolution: to the rise of modes of 'governance' that are concerned with the management of self-steering networks transcending conventional public/private boundaries; to the rise of new systems of 'soft' bureaucracy that dispense with the hierarchies of Weberian administration; to the rise of soft law as a successor to command law; and to the displacement of the ambitious projects of economic and social control that are the characteristic product of high modernity by more modest projects of strategic steering.

A simple starting point is, therefore, to look at what a real existing regulatory state looks like in the light of this orthodoxy. The American regulatory state has copyright on the phrase by virtue of its historically pioneering role, by virtue of the dominant position of American scholarship about that regulatory state, and by virtue of America's dominant place in the global system. And the history of the American regulatory state fits little of the scholarly orthodoxy. Its history since the Progressive origins is one of the expansion of interventionist domains; of the growth of a dense and elaborate jurisprudence; and of the multiplication of the pathologies of the very kind of command from which regulatory states are supposed to be an escape. Of course, much of the new governance and steering literature is precisely a product of the perceived American crisis. But in the light of that crisis we are entitled to say one thing, and ask another: to say that whatever new forms are developing, they cannot be 'the' regulatory state, but merely 'a' new regulatory state; and to ask why, if the teleology of the regulatory state is so oriented to withdrawal and steering, the American form has taken such an interventionist, command like turn?

An obvious answer to this last question is that the United States of America has its own history of exceptionalism, and that the regulatory state developing elsewhere is indeed one that fits the governance image. That makes the images of the 'European regulatory state' and the 'smart' regulatory state examined above particularly important, because in their different ways they are indeed congruent with images of governance and steering: the European because, in the hands of Majone, it emerges as a kind of reincarnation of Madisonian government; the smart, because it suggests that regulatory states are selecting more efficiently than in the past from a range of regulatory instruments, and that this selection widens the range of rule beyond command and hierarchy. These sections of the chapter amount to sketches of hypothetical understandings of what has been going on in Britain during the 1970s to the 1990s; and the discussion of the risk society and regulatory society is intended to sketch a very different kind of hypothetical understanding, one that, in principle, promises to help account for the hyper-innovation of recent decades. But my argument in the pages that follow is that none of these hypothetical understandings works. The final substantive section of the chapter has formed a link to the chapters that follow. And what follows will show that there is not a single regulatory state in Britain, but at least two; it will show that the second, present version has grown out of the crisis of the first; and it will show that the crisis is not just a crisis about regulation or regulatory effectiveness, but is part of a wider crisis of the state in Britain.

I now turn in more detail to these historical matters.

3

Creating Club Regulation

REGULATING WITHOUT A STATE

Regulation is not a modern invention. There is ample evidence both from the distant and more recent historical past of many elaborate attempts at both economic and social regulation: of monopoly, for example, traceable back over 4000 years to the Babylonian era. Price controls and controls over production for social purposes can be traced back at least to Roman times.[1] A large literature also documents the regulation of both economic exchange and social behaviour in pre-industrial Britain. In medieval England, for instance, the creation of markets and entry into exchange relations was a concession that arose from customary understanding or by explicit grant from public power. Freedom of trade, in Ogus's words, 'was perceived as a "privilege" which in relation to, for example, markets was normally to be granted in charters and licences'.[2] Hence, the widespread organization of labour into guilds that attempted to exercise control over entry and price, the extensive prescription in various public pronouncements of the obligations of workers to employers, and the establishment of local markets through the grant of Royal Charters.

All this, however, took place in a society that had no 'state' in any understandable sense of that word. The building of a modern state apparatus in England is conventionally identified with the 'Tudor Revolution in Government'.[3] The revolution created a 'New Monarchy' that 'concentrated authority' and subjugated institutions of civil society like the Catholic Church.[4] We have ample documentation of how pervasive in the Tudor period was the reach of official regulation of economic life: under the Tudor monarchs alone, about 300 statutes were passed governing economic life.[5] Regulation stretched to the creation of monopolies authorized and protected by Royal power: for instance, to encourage foreign trade and exploration; to the protection of home industries against foreign competition, as in restrictions on the import of goods as varied as daggers, cloth, and saddles. It even stretched to the use of what in modern language we would call public procurement to create employment and foster home industries: even in the eighteenth century the Royal Dockyards were by far the largest single employer in Britain.[6] Above all, from the Tudor period we can date an ambitious mix of social regulation and the regulation of labour conditions. These included an attempt at a comprehensive regulation of the linked conditions of unemployment and poverty, notably in the Statute of Apprentices (1563) 'a general and pervasive labour code which survived for over 200 years'.[7]

Yet, 'the Tudor revolution in government was only revolutionary in English terms.'[8] In other words, it left the state with comparatively poor bureaucratic and financial resources. Even by 1830, 'by continental standards England's central government seemed absurdly small.'[9] By contrast, in civil society there were diffused extensive regulatory mechanisms, including a large magistracy drawn from local gentry and a web of what Arthurs calls 'customary law', modes of adjudication with origins in a wide range of traditional institutions of civil society beyond the conventional domain of government.[10] These are all good reasons why it makes no sense to speak of a regulatory state. 'Regulations' took the form of a shifting mix of royal proclamation, some legislation (which was often not published), and exercises of power by local elites, some of it customary.[11] Enforcement depended on a mix of cooperation by local elites and the operations of civil society—for example, through giving informers incentives to report breaches of regulations. Finally, as might be inferred from this, enforcement of regulations was commonly ineffective. Not only were the bureaucratic means of enforcement usually missing, but even the most basic information about regulation was non-existent: it was not until early in the nineteenth century, for example, that there even existed a consolidated public list of statutes.[12] For the eighteenth-century, Haas's account of the attempted regulation of conditions in the Royal Dockyards shows a picture of ineffectiveness, corruption, and absence of even the most elementary information.[13]

We can, thus, speak of the existence of a regulated economy in pre-industrial England, but we cannot speak of a regulatory state. The beginnings of this are observable as a consequence of the great revolutionary event in modern British history: industrialism.

INDUSTRIALISM, FEAR, AND CLUB RULE

The challenges of industrialism have been aptly and famously summarized in Hobsbawm's picture of the 'two revolutions': the social disruption occasioned by the sheer ferocity of industrial change; and the political challenge to the old order represented by the French Revolution.[14] The two were connected in early nineteenth-century Britain since many of the social forces unleashed by industrialism were inspired by ideologies, in turn, released by the French revolution.

Why and how the two revolutions led to the changes in the character of the state in Britain in the nineteenth century virtually occupies the whole historiography of the period, and are, therefore, beyond our modest scope. But three kinds of novelty are particularly important because they lay at the heart of regulatory change. The first was novel ideologies. It is the rise of these new ideologies that lies at the heart of many of the puzzles and controversies surrounding the revolution in economic and social regulation that came over Britain, especially in the first half of the nineteenth century: for instance, the debates about how far landmark reforms such as the Poor Law Amendment Act of 1834 are best understood as acts of laissez-faire liberalism or as precursors of a new collect-ivism.[15] The problem at its simplest may be put as follows. The most important new ideologies in the economic sphere were ideologies of economic liberalism, which attacked many of the old regulatory restraints; yet, as cases like the new Poor Law showed, the actual reforms they inspired seemed to lead in the direction of more central state control.[16]

A second novelty involved changes in the scale of economic activity, coupled with changes in the technologies of production. Perkin crisply summarizes these. They involved 'the gradual replacement of the domestic system by the factory system'. These 'increased the size, complexity and degree of organization of the real unit of production'.[17] They led directly to the range of regulatory problems that produced so much institutional innovation throughout the nineteenth century: problems of regulating the new factories, especially in the interests of some notion of safety; problems of regulating the impact of the new technologies on the physical environment; problems of regulating the quality of production, as in the goods and services offered in the new markets of industrialism.

Finally, the third novelty lay in the creation of new social and economic groups, and, therefore, new interests in the regulatory process. A central theme of what follows in our substantive account of regulatory reform will not only be about the clash between new groups and interests, most obviously between workers and the new capitalists, but it will also be about the organization and regulation of new occupations that grew out of industrialism—most obviously, in what follows, new professions or newly reorganized ancient professions.

These forces—new ideologies, new technologies and forms of production, and new social and economic interests—thus helped drive the reconstruction of regulation, helping shape a Victorian regulatory state. But there were also more immediately political forces that provided important parts of the context of the new regulation. They, in turn, can be summarized as involving three revolutions: the revolution in government itself; the legal revolution; and the fear of popular revolution.

The Victorian revolution in government (to borrow MacDonagh's phrase) was, in part, a revolution in scale of central control.[18] In 1830, 'administration' meant government through local elites by mechanisms diffused through civil society.[19] But in the next 40 years, in Parris's words, there was created 'a new pattern of central administration'.[20] That centralization was accompanied by the growth of bureaucratic resources, both in numbers and capacity, the latter signalled by the growing professionalization of local government and by the shift to formal merit in recruiting and promoting in the central civil service.[21] A more subtle but equally important aspect of professionalization is one identified by Macdonagh, in his landmark studies of the revolution in government: there was a great increase in both the quality and the quantity of the data which govern-ment began to assemble about the society which it was attempting to regulate.

Much of the Victorian regulatory revolution was a revolution in inspection, and it was the improvement in social data that made much of this inspection possible.[22]

These changes could be summarized as involving the rise of a specialized set of state institutions marked off from civil society, by contrast with the complex system of tessellation that had hitherto prevailed. This growth of specialized public domains also marked the second great contextual change, the displacement of the ideologies and institutions of customary law by specialized, centrally created legal institutions, and the development of a distinctive ideology to support these centrally created institutions. Arthurs summarizes his study of this process as it began in the 1830s: 'there was increasing reliance on legal professionals as the standard bearers of formal law and of "law" as the vehicle of certainty, impartiality and dignity.'[23] The shift echoes through the regulatory history of the century: it helped fashion the hegemony of one key profession, the law; and as we shall see shortly, it created tremendous apprehensions for business interests used to controlling their own affairs by custom and self-regulation.

These apprehensions were linked to larger fears, and these fears mark the third key contextual feature that should interest us. Victorian politics was dominated by the problem of how to integrate, or successfully exclude and control, the great new class interests created by industrialism. In particular, it was dominated by fears about the frightening spectre of popular government represented by the newly created working class.[24] The narrower domains of regulation were closely shaped by these fears, and in particular by the problem of how to create regulatory institutions that could allow powerful interests to continue to control their own affairs should the threat of popular rule ever be realized. Club regulation developed in the nineteenth century to cope with this problem, and was consolidated against the rise of formal democracy early in the twentieth century. In this manner, as we shall see, the early attempts to protect elites from democratic threats continue to shape regulation in modern Britain.

THE VICTORIAN REGULATORY STATE

Like many periods, 'the Victorian age' is an elastic notion: it arguably began before Victoria ascended the throne, arguably ended before she died, and as far as public policy, especially regulatory policy, is concerned, certainly had little or nothing to do with her. The shorthand nevertheless conveys something important about regulatory history: that in the half-century or so from the 1830s to the 1880s there took place a large-scale construction (and in some cases reconstruction) of regulatory institutions. The couple of decades up to the mid-century were, in particular, years of extraordinary institutional creativity. Between 1833 and 1850 there was created, to name but a selection: the Factory Inspectors; the Poor Law Commissioners; the Prison Inspectorate; the Railway Board; the Mining

Inspectorate; the Lunacy Commission; the General Board of Health; the Merchant Marine Department; and the Charity Commission.[25]

I call all this for shorthand the creation of a regulatory state because it created, or in some instances reorganized, public institutions as regulatory bodies; it shaped a very particular kind of boundary between public and private regulation, and in so doing may be said to have been critical in defining the nature of the Victorian constitution; and it elaborated legitimizing ideologies that were to shape regulatory behaviour and institutions to the end of the twentieth century. Victorian regulatory innovation was rich, diverse, and extended over time. Sketching it in the summary manner attempted here demands extreme selectivity in choice of material. I focus on three areas. The first I call in summary 'industrial regulation', and the choice is probably the most self-evident of the three. From the 1830s there developed successive waves of control directed at the new industrial economy and society. As this name implies, these waves were a response to the consequences of industrialism—consequences that encompassed workers, consumers, and the wider physical environment of the whole community.

The substantive importance of these developments is obvious. Their analytical importance for this study will unfold in the description, but in summary: the single most revealing common feature of industrial regulation, as we shall see, was its cooperative character. Though formally based on statute, and on the appointment of independent public inspectorates to enforce the law, the practice of regulation soon developed into something very different: the law was marginalized; resort to sanctions was rare; and there developed an overwhelming stress on fostering trust between regulator and regulated.

The second domain examined here covers professional regulation. What are sometimes conventionally called the ancient professions—the church, the law, medicine—of course already existed before the industrial revolution, but the nineteenth century saw the establishment of a new pattern of professional regulation, one that both reformed some of the ancient professions and established a network of new ones. A widely imitated pattern was set by the Apothecaries Act of 1815, which established some statutory backing for control over education, licensing, and discipline.[26] But despite the formality of legal authorization, the professions, whether new or newly organized, exhibited a powerful ideology of self-regulation: legal authorization went with a light touch from the state, an emphasis on cooperation within the profession itself and a distaste for the imposition of sanctions. The substantive importance of this part of the regulatory state lay in the central role that occupations called professions increasingly occupied in nineteenth-century economic life: 'new professions proliferated, and organized themselves to demand the same kind of status and independence as the old: the civil engineers in 1818, the architects in 1837, the pharmacists in 1841, the mechanical engineers in 1847, and so on.'[27] The analytical importance lies in the summary above: in the way the pattern of cooperative regulation, evident in the case of the industrial regulation, was replicated here.

The third domain of cooperative regulation directs us to the special nature of British self-regulation in the financial markets, historically the most powerful part of the British economy. Above all, there developed in the Victorian era a distinctive City of London regulatory style: it rested on the internalization of cultural norms and the exercise of subtle social controls, rather than the imposition of overt sanctions—still less on the imposition of legal sanctions.

The next three sections of the chapter trace the origins of this common regulatory culture in the three very different domains of industrial inspection, professional regulation, and the regulation of financial markets. The historical conjuncture of three factors—the timing of British economic development, the timing of British political development, and the timing of the appearance of regulatory institutions—resulted in the dominance of a particular pre-modern ideal. This can be summarized as the ideal of a 'gentleman'; and it was the notion that economic actors were 'gentlemen', with claims to a particular style of treatment by regulators, and with claims to gentlemanly standards that could deliver effective regulation without adversarial controls, that gave rise to, and then institutionalized, cooperative regulation.

Industrialists and Gentlemen

By the last quarter of the nineteenth century, the cooperative style of regulation was institutionalized across the British system of industrial inspection. The process of institutionalization can be traced in the historical origins of four particularly important nineteenth-century inspection systems: the Factory Inspectorate, concerned with the regulation of the characteristic institution of industrialism; the Alkali Inspectorate, the most important ancestor of modern air pollution inspection; the Railway Inspectorate, concerned with safety regulation on the most important nineteenth-century innovation in transport; and the inspection of food purity.

Modern factory law begins with legislation of 1802 (strictly, the Health and Morals of Apprentices Act), a law conspicuous by the absence of any organized system of inspection or enforcement: a typical product, in other words, of the culture of pre-industrial regulation. The Factory Act of 1833 is the first example we have of regulation occasioned by industrialism backed by a system of inspection and inspectors.[28] The cooperative style was soon established. There were four inspectors and the first instructions issued by the inspector for the Midlands to superintendents who visited factories was typical: 'Your best chance of success will be a courteous and conciliatory demeanour towards the mill-owners; and by impressing on their minds that the object of your visits is rather to assist them . . . than to fish out grounds for complaint.'[29] Even this initial early turn to a cooperative style was soon moderated further: there was a sharp decline from even the early modest levels of prosecutions after the late 1840s, the inspectorate openly embracing a philosophy that stressed negotiated compliance over prosecution.[30]

This pattern was replicated in the history of the Alkali Inspectorate, the first great effort (inaugurated in the 1863 Alkali Act) to establish an inspection system to regulate environmental pollution. The first Chief Inspector, Angus Smith, founded a dynasty: his own term of office lasted until 1884, and he trained the three successive Chief Inspectors whose tenure stretched to 1920.[31] After a decade of working the Act, Angus Smith summarized his style of enforcement as follows— or, rather, summarized two styles in terms that left no doubt as to his preferences: 'There are two modes of inspection, one is by a suspicious opponent, desirous of finding evil, and ready to make the most of it. The other is that of a friendly adviser, who treats those whom he visits as gentlemen desirous of doing right.'[32]

Railway safety inspection, after the appointment of the first Inspector General in 1841, showed an even more marked turn to conciliation. Both Parris and Alderman paint a picture of the avoidance of compulsion in implementing regulations; of informality and closeness in social relations between inspectors and companies; and even of the existence of business connections between inspectors and companies.[33] A remark by Parris is especially telling: 'the most striking feature of the records of the Railway Board is the number of serious accidents passed over without enquiry.'[34] The whole period from 1840 to 1870 is summarized by Gourvish thus: 'supervision was general and exhortative rather than mandatory.'[35] Dobbin has illuminatingly explored the wider ideological roots of this abstentionist tradition in his comparative study of railway policy in the nineteenth century. In the British case, it arose from a presumption that company autonomy from external state interference was the prime value that should guide economic policy—a presumption of autonomy that, as we shall see in later chapters, has also shaped the wider system of business self-regulation and company law.[36]

Paulus's study of the control of food and drug adulteration shows a similar pattern: the absorption of the regulatory issues into the routines of the economic community itself. Until the passage of a landmark Act in 1875, the issues had been the subject of agitation turning on the defence of mass consumers who innocently consumed adulterated and/or dangerous products. From the last quarter of the nineteenth century, adulteration was transformed into an issue to do with the regulation of economic competition. From being a crime against the consumer and public interest, it became a tactic in economic competition to be fought over by competing business interests:

the State and business interests slowly evolved a modus operandi that did not cause harm to either. Although strict liability provisions were used, certain kinds of adulteration practices diminished only to be replaced by others. The general refusal on the part of magistrates to fine adulterators appreciably aided in balancing the effects of the Act. Convictions were secured but offenders were not criminalised ... The intended and unintended offence became part of the cost of doing business and was soon accepted by all factions in a rather perfunctory manner.[37]

The effect was both to routinize any regulatory offence, washing off all moral stain, and to shift the actual enforcement process into arenas dominated by producers themselves: 'Food adulteration as it affected the public was no longer an important problem. The issue had shifted: how food adulteration affected the interests of producers, manufacturers and sellers of culinary articles became the central problem to be solved.'[38]

Why did industrial regulation take the turn described in these thumbnail sketches—away from the adversarial world of the criminal law and towards a world of consensus and cooperation? There are plainly a number of historically contingent reasons that help explain what was going on, and they link to a range of well-known analytical accounts of the forces that shape regulatory systems. Above all, they reflect two linked factors: the balance of power between different actors in the regulatory process and the balance of resources between them.

Power relations were plainly important because much of what was at issue in the early history of industrial regulation was the attempt to curb the power of business interests who simultaneously dominated the wider political and economic systems. What is more, it was an attempt at control in a legal system that historically had cordoned off business regulation from the legal system into its own systems of self-control.[39] Sometimes this domination was crude and obvious: railway interests, for example, were powerfully represented in both Parliament and Cabinets throughout the second half of the nineteenth century.[40] Sometimes, the presence of powerful interests frustrated the development of any system of safety regulation of dangerous new technologies. For instance, steam boiler explosions, the result of inadequate inspection of an increasingly powerful and widely used technology, killed an average of over seventy people a year from the 1840s onwards. Yet legislation—and that limited in its scope to investigations after explosions had occurred—was not placed on the statute book until 1882. The rejection of compulsory inspection was due to the lobbying power of companies and insurance societies that had a commercial interest in the existing, ineffective, system of voluntary inspection.[41] When legislation was put on the statute book, its enforcement depended on arms of the state that were often controlled by the regulated interests. Magistrates, for instance, were crucial both to successful prosecution and the imposition of penalties in factory law and in food purity law; in both cases the magistracy was dominated by the very groups—the millocracy and the shopocracy—from whom offenders were drawn, and securing prosecutions and appropriate sanctions was correspondingly difficult.[42] Above all, the fact that regulations were being imposed on powerful economic interests meant that regulatory doctrines had to be shaped around the needs of those interests. In the case of pollution control, this explains the emergence and endurance of the single most important enforcement doctrine: that regulation must be about the search for 'best practicable means' of controlling pollution in cooperation with enterprises, and not about the imposition of fixed emission standards. The development of the 'best practicable means' doctrine was central to the task of gaining industrial confidence in the first decade of the life of the Alkali Inpectorate following the Act of 1863; in the longer run, it became 'the signature tune for the flexible, empirical style of pollution-control in Britain'.[43]

These power inequalities were reinforced by inequalities of resources, especially in the early decades of the life of the Victorian inspectorates. Effective regulation demands that someone, somewhere, expend resources to conduct surveillance and to enforce regulatory breaches when surveillance reveals their occurrence. In regulating whole industries, the resources required are, in principle, huge. In an age when the bureaucratic state with large administrative resources was a novelty, regulatory institutions were poorly resourced. That was true even in cases when the regulation was conducted by the central state itself: for instance, the Joint Stock Companies Act of 1844, 'inspired largely by evidence of insurance fraud, led to the creation of a staff of two, a registrar and his assistant, to try to keep track of many hundreds of companies.'[44] The disparity between the scale of the regulated industries and the numbers of inspectors is a constant theme in the early history of industrial regulation.[45] In some instances, the pioneering character of regulation meant that even the basic data required for surveillance did not exist. For instance, a critical purpose of early factory law was to regulate the employment of children of prescribed ages. That task presumed the existence of what was actually missing in the early decades of regulation— a systematic registry of births.[46] The synoptic gaze of a regulatory state could hardly function unless it had something to gaze on. Behind these immediate problems lay the fundamental fact that there was a huge disparity in resources— in personnel, information, and technical expertise—between regulators and regulated, and this inevitably meant that regulation could not be conducted without the cooperation of the regulated industries. The Victorian revolution in inspection and data gathering was indeed impressive; but it was still puny compared with the social range demanding surveillance.

Considerations of power and resources help make sense of the origins of cooperative regulation because of the timing of British regulatory development. It is hardly surprising that systems of regulation that developed before the rise of modern democratic politics, in a society where government was controlled by an alliance of aristocratic and bourgeois interests, should have taken the path of cooperation and conciliation with powerful industrial interests. But that observation alone cannot explain the endurance of this regulatory style, for the developments of the twentieth century—the rise of democratic politics, the emergence of a state with substantial bureaucratic resources, and the development of a labour movement with strong political and industrial wings—plainly altered the environment in which regulation was conducted. A third set of factors was at work, and they lie behind the successful institutionalization of the club system, which I discuss later in this chapter. In part, the explanation does indeed lie in the ability of institutions to transmit to successive cohorts their standard operating procedures: the 'signature tune' of best practicable means in the Alkali Inspectorate is one instance of that. But a more fundamental feature of the meaning ascribed to industrial regulation explains the endurance of the culture of cooperation. It takes us directly to the importance of the 'gentlemanly ideal' in shaping regulation, and it emphasizes the traditional, pre-democratic ideologies that supported club rule.

The crux of the matter was the inevitability of regulation and inspection and the threat this posed to business interests. In a few instances—as in the case of steam boiler safety summarized above—entrenched interests were powerful enough to resist statutory control. But the rise of regulation in Victorian Britain shows that there were irresistible structural forces creating a new regulatory state that was embodied in statute. These new laws threatened to criminalize economic activity—to create whole new fields of, not merely white-collar, but 'gentlemanly' crime. As one outraged mill owner remarked about the role of Inspectors under the 1833 Factory Act: 'does the Inspector suppose that it is no punishment to a *man*, we will say nothing of a *gentleman of education and standing in society* equal to himself, to be dragged into a court of justice, tried and condemned, and to have his name entered on a register of convicts?'[47] The threatening spectre of law also reflects the importance of the revolutionary legal changes described by Arthurs: the rise of ideologies of legal standardization and centralization were immensely threatening to business interests used to controlling their own affairs by customary law and self-regulation.[48]

How could this undesirable state of affairs be avoided? In part by means that we have seen already in the case of the laws on food adulteration: by constructing regulatory offences as mere technical breaches of rules designed to regulate competitive conditions between industrial interests, and by thus separating them from the world of the criminal law altogether. Carson's studies of an even more sensitive regulatory field—that created by factory legislation concerned with employment conditions and workplace safety—explore the process in more detail. Observance of rules was assumed to be the normal state of affairs since the subjects of regulation were gentlemen who could be trusted; most breaches of rules were thus viewed as mere formal or technical irregularities; and sanctions were reserved for a deviant minority.[49] In this way, to appropriate Carson's term, factory crime and other regulatory crimes were 'conventionalized': were separated from the criminal law and were enforced largely through persuasion, bargaining, and warning.[50] It is worth quoting Carson because he illustrates the tension between the powerful structural forces creating regulatory intervention and the prevailing powers and interests:

there was an internal dynamic or logic within the emergent order of industrialization pointing firmly toward, rather than away from, legislation . . . this impetus notwithstanding, the most significant forms of factory crime in this period were firmly embedded in the structure, organization, and ideology of the relevant productive processes.[51]

As we shall now see, this conception of the special regulation of a 'gentlemanly' activity also shaped the emerging style of professional regulation.

Professionals and Gentlemen

Professionalism is a mode of regulation that is simultaneously a way of controlling competition in labour markets, a form of social stratification, and an avenue of collective social mobility for the members of an occupation. The nineteenth century was the critical period in the development of this regulatory strategy in

Britain: to be more precise, in Perkin's words, 'the mid-Victorian age . . . . was the key period for the emergence and consolidation of the leading professions.'[52] At its core the strategy had three elements, all present in the Apothecaries Act of 1815, which, as I noted earlier, is recognized to have supplied a widely imitated pattern.[53]

The first was, precisely, the resort to legislation to provide a backstop to the powers exercised by the organizing occupation. The second was the use of 'qualification' as a mode of control over entry to the market: as Millerson's study shows, most of the occupations that now successfully claim the label of profession (and many that have not fully managed to make the claim) originally established qualifying status in the nineteenth century.[54] Qualification had a dual function: it asserted the occupation's claim to possession of a systematic and distinctive body of knowledge that could only be revealed by success in some qualifying tests; and institutionally it established, through control of syllabus and testing arrangements, a means by which entry to the occupation could be controlled. The third element in the historic strategy of professionalism was the development of codes, including ethical codes—a development central to market control both because it helped foster trust among potential consumers and because it delimited areas of legitimate and illegitimate competition. The Apothecaries Act was of pioneering importance again because it established a widely imitated pattern: conferring on a self-governing occupation control over entry, of title, and of terms of competition between members, and using the power of the law to buttress those controls.[55] In the succeeding decades, this model encompassed the organization of traditional professions to exploit new markets (medicine), new professions created by the technologies of industry (engineering), and new professions created by the novel demands of new forms of business organization (accountants and actuaries). Our modern, Weberian, understanding of professionalism pictures it as a quintessential example of social closure.[56] But the form of social closure that it represented in nineteenth-century Britain had a number of distinctive features, all of them congruent with the emergent cooperative culture of regulation. Although the power of the state was used to help enforce closure, subsequent intervention by the state in the details of regulation was typically slight. The characteristic culture of professional government was collegial: in other words, it stressed the equality of members of the profession rather than the hierarchies of professional government.[57] The cue for this came from the older professions that, already existing, were institutionally reorganized in the nineteenth century. In part, as a reflection of this collegial style, the codes that the newly emergent associations developed were typically general and skeletal rather than detailed—a contrast with, for instance, the United States of America noted by Millerson.[58]

Three particularly striking instances of the characteristic mode of regulation are provided by medicine, by accounting, and by actuaries. They are striking because they represent very different parts of the new professional domain. Medicine was an 'ancient' profession whose technologies and market opportunities were transformed by both the technological innovations of industrialism and the new social structures of an industrial society. Accounting, as we shall see, was in essence a regulatory creation: in other words, an occupation (or, more accurately, a conglomeration of occupations) brought into existence by the regulatory requirements of the new economic world created by industrialism in nineteenth-century Britain. Actuaries are remarkable because the highly technical nature of their skills might have been expected to lead to an 'ungentlemanly', more meritocratic, and open mode of regulation; but even here, as we shall see, the gentlemanly ideal triumphed. What is, therefore, remarkable about all three is that, despite their very different routes to professional organization, they each exhibit clearly the culture of cooperative regulation and the gentlemanly assumptions that underlay it.

Medicine, of course, was an 'ancient' profession with the defining English marks of the ancient: an emphasis on the importance of social rather than technical skills as a condition of qualification; roots in the ancient universities; and, in its most prestigious parts, a set of institutions—notably the Royal College of Physicians dating from 1518—closely connected with the metropolitan state elites.[59] The Medical Act of 1858 was the defining moment. It organized a modern profession to take advantage of the opportunities (and threats) posed by the new markets in medical consumption, and the new technologies of medical care, created by industrialism. It did this through the device of registration and through the creation of an institution (originally, the General Council on Medical Education and Registration, but universally abbreviated to the General Medical Council), which controlled registration. Legislation was both instrumentally and symbolically the sign that state power now stood behind those who controlled the Council. Control over registration also gave control over the title of doctor—the key sign of competence to clients—and by extension gave control over the terms of qualification (by supervision of the medical curriculum) and control over professional ethics, breaches of which were the grounds for being struck off the register.[60] This system rapidly settled down to a pattern, which lasted for a century, until the profession entered a new period of turbulence in the 1960s. Having invested the Council with statutorily backed powers, the state withdrew from the regulatory arena. There were virtually no interventions in the regulatory system for a century, and those few occurred only on the rare occasions when the Council itself requested them: the inquiry by the Merrison Committee into the regulation of medicine in 1972 was the first for a century.[61] Although the rules of nomination to the Council could, in principle, have allowed external institutions (the universities and the central state) to impose a majority of lay people on the Council, it was, in practice, dominated by doctors, and not until 1950 was there any statutory provision for lay membership.[62] The composition of the Council itself institutionalized a collegial system of regulation in which the Council refrained from any attempts at detailed control over the institutions under its surveillance. Thus, the Council was formally responsible for supervising and approving the medical curriculum in the universities; but even in the 1970s the Merrison Report found that it had virtually given up the business of inspection.[63] The Council extended this collegial culture to the formulation and enforcement of ethical codes on individual practitioners. The rules of professional conduct and misconduct were dominated by a concern with how doctors should treat each other, rather than with their conduct towards patients. Thus, the rules governing the etiquette of relations with other medical professionals—concerning, for instance, the conditions under which doctors could give a second opinion on a medical diagnosis—were detailed and strongly enforced.[64] Nor was this surprising. It was entirely consistent with the collegial conception of professional regulation, which developed from 1858. Professionalism in medicine involved the organization of an elite college of equals, and in this collegial culture detailed control over the professional judgement of the doctor, once admitted to the collegial community, was inappropriate. The fundamental purpose of regulation was to regulate relations between members of the collegial community and to preserve its solidarity. And as in any collegial conception of social life, regulation depended on harmonious, cooperative relations.

The rise of collegial, cooperative regulation in accounting is perhaps even more striking than in the case of medicine. Medicine could look backwards to its ancient origins, and indeed in institutions like the Royal College it already had a template of collegialism. By contrast, while the archaeology of modern accounting systems can be traced to the eighteenth century, the organization of the profession in the nineteenth century involved the separation of the occupation from a long trail of low-status jobs like bookkeeping.[65] More important still, the profession was the product of state regulation of companies. Two stages in that regulation were critical. The Bankruptcy Acts of 1831 and 1849 made discharge from bankruptcy conditional upon the report of an official assignee, typically an accountant.[66] The Companies Act of 1862 is usually labelled 'the accountant's friend' because, in establishing the position of official liquidator in company failure, it created a large market for any group that could claim expertise in accounting failure.[67] With over 13 000 insolvencies over the following 20 years, the act created a lucrative market. The legislation of 1855, which introduced limited liability, created an even more significant market in audit through its provisions for financial reporting—more significant because it was detached from the specialist area of company failure and was a source of recurrent business from prospering firms.[68]

The creation of these new markets spurred professional regulation for two linked reasons: to regulate competition by excluding the 'unqualified'; and, by this exclusion, to foster consumer confidence in the services of accountants. Separate movements to create regional associations culminated with the grant of a Royal Charter and the formation of the Institute of Chartered Accountants in 1880.[69] But from the beginning professionalization was not only marked by an emphasis on the importance of self-regulation independent of the state, it also rejected detailed prescriptive rules, which would have controlled the occupational practices of accountants. The most striking instance of this is the historical refusal to prescribe what might be thought to be the heart of the accountant's art—a single set of accounting conventions and practices. Summarizing his historical review of UK conventions, Willmott writes: 'a variety of accounting conventions and practices were recognized, and it was left to the "expert" judgement of the accountant to determine which convention to apply.'[70] As late as the 1920s, the Institute of Chartered Accountants was resisting any prescriptive form for company accounts. The nineteenth-century regulatory history of accounting is remarkable because, since the profession was the product of state regulation, one might have expected it also to be the creature of the state. But the reality was different: the model of independent collegialism, involving both independence from the state and a 'light touch' system of internal collegiate controls, was established.[71] Kynaston perhaps exaggerates— but not by much—when he describes company annual accounts of the late nineteenth century as 'a world of systematically concealed or distorted financial information'.[72] It is an instructive background to the problems facing auditors and accountants in the twenty-first century, which we discuss in Chapter 4, that their key nineteenth-century role was to bamboozle, not enlighten, investors.

The common feature linking a reorganized 'ancient' profession, medicine, and a product of the age of state regulation of the new domain of company law, accounting, is, therefore, the development of the characteristic features of cooperative regulation. The state endowed regulatory institutions with authority, but then practised the lightest of light touch controls; the self-regulatory institutions themselves, in turn, adopted collegial regulation—a style that presumed control among an elite of equals, was designed to foster collegial solidarity, and relegated hierarchical controls and the exercise of sanctions to a marginal role. The two professions are chosen here as illustrations precisely because they represent very different historical routes to professionalism, yet exhibit this common cooperative culture. A remark by Reader about the older professions thus has a more general application: what they seem to have conceived of themselves as doing, he remarks, 'was admitting educated gentlemen to small, self-governing groups of their social equals'.[73] The spread of Royal Charters is particularly revealing in this respect. Before the changes in company law that allowed incorporation, a Charter was a legal necessity. Afterwards it ceased to have any functional significance, but its symbolic importance—precisely as a sign of the gentlemanly distance from trade—became critical.[74] Hence, the late nineteenth-century flood of occupations acquiring Royal Charters: Accountants 1880; Surveyors 1881; Actuaries 1884; Chemists 1885; Journalists 1890; Patent Agents 1891; Librarians 1898.[75]

The idea of a profession as a college of gentlemen, preferably sanctified by grace of the Royal touch, raised the status of occupations that were being created, or reshaped, by industrialism. It associated new occupations, by reflection, with the prestige and institutional connections of two of the three ancient professions, law and medicine. But, in the case of accounting, it involved something more than the symbolic search for gentlemanly status or the ideological mystification of sanctification by Royalty. The rise of accounting involved not only a struggle for control within the occupation itself, but also fierce struggles for business with lawyers, notably in the lucrative fields of insolvency and bankruptcy administration.[76] Faced with a struggle with a quintessential ancient profession, the acquisition of the status of a college of gentlemen, accompanied by royal sponsorship, was a key weapon in the competition for custom.

This stress on the gentlemanly ideal, and the way it legitimized professional freedom from state control, is revealed with remarkable clarity in our third case, actuaries. It is remarkable because the actuarial profession emerged in the nineteenth century as the claimed possessor of highly technical skills of estimation, which were vital to the prudential stability of the new insurance industries, and it might, therefore, have been expected to be more modern in its regulatory ideology. Yet, Porter has shown how, faced with Parliamentary pressure to systematize actuarial knowledge and subject insurance companies to explicit rules, the spokesmen for the new profession retreated behind the gentlemanly ideal. In their responses to Parliamentary questioning, an emphasis on the importance of 'character' is 'repeated like a refrain' in the remarks of the defenders of the profession.[77] Quoting a series of Parliamentary witnesses, Porter continues:

Since we must depend on the skill and integrity of the actuary to prepare the data, he might as well be trusted to make the final calculation. Actuaries are 'gentlemen of character', reported William Farr, and the government should leave the preparation of accounts to them. No quantitative measure of solvency can be adequate, insisted Francis Neison . . . There is always 'special knowledge beyond the accounts, not appearing in the books of the institution'.[78]

Accountancy and the actuarial profession are particularly relevant illustrations here for an additional reason: because their regulation overlapped with the third domain examined now, the regulation of the financial markets in the City of London.

Financiers and Gentlemen

A large literature demonstrates that the City of London is special in the British economy: in its global orientation; in its weight in the global financial system; and, as we shall now see, in its system of regulation.[79] The City has historically been the single most important example in the domestic economy of what is summarily called self-regulation. Until the institutional upheavals of the last 15 years—discussed in Chapter 4—regulation of City markets was a study in cooperative regulation. Although there naturally existed important differences of nuance between different markets, key features recurred: the law was of marginal importance; non-legal codes, even where they existed, generally provided broad guidelines rather than detailed rules; and, in consequence, regulation was supposed to be the product of internalized cultural restraints and the subtle exercise of social controls. This summarily describes the historical mode of regulation in securities markets, especially in the Stock Exchange; in banking markets, both in retail and in merchant banking; in the money markets; and in important commercial markets like the reinsurance markets.[80] And, more than in any part of the British economy, the City developed an explicit ideology of cooperative regulation to support its institutional practices. That ideology emphasized the supposed benefits of a cooperative style, elaborated the grounds for not creating a distinct cadre of regulators, and stressed flexibility and negotiated compliance. It also managed what professions could rarely do: it institutionalized this entire system in club-like bodies such as the Stock Exchange and the Corporation of Lloyd's.[81]

Many institutions and markets critical to the City system of self-regulation had ancient histories: for example, the Bank of England, which, as we shall shortly see, was the linchpin of the whole system, dated from 1694. But like much else in British economic regulation, the 'traditional' City system was the product of the Victorian climacteric: it was largely invented in the middle and later decades of the nineteenth century at the moment when the City was also becoming a linchpin of the global financial system. That invention was then elaborated into a stable institutional system with a legitimizing ideology in the first three decades of the twentieth century.

The Victorian story of City regulation is partly the story of the adaptation of particular institutions and markets, and partly a grander story of the rise of the Bank of England as the manager of the interests of the wider City system. For instance, in securities, the legal reforms that created joint stock companies simultaneously created opportunities for market expansion by existing exchanges and, through a succession of scandals, pushed these exchanges into reforms.[82] By the turn of the twentieth-century, stock jobbing, once an occupation occupying the same sort of cultural and socially marginal reputation as racecourse bookmaking, had become a respected occupation for gentlemen. The definitive sign of its integration into an upper-class world came with the first old Etonian jobber in the 1890s.[83] Even as early as the 1870s, the ideology of light touch self-regulation was already well established. Here is a Royal Commission on the Stock Exchange in 1878:

The existing body of rules and regulations have been formed with much care, and are the result of long experience and the vigilant attention of a body of persons intimately acquainted with the needs and exigencies of the community for whom they have legislated. Any attempt to reduce these rules to the limits of the ordinary law of the land, or to abolish all checks and safeguards not to be found in that law, would in our opinion be detrimental to the honest and efficient conduct of business.[84]

But the most important key to wider development of the system of regulation lay not in the particular markets but in the transformed regulatory role of the Bank of England. The most important transforming forces were structural. From the 1820s to the 1890s, the instability of the new banking worlds in the City created by the booming domestic economy, and by the City's central role in the wider global system, led to a succession of banking crises.[85] Out of these crises the Bank virtually invented itself as a modern central bank. It emerged as the manager of systemic crises, and by extension the prudential regulator of the banking system in times of normality. The consummation was the Bank's role in organizing the rescue of the House of Baring in the great crisis of 1890.[86] The single most important feature of the Bank's role from our point of view was that it took place largely beyond the law, and indeed formally even beyond the boundaries of the state, since at that time the Bank was legally a privately owned institution, and in practice one largely controlled by a particular segment of the City elite, merchants and merchant bankers.[87] Because the Bank neither had, nor sought, the formal authority of the law in this critical sphere of financial regulation, the familiar traits soon emerged: control through informal pressure; stress on the informal willingness of institutions to cooperate; and avoidance of any adversarial confrontation in favour of the private exercise of informal pressures and reliance on internalized cultural controls. In some cases, this regulatory role just emerged as a by-product of the Bank's market operations. For instance, in managing the overnight money market in London, the Bank developed close working relations with the Discount Market, culminating eventually in the organization of the Discount Houses into a self-regulatory cartel.[88] Until the 1970s, indeed, the Bank's supervisory duties were run as a by-product of its Discount Office.[89]

As the Bank's regulatory importance grew, another critical feature of club regulation in the City developed: the Bank became the mediator between the City and the central institutions of the state. This role was the key to the development of the distinctive City form of regulation, for without the Bank as mediator it was inevitable that regulation would have taken an alternative route—via the statute book. It was the Bank's success in establishing itself as the expert on control in the City, and as the mediator between the City and departments like the Treasury, that ensured that it could claim the right both to represent the City in Whitehall and Whitehall in the City.[90]

The development of this distinctive City style of regulation had its roots, in part, in conditions that we have already encountered in the cases of industrial inspection and professional regulation. The timing of British economic and political development was again crucial. The development of an industrial economy; a system of corporate ownership based on joint stock companies; a complex banking system woven into both the domestic economy and the developing global financial system: all produced immensely powerful pressures for regulation. The most obvious manifestations of these pressures were the series of great Victorian financial crises: the great frauds, and above all the systemic crises in banking in 1825, 1847, 1866, and 1890.[91] The publication of Bagehot's *Lombard Street* in 1873 marked the classic statement of central banking as a practical art.[92] As in the case of industrial inspection, regulation was now unavoidable; the only issue concerned how it was to be done. The regulatory capacities of the Victorian state in the financial sphere were pitiful; by contrast, the Bank of England had performed a semi-public role virtually since its foundation. But the Bank's own regulatory resources were also primitive. It was inventing modern central banking, but had none of the resources of a modern central bank. Until Montagu Norman's long tenure (1920–44), it lacked even a permanent governor and it neither possessed, nor desired, statutory power over the markets. Looking back at its nineteenth-century history in 1931, the Macmillan Committee put it succinctly: 'Historically the principles of central banking were established empirically long before they received theoretical formulation.'[93] All these factors pushed the regulatory system in the direction of an informal cooperative style.

But that style could only work by setting limits to competition. Unacceptable competition—to the point in some cases of fraud—was what lay at the root of the problems, which brought about pressure for regulation in the first place. The brutal, ferocious competition that had simultaneously built the City and pushed it into a series of systemic crises had, by the turn of the century, been transformed into a more gentlemanly model that was taming excessive competition.[94] To support this gentlemanly culture, ascription in recruitment became an important underpinning mechanism. Lisle-Williams documents the importance of dynastic succession from 1850, and shows how these dynasties, in turn, were incorporated into surrounding aristocratic elites. In the period 1850–90, there occurred, Lisle-Williams writes:

the revival and selective reconstitution of the gentleman, a social type which was hegemonic within the propertied class. It was this ideal and the constellation of values associated with it that were grafted onto the social organization of the City by the merchant banking families in the later Victorian era.[95]

Industrial inspection, professional regulation, financial regulation: all were laid down in the Victorian era. But how did they manage to outlive that age?

EMBEDDING THE VICTORIAN REGULATORY STATE

What I have here been calling the 'Victorian regulatory state' was not a settled creation, and for the most obvious of reasons: the period of creation was not of a single piece. If we stick literally to the image of a Victorian era, then the Britain of 1837 was very different from the Britain of 1901. Not only was Victorian England a place of immense social and administrative change—it faced change of a particularly challenging and revolutionary sort. The twin challenges of democratic politics and working-class organizations seemed particularly threatening to large sections of the political elite.[96]

These threats were, of course, fully realized early in the following century. By 1918, over half a century of electoral reform had produced something close to universal adult suffrage. And in the General Election of December that year, the Labour Party rose as the main opponent of the Conservatives, marking the emergence of labour as a major political force. The war itself had caused a great surge of state intervention. In 1918, therefore, Victorian nightmares of popular revolution came to life: a large state, near universal adult suffrage, a popular working class party using the rhetoric of socialist utopianism. Yet the outcome in practice resembled Burke's verdict on 1688: not a revolution achieved, but a revolution averted.

Averting this revolution involved work well beyond the concern of these pages: defending the social order is a major theme of British politics in the early decades of the twentieth century. But embedding the institutions and practices of what we have been calling Victorian regulation was an important contribution to the process. Victorian regulation could not simply be transplanted to the very different world of the twentieth century. 'Embedding' is a consciously chosen image: to successfully embed the old system in the new world of formal democracy often meant reshaping it to fit new surroundings. Nevertheless, one of the great political achievements of the first half of the twentieth century was to arrive at its mid-point with many of the key cultural understandings and institutional practices of the old club regulation still intact.

Embedding Self-Regulation in the City

By the beginning of the twentieth century, the culture of the City elites—gentlemanly restraint, ascriptive recruitment, and the economic closure of privileged markets—fostered a style of regulation that emphasized informality, collegiality, and cooperation. But the first three decades of the twentieth century witnessed great economic and political changes in the City's environment, and these made the maintenance of this style of regulation even more vital. The dominant regulatory culture had been created during the period of the City's—and Britain's—ascendancy in the global financial system. The First World War, British economic decline, and then the great world depression dealt fatal blows to that ascendancy. The inter-war years, in particular, were periods of great stress in the City, and the reaction—led and managed by the Bank of England—was further to suppress competition and strengthen cartels. This forged an even closer connection between economic practices and regulation. In the organization of markets, supplemented by informal pressure from the Bank of England, lay the essence of the regulatory system. Admission to the stock exchange, to the Discount Market, to the Accepting Houses Committee (the elite of merchant banks founded in 1914) entailed observance both of the rules of business and the norms of gentlemanly behaviour.[97]

If economic developments strengthened cooperative regulation, political developments made its maintenance vital. Late Victorian England saw the beginnings of democratic politics: successive extensions of the franchise; the rise of radical Liberalism; the organization of the industrial wing of the labour movement; and the challenge to Liberalism from labour's political wing. These developments, especially when accompanied by a rhetoric of utopian socialism, were immensely threatening to City markets.[98] The ideology of cooperative regulation now began to perform an important role in protecting City interests from the threats of democratic politics, for this ideology precisely rejected the processes associated with parliamentary democracy—notably the passage of regulatory laws, with all the potential for interference in markets that this opened up, and the potential demands for parliamentary oversight that it might entail. But providing this protective bulwark demanded a more active and organized role for the Bank of England. Under the governorship of Montagu Norman (1920–44), this transformation took place.[99] The Bank became partly professionalized. The symbol of this was the transformation of the Governor's own role from that of someone selected from the City to serve a short period of office to a permanent figure who dominated the City for over 20 years. Not all the City's attempts to defend itself were successful: it took a considerable mauling, for instance, in the hearings of the Macmillan Committee.[100] But its achievements were still considerable. The two landmark official enquiries in the age of club government in the twentieth century endorsed self-regulation and City autonomy. Here is the Macmillan Committee, the most important official inquiry into the financial system of the inter-war years, writing in 1931:

An important thing to bear in mind is that financial policy can only be carried into effect by those whose business it is. We have in this country a great financial and banking organization with great experience and traditions. It is through and with that organization that we have to work, for they alone are the repositories of the skill and knowledge and they alone possess the equipment necessary for the management of our financial affairs.[101]

And here, nearly three decades later, is the picture painted by the Radcliffe Committee, writing in this instance of the particular relations between the Bank of England and the clearing banks, the heart of the mechanism by which monetary policy was operated:

The Bank of England is in continual touch with the clearing banks both on operational matters and on questions of policy . . . It is on this relationship, and on the mutual trust and confidence that are the basis of the relationship, rather than on formal powers or the regular provision of statistical information that the Bank has relied in seeking to inform itself about and influence the clearing banks.[102]

This description of the relations with the clearing banks is particularly instructive. The clearing banks had originated outside the City's magic circles, developing from provincial origins. In some instances—the most notable being the Midland Bank, before 1914 the largest bank in the world—they were closely connected to the manufacturing sector.[103] But the wave of banking amalgamations immediately after the First World War consolidated clearing banks into a metropolitan cartel: a small number of institutions controlled from London and safely integrated into the club world of the City.[104]

The successful embedding of the Victorian system in the very different world of the twentieth century was largely the work of the Bank of England. That success had components that may crudely be distinguished as institutional, economic, and ideological.

Institutionally, the Bank transformed itself in the 25 years or so after 1914 and did so in ways vital to the preservation of club regulation. The Bank, partly because of its central role in managing the state's debt raising needs, emerged as a key institution within Whitehall, whereas before the First World War it had largely operated in isolation from the central machinery of the state.[105] The acquisition of a central role in Whitehall, based as it was on the Bank's ability to manage the financial markets, also gave it authority to act in another key role: as the intermediary between the central state and the city markets. From this period there grew up an understanding, which endured for more than half a century, that the Bank would be the virtually sole intermediary between the City and the central state, and that this intermediary role would essentially be practised in an informal, uncodified way.[106] The acquisition of this key institutional role was accompanied by important internal changes to the organization of the Bank. The most important is signified by the long career of Montagu Norman as Bank Governor. Norman's domestic achievement was internally to professionalize many of the Bank's operations. He also imprinted on it a particular style of working. This style grew out of his own temperamental dislike of intellectualizing the grounds of policy, but it fitted the need to embed the old Victorian system: dislike of formal methods of doing business; a corresponding emphasis on the importance of personal connections; a dislike of politics and politicians, especially of their presence in the City; and fierce defence of the role of the Bank as the main manager of both the City's interests and its regulatory practices. It amounted to privileging tacit knowledge over the explicit knowledge of 'experts'.[107] As Norman himself put it in his evidence to the Macmillan Committee in 1931: 'I do not attach importance to great elaboration of statistical information.'[108] Nor was this just a product of Norman's own quirky instinctiveness. Nearly 30 years later, one of his successors, responding to debate about the Bank's mode of operation prompted by the hearings of the Radcliffe inquiry into the workings of the monetary system, dismissed the utility of systematic research with the observation that 'the Bank of England must be a Bank and not a study group'.[109]

The club world was reinforced by economic changes mostly prompted by the Bank in the quarter-century after 1914. There occurred a large-scale cartelization of City markets, in part because of the economic pressures arising from the destruction of the old open international financial system in which the City had prospered and, in part, because of the world slump after 1929. The Bank sponsored cartelization as a way of maintaining stability in markets; but cartelization also reinforced self-regulation, by forging a connection between membership of self-governing 'clubs' and the economic privileges arising from membership of the clubs.[110] The outcome solidified the club structure. As the central bank Governor put it in evidence submitted to the Radcliffe Committee at the end of the 1950s: 'If I want to talk to the representatives of the British Banks, or indeed of the whole financial community, we can usually get together in one room in about half-an-hour.'[111] The connection between club regulation and cartelization was, as we shall see, to prove fatal to the club system from the 1970s onwards.

The institutional and economic structures of club regulation were underpinned by systematizing the Victorian regulatory ideology. It is not surprising that this happened. Before the advent of formal democracy, the rise of labour, and the development of an interventionist state, the ideology could remain implicit, since it was born in an era when business values were hegemonic and the state's own ambitions and resources were limited. At a number of points in the twentieth century, by contrast, the City found itself on the defensive, having explicitly to justify its regulatory practices. It was on these occasions—for example, in evidence to the great enquiries into the financial system—that the ideology of self-regulation was systematized, in a way hardly necessary in the Victorian era. The key defence against the threat of democratic politics was the independence of the City's main protector, the Bank of England. In his evidence to the Macmillan Committee in 1929, the Deputy Governor outlined the official grounds for Bank independence from democratic government:

I think I may claim that it is an accepted principle that (the Bank) should be free from political pressure . . . . It has duties to the Government of the day undoubtedly, provided it is, as I suggest it should be, the banker of the Government, but its duties in that respect are the ordinary duties of banker to client. It should be free from being required to submit to political pressure and to subordinate sound finance to the dictates of political expediency. For that reason, as I say, we feel that it should be free from political control.[112]

The systematized ideology amounted to a rationalization of the practices of the Victorian era: an emphasis on the importance of practical knowledge as the key to effective regulation, thus privileging actors in markets in the regulatory process over any outside 'experts'; an emphasis on the importance of regulation created and administered by actors in markets themselves, on the grounds that this was most likely to encourage full-hearted compliance with rules; and an emphasis on the superiority of such systems of regulation over more legally based modes in responding flexibly to the changing character of markets. Marginalizing the law also marginalized Parliament and the democratic forces that Parliament threatened to mobilize. And marginalizing law, Parliament, and democracy was, as we shall see later in this chapter, also a key to the wider character of club government in Britain.

Embedding Self-Regulation in the Professions

In one obvious sense, the professions were more vulnerable to the threat of external regulatory control by the twentieth-century state than was the City: they possessed no institution comparable to the Bank of England, which could simultaneously protect against the state, act as a stimulus to collective action, and systematize an appropriate regulatory ideology. And, indeed, in the twentieth century, the experience of different occupations claiming the label 'profession' was highly varied. Much depended on the dominant client group that the occupation served. For instance, the failure of teaching to develop strong institutions of self-regulation, and the fact that it was regulated by an inspectorate of the central state—albeit an inspectorate that practised remarkably light touch controls—reflected the fact that the profession was almost from the beginning a client group of the state.[113]

What was nevertheless remarkable until well past the second half of the twentieth century was the extent to which the Victorian regulatory settlements for key high-status professions—medicine, law, accounting—'held' and the extent to which these settlements provided both an institutional template and a regulatory ideology that was widely copied. This is the theme to emerge most clearly from the only systematic comprehensive account of professional regulation in the years between the two world wars, that conducted by Carr-Saunders and Wilson. The date of publication, 1933, is particularly helpful because it covers the moment when the embedding of the old Victorian systems was complete. Three themes emerge: the persistence of the collegial, anti-hierarchical model of internal professional government; the widespread autonomy from external control in the practice of professional government; and the weak and limited character of public, especially Parliamentary, control, despite the fact that these institutions were typically wielding power originally derived from Parliament.[114] The successful embedding of the Victorian pattern of professional regulation is all the more remarkable in view of the fact that many of the occupations that had originally developed as liberal professions—that is, small entrepreneurs making a living from cash transactions with individual clients—in the twentieth century began to derive all, or a substantial proportion, of their incomes from the state. Indeed, in general, the twentieth century saw the large-scale decline of the liberal professional and the incorporation of professions into large bureaucracies, either private or public sector.[115] The economic setting of the medical profession, for instance, had been transformed by the foundation of the National Health Service in 1948. Yet, almost a quarter of a century later, the report of the Merrison Committee into the regulation of the profession still defended the Victorian ideology of professional self-regulation.[116] The economic setting of the law had likewise, by the 1980s, been utterly transformed, by the rise of corporate law and by the rise of the state as a major source of income in the form of legal aid; yet, Abel could still, in that decade, characterize both the English Bar and solicitors as late nineteenth-century creations.[117]

The striking endurance of the Victorian professional settlement was due to three factors. The first might best be summarized, quite simply, as spillover—especially as spillover from the successful institutionalization of self-regulation in the City. The ideology of self-regulation that developed to legitimize the Victorian regulatory settlement both contributed to, and benefited from, the wider British regulatory ideology. We have been examining the different regulatory domains independently, but, of course, in practice neither their operation nor the development of their ideology took place in this fashion. The City's defence of self-regulation transcended financial markets themselves, important as they were, for the social ascendancy of the City gave to its regulatory ideology a wider prestige. There was also obvious overlap between, for example, some professional elites, such as those of the elite of commercial law, and the elites in the City; and there was in some cases an obvious overlap in occupational jurisdictions, as, for example, in the case of accounting and the law.

A second factor is that at least some of these professions were particularly well placed to defend their autonomy against outsiders. The obvious examples again are law and medicine. The judiciary and high-status corporate bodies, like the Inns of Court, controlled key aspects of the regulation of the legal profession.[118] An even more striking instance, because it represented open defence of professional prerogative, was the settlement won by the medical profession when the National Health Service was established. Not only was the nineteenth-century structure of regulation organized around the General Medical Council left largely intact, both General Practitioners and consultants were also able to establish an 'arms length' relationship with the state, for instance, through a special employment status that preserved the traditional independence of the liberal professional.[119]

The success of doctors in preserving much of the Victorian regulatory settlement at the foundation of the National Health Service also sprang from a third factor, the most fundamental of all: the central role that professionals came to play in the world of the interventionist state in the twentieth century. The new world of the interventionist state created dangers for professional autonomy, but it also offered opportunities. Perkin has charted the way the discourse of professionalism—of impartial expertise brought to bear on social problems—came to dominate debates about social reform in the first half of the century, and thus shaped the welfare state settlement of those decades.[120] The welfare state was a professional state: it depended on professionals both for the expertise needed to formulate policy and to deliver that policy—a dependence illustrated to perfection by the National Health Service. Thus, for the Victorian professional settlement, the rise of the interventionist state in the twentieth century was a double-edged sword: it represented a threat, but also offered opportunities because the state relied so heavily on expertise, and professionals were recognized as key holders of expertise. Even professions that were successfully incorporated into the state apparatus—like teachers—managed to negotiate a considerable area of occupational autonomy in the first half of the twentieth century, and some more prestigious parts of the education system were able to use their strategic position in the club system to enjoy a particularly privileged autonomy.[121] The most obvious examples of the latter are provided by the twin cases of the old universities and the elite of the scientific research establishment that were able to use institutions like the University Grants Committee and the Research Councils to secure public funding without any serious public accountability. It is striking that these institutions of professional protection were developed in the very years when club regulation faced its greatest threats: the original prototype of a research council (for medical research) dates from 1913, while the UGC was founded in 1919.[122] (I examine these last two cases in more detail in Chapter 6.)

Embedding the Inspectorates

We have seen that even when the Victorian regulatory state developed the formal apparatus of state regulation—through inspectorates empowered by law—it nevertheless practised something that approximated to self-regulation: that is to say, it developed a style of cooperative regulation that disavowed sanctions, especially legal sanctions, in the inspection process. That style was well embedded throughout the first two-thirds of the twentieth century. A succession of inspectors, from a variety of domains, throughout this period virtually repeated word for word the regulatory philosophy of the Victorian founders.[123] Indeed, as recently as the beginning of the 1970s, this is what the Robens Committee was being told by 'the responsible government departments and inspectorates' across the whole range of health and safety. They

tended in their evidence to describe their primary functions in terms of improving standards of health and safety at work, rather than in terms of law enforcement as such. While inspectors regard the threat of legal sanctions in the background as important, in practice they find that in most cases advice and persuasion achieve more than duress. They have learned from experience that recourse to legal sanctions is only one means of achieving objectives of safety legislation, and that it is rarely the most apt or effective.[124]

As this observation demonstrates, the 'official' view was that cooperative, informal regulation was demanded as a condition of effective enforcement. But this notion that it was a functional adaptation to the needs of regulation was ideological mystification. Vogel's comparative study of Anglo-American environmental regulation, which was based on fieldwork done when the club system still endured, concluded, after a close examination of the evidence on effectiveness, that 'there is no evidence that either nation's policies have been particularly more or less effective; that is to say, depending on one's point of view, they have been equally effective or equally inadequate'.[125] The differences were not due to functional requirements—they were, as Vogel says, due to politics.[126] This argument is reinforced by the many failures of the British system, which were themselves reflections of the embedded culture of cooperative regulation. For instance, the regulation of the health of those working with asbestosis showed how the cooperative system could operate with indifference to manifest dangers.[127] Carson's study of the regulation of safety in the North Sea oil exploration industry also showed an elementary failure to perform obvious inspections and enforcements.[128] As far as cooperative regulation was concerned, therefore, effectiveness had nothing to do with its persistence.

The endurance of the Victorian system in the case of the two other domains examined here was explained largely by reference to particular features of those domains: in the case of the City, by the emergence of the Bank of England as a key organizing institution for the City; in the case of the professions, by the way the very interventionist state that might have been thought to threaten professional autonomy in fact buttressed the Victorian system because it needed the expertise of the professions to realize its interventionist ambitions. In the case of the Inspectorates, some of the explanation must lie in the ability of institutions, once an organizational culture was established, to transmit that culture to successive cohorts of officers. This kind of transmission is, for instance, plainly observable in the case of the Alkali Inspectorate: 'in 1950 . . . . Its style of working was in the tradition set by Angus Smith: pragmatic, flexible, forbearing in difficult cases, strict where strictness was justified.'[129]

Nor was this merely public ideology; it permeated the practice of inspection. While naturally there were differences between different inspectorates, the attachment to a cooperative philosophy and practice was remarkably consistent. Hawkins's ethnographic study of the enforcement of water pollution law, based on fieldwork done in the mid to late 1970s, presented a regulatory culture where law was a 'last resort'.[130] Hutter's studies of the Health and Safety Executive, based on field work from the early 1980s, and of the Railway Inspectorate, based on field work for the end of that decade, likewise stressed the centrality of cooperation both at site and industry level.[131] The history of school inspection is particularly striking, for in the nineteenth-century it had indeed developed an unusually inquisitorial inspection style with the inspector as a 'tester and enforcer' in the pursuit of value for public money.[132] But from the end of the First World War, Matthew Arnold's patrician hostility to inspection as the measurement of attainment triumphed; inspections became both infrequent and cooperative in style.[133] Rhodes's survey of the whole inspection system, incorporating evidence up to the end of the 1970s, concluded: 'Prevention rather than detection, persuasion rather than coercion, friendly advice rather than the heavy hand of the law—these are the characteristic ways in which enforcement inspectors behave.'[134]

The small scale of the system helped to transmit these values through successive cohorts. Club regulation worked best when the club numbers were small, and this was a condition amply fulfilled in the case of the inspectorates. These were communities where the participants were sufficiently small in number to forge personal relations and to communicate informally. If we take what in many ways was the heart of industrial regulation in Britain—the central government inspectorates concerned with the regulation of health and safety—the total numbers of all inspectors in 1960 was only 750; and some of these, such as the 70 concerned with health and safety inspection in agriculture, were combining their duties with very different ones concerned with agricultural wages.[135] The world of environmental inspection was similarly small in scale: as late as the 1980s, 'the central air pollution inspectorate numbered, at most, only a few hundred people'.[136]

But there was a more fundamental reason still for the persistence of the Victorian settlement within the Inspectorates, and this reason both links our discussion to the wider character of the British state and begins to anticipate some of the reasons for the breakdown of the whole Victorian settlement from the 1960s onwards: it exactly fitted the wider culture of club government, especially in the metropolis. Nor is that surprising; the surprise would be if there were some fundamental disjuncture between the Inspectorates and the wider civil service. The ideology of cooperative regulation was of a piece with the wider, well-established administrative culture: a culture that valued the civil servant as a source of policy advice to ministers, a generalist able to roam widely and analytically over a range of policy problems, rather than an expert in particular fields of administration.

Being a success as a senior civil servant involved mastering, through long experience in a small world of Whitehall, the nuances of elite political culture. 'Expertise' came with experience. The elite of the civil service had little capacity, and desired little capacity, to intervene directly in the detailed delivery of policy.[137]

This outcome—the rise to hegemonic status of a mandarin, club culture—is connected to one of the great mystery stories of the original Victorian regulatory system, for one part of that original inspection represented a 'road not taken' in the development of the regulatory state. After the mid-1830s, the Victorian state turned to the device of independent regulatory commissions, for regulatory domains as different as social policy (the Poor Law) and the new industries (for instance, railways).[138] In short, there existed the potential for the rise of powerful regulatory agencies of the sort that came to characterize the American regulatory state in the twentieth century. By the 1870s, this had shrunk to a single domain—the Railway Commission—and by the early twentieth century, this had shrunk in turn into the Railway Rates Tribunal, charged only with the administration of price controls in a cartelized, declining industry.[139] Many contingent factors explain the death of this alternative form of the regulatory state: for instance, in the case of the Poor Law Commissioners, revulsion against the ferocity of the social regime they were administering.[140] But, fundamentally, what destroyed them was the power of traditional constitutional ideologies, notably those that insisted on the central department with a ministerial head as the only proper way of organizing public regulation. In this way, the regimes of inspection were drawn into the control of the metropolitan elite in Whitehall.[141]

My argument in summary is, therefore, as follows. Key features of the wider administrative culture—the rejection of involvement in the detailed implementation of policy, the stress on knowledge acquired by experience over formal rules, the reliance on the wider institutions of civil society actually to deliver policy—were congruent with the ideology of cooperative, consensual regulation practised by the inspectorates for much of the twentieth century. This wider administrative culture was rooted in the system of club government that dominated metropolitan politics in Britain. This was the final important mechanism in embedding the Victorian settlement for the first six or seven decades of the twentieth century.

THE COMING CRISIS OF CLUB REGULATION

Regulation is nothing new in Britain. There was an extensive system of regulation in pre-industrial England, shaped by forces that will be entirely familiar to any modern observer: the competition between rising and falling industry; the efforts of domestic interests to use public power to protect or expand markets at the expense of foreign competitors; the need to manage social problems to protect the existing social order. But while these are modern in style, the means to realize them were pre-modern and thus ineffective. Industrialism marked a watershed in both the scale of regulatory ambitions and in the means of their realization; what we conventionally define as Victorian Britain was the era when both scale and means were combined. A distinctive Victorian regulatory state was created, and it proved extraordinarily resilient: as late as the 1960s, we could still see its essential outlines. It turned up, and persisted, in the most unexpected places. What could seem more exposed to the adversarial world of democratic politics, for instance, than the regulation of industrial relations, striking as it did at the heart of class relations in a society where class was the dominant organizing mode of politics? Yet, as late as the 1960s, key assumptions of club regulation, notably the insistence on informality, cooperation, and freedom from state control, still guided policy in industrial relations. Here is the summary given by the Donovan (Royal) Commission into trade unions and employers' associations of the state of the regulatory art in 1968:

Until recent times it was a distinctive feature of our system of industrial relations that the State remained aloof from the process of collective bargaining in private industry . . . This abstentionist attitude has reflected a belief that it is better in the long run for the law to interfere as little as possible in the settlement of questions arising between employers and workmen (sic) over pay and conditions of work. Parliament has long been committed to the view that the best means of settling such questions is voluntary, collective bargaining.[142]

The fate of Donovan—the fact that the Commission was wracked by internal divisions, and the fact that the analysis of the majority Report was swept away in the events of the early 1970s—was indeed one early sign of the decay of the club system.[143]

The character of the Victorian regulatory state, and of its twentieth-century legacy, was critically linked to the timing of its development. Like so much else in the evolution of British institutions, the fact of early industrialism was crucial. The Victorian regulatory state was created in a world where formal democracy existed only as a frightening spectre, and where oligarchies, both local and national, controlled politics; where business was a hegemonic interest and, therefore, where the crucial struggles were between different factions of business; and where the state had few of the fiscal and bureaucratic resources that it acquired in the twentieth century. The early decades of that century saw challenges to the system of club rule: the extension of formal democracy; the rise of the Labour Movement, itself a muffled echo of the frightening threats to the established order from the revolutionary socialism that swept across large parts of Europe; the growing scale of state intervention; cultural changes—like the decline of established religion and the changed condition of women—that threatened traditional hierarchies. Embedding Victorian regulatory institutions and practices in the twentieth century helped provide defences against these developments: it privileged the tacit knowledge of insiders over systematic public knowledge and it insulated regulatory worlds from those of parliamentary and electoral politics. Viewed thus, the persistence of these patterns into the era of democratic politics is hardly surprising: they were needed to provide protection from democracy. In this way, the great Victorian apprehensions about the revolutionary consequences of popular rule were averted.

Institutionally and ideologically, the system of self-regulation was at the heart of all this. Its watchwords—informality, flexibility, cooperation—summarized the dominant British regulatory ideology. The club-like structure of so much self-regulation in the professions and in the City was the institutional epitome of this wider system of club government. The scale and reach of the system of self-regulation was the key to insulating interests from democratic control, for easily the most effective form of protection was to organize an activity out of politics altogether, by defining it as belonging to the domain of self-regulation. But this was a strange, historically fragile settlement: oligarchy designed to provide protection against democracy. It was bound to pitch into crisis sooner or later. When the crisis came it was particularly deep in the worlds of self-regulation. This is the subject of Chapter 4.

4

Transforming Self-Regulation

THE MOSAIC OF SELF-REGULATION

Understanding how self-regulation is changing presumes something obvious: that we understand what self-regulation itself amounts to. But, in practice, 'self-regulation' is hard to clarify, and for a revealing reason. It is more than an institutional arrangement; it is a regulatory ideology mobilized to legitimize any number of particular institutional arrangements. We commonly find the language of self-regulation used in self-descriptions of regulatory arrangements in very different market economies: in a traditionally juridified economy like that of the Federal Republic of Germany;[1] in the system of securities market regulation set up in the United States of America under the Securities and Exchange Commission in the 1930s, which is commonly described as self-regulation under SEC oversight;[2] and even in very different arrangements within a single jurisdiction, as in the practice of describing financial regulation in London both before and after the major reforms in the 1986 Financial Services Act as examples of self-regulation.[3] Some of the practical difficulties in organizing the material in this book are indeed themselves revealing about both the problem of delineating the boundaries of the self-regulatory system and the function that this lack of clarity serves. As we will find in Chapter 6, some of the domains examined there, notably those concerned with what has conventionally been called 'quasi-government', might as easily have been examined in this chapter; and that difficulty in deciding whether to assign a domain to the sphere of 'state' or 'self' regulation precisely arises from constitutional silences and obscurities that help occlude lines of public accountability.

The existing attempts to lay out the nature of self-regulation emphasize these conceptual problems. Baggott organizes self-regulatory systems by one predominant variable, degree of formal organization. Viewed thus, self-regulation ranges from entirely informal sets of practices to those that, involving direct control of regulatory systems by central government, shade off into systems of state control.[4] The key feature of his scheme is that assigning any particular real institutional system a place on the spectrum is a highly judgemental business. Ogus, by contrast, sketches three kinds of variations, in principle, therefore, offering a three-dimensional classification system: degree of autonomy from the state; degree to which rules have legal force; and degree to which regulatory institutions have a monopoly of control over entry to a market—one might say, in Weberian terms, degree to which they are able to enforce closure.[5]

It is, thus, easier to create systems for classifying self-regulation than to separate it definitely from other modes of control. It is, in particular, plainly possible—as Ogus's exercise shows—to create a general classification of systems of self-regulation that applies in a wide range of jurisdictions. Indeed, some of the work examined in Chapter 2—notably the theories of enforced self-regulation and coregulation developed by Braithwaite and collaborators—does something even more ambitious: it assimilates classifications of self-regulation to more general classifications yet of modes of regulatory activity.[6] But since our interest is Britain, it is most sensible to build description around the British system and its distinctiveness. And the question of distinctiveness immediately directs us to a key comparative question: how is the British system unusual when compared with that of other nations?

The merit of thinking comparatively is that it not only clarifies what has been unusual about British self-regulation, but provides a key to understanding how it is changing. That historic distinctiveness is indeed well established in the literature. Britain is, in Baggott's words, 'a haven for self-regulation'.[7] In this haven, self-regulation of markets—in labour, in products, and in services—has taken a very individual direction: in a phrase, it has been uniquely informal.[8] Specialized regulators have been rare; instead, regulation has commonly been done as a kind of by-product of market activity.[9] Self-regulation in Britain has also traditionally been distinguished by another kind of informality: the British have been reluctant to codify rules in detail, and correspondingly reliant on trust and implicit understandings.[10] Finally, self-regulation in Britain has taken an unusual legal form: private associations, often entirely unknown to the law, have been central to many of the most important systems of self-regulation; and the law itself has historically played no role, or only a residual one, in the life of self-regulatory systems.[11] None of this is surprising: it is exactly what we should expect given the wider features of club government described in Chapter 7.

A summary way to express all this is as follows. Self-regulation in the British system can be described in terms of three variables: the degree to which systems are institutionalized, that is, are built around specialized institutions of control; the degree to which they codify their rules, that is, make them explicit rather than simply relying on tacit understandings; and the degree to which substantive rules and procedures are juridified, that is, are expressed in the language of the law and integrated with the wider legal system. The language of institutionalization, codification, and juridification revealingly isolates what has historically been comparatively distinctive about self-regulation in Britain: low levels of institutionalization, codification, and juridification have marked the system.[12]

This summary admittedly involves huge simplifications. To state the obvious: not all systems of self-regulation in Britain are equally institutionalized, codified, and juridified. At one end of the spectrum, we can find pretty pure examples of what Collins calls club markets: that is, informally organized regulatory systems that are simply the by-product of trading in particular goods and services.

The classic, often cited, instance is the Liverpool cotton broking market in the nineteenth century.[13] In these pure club markets, there is barely any separation between regulatory organization and the daily conduct of business. Deals are struck on the basis of trust, rules are understood even when unstated, law and the state are irrelevant. The club creates high cultural and social integration; expulsion provides a last resort sanction. Regulation is woven into the fabric of civil society.

At the other end of the spectrum, we can find historically well-established systems in Britain—some of the best examples are in parts of the banking industry, in parts of insurance, and in some professions—where there has long been a comparatively high degree of specialized regulatory organization, where rules of behaviour have been elaborate and explicitly codified, and where statute has been important in providing both a legal framework and a 'last resort' power to support self-regulatory bodies.[14] All this is only to state the obvious: that in a complex economy no single regulatory template will fit everything.

The world of self-regulation in Britain is, therefore, a complex mosaic. But the following pages show that during the 1970s to 1990s this mosaic has been rearranged according to a consistent pattern. Wherever we look, we find a growth in the extent to which the systems of self-regulation are institutionalized, codified, and juridified. The observation is true whether we speak of markets in labour, in products, or in services as different as financial services or cultural services like art and sport. This transformation of the British system can be convincingly demonstrated. But that still leaves big questions unanswered: what are the sources of the transformation; and what does this transformation of a key part of the whole system of regulation tell us about the changing role of the state in the regulatory system? We need to clarify these questions before turning to the institutional details.

UNDERSTANDING TRANSFORMATION

How might we account for the decline of the unorganized, uncodified, and unjuridified British system of self-regulation—and its replacement by more formally organized, more elaborately codified, and more legally bound and state-controlled systems? The puzzle exists at both an analytical level and at the level of everyday policy language. The analytical puzzle has already been flagged in Chapters 1 and 2. The dominant analytical paradigm for the modern regulatory state pictures it as an institution concerned with steering self-regulating networks; yet, the changes documented in the following pages actually amount to the replacement precisely of such autonomous self-steering systems by more hierarchically controlled institutions.

The puzzle exists at the level of everyday policy language because the transformation has happened in a period when *self*-regulation—as a doctrine that actors in markets should control their own affairs—was seemingly being strengthened by the rise of ideologies of *de*regulation in Britain during the closing decades of the twentieth century. The transformation, therefore, marks not only a breach with historically established practice, it also seems to defy the spirit of the times. Some of the main arguments for deregulation—a dominant symbol of our time—are in effect arguments for more self-regulation. They assert that control of markets by independent public agencies is often ineffective because it is not conducted by those with practical experience; that control by the law is too rigid for markets that need to adapt flexibly, often at short notice; and that regulation is most likely to be done in a cost-effective way when controlled by those who themselves directly bear its costs. Much recent advocacy of more light touch regulation in Britain has, thus, involved the attempt, not simply to abolish controls, but to shift regulatory authority and responsibility away from public officials and agencies, towards actors and institutions in markets themselves.[15]

I begin the job of puzzling out these anomalies by juxtaposing two powerful general accounts of the nature of changes in systems of self-regulation. One is most commonly found in political science; the other has heavily influenced lawyers who have examined self-regulation.

The best way to introduce the first of these is to begin with a simple mental experiment. Imagine a society where self-regulation was always conducted by private, informally organized institutions; where the rules were rarely codified; and where neither the state nor the law had much part to play in the self-regulatory system. We would be looking at an ideal-typical model of pluralist regulation. And, indeed, later in the chapter we will come across a historical working example of this model—the system of regulating sport, a system presently in decline. Now, imagine by contrast a society where regulatory bodies were formally organized in a hierarchical fashion; where rules were codified elaborately; where those rules were mostly embodied in law; and where the authority of the enforcing institution was backed by the power of the state. We would be looking at a society organized along the principles of statist corporatism of the sort classically anatomized originally by Schmitter and collaborators: one where 'the constituent units are organized into a limited number of singular, compulsory, non-competitive, hierarchically ordered and functionally differentiated categories, recognized or licensed (if not created) by the state and granted a deliberate representational monopoly.'[16] That pretty accurately catches the drift of change in self-regulation in Britain in recent decades. Here, then, is an alternative way of summarizing the transformation of self-regulation in Britain, and one that sharply expresses the sense of anomaly in the whole process: in the age of liberalism and deregulation, and in the age of uncoupled hierarchies and self-steering by autonomous systems, we have actually witnessed the consolidation of corporatist regulation. Invoking pluralism and corporatism emphasizes the importance of the change sketched in this chapter, for on this account the transformation of self-regulation in Britain is more important even than an alteration in modes of economic regulation: it is a fundamental alteration in the nature of the Constitution, because it is a fundamental alteration in the relationship between civil society and state power.

Now, consider just about the most influential analytical account of these changes offered in the legal literature on regulation: that derived from theories of the autopoietic character of regulatory systems. On this account, we are witnessing a 'constitutionalization' of self-regulation, to adapt a phrase of Black.[17] This process of 'constitutionalization' allows us to picture the changes along the three dimensions in very different terms from the images of inexorable increases in state control outlined above. Instead, it views them as consistent with models of coregulation or of enforced self-regulation proposed by writers like Braithwaite and collaborators.[18] The changes are a response to the autopoietic character of different social sub-systems, like the law and the economy. The theory of autopoiesis is derived from cybernetic theory. In conditions of great complexity, regulatory systems—especially those embedded in highly developed institutions and in communities, like those of professions—have their own elaborately developed life. In the manner of cybernetic systems, communications with the external world—with other sub-systems—are mediated by these highly developed institutional structures and cultures. The development of more formally organized systems of self-regulation can, thus, be viewed as a functional response to the problems of reconciling the worlds of different sub-systems in conditions of high complexity. It is functional because the alternatives are either deregulation or an increasing turn to command, with all the limitations and perversities of those two modes.[19] Writing with reference to law, Teubner puts it as follows:

Society is understood as a self-regulating system of communication. It is made up of acts of communication which generate further communications. Specialized cycles of communication have developed out of the general cycle of social communication. Some have become so thoroughly independent that they have to be regarded as second-order autopoietic social systems. They have constituted autonomous units of communication that, in turn, are self-reproductive. They produce their own elements, structures, processes, and boundaries. They construct their own environment, and define their own identity. The components are self-referentially constituted, and are in turn linked with one another by means of a hypercycle. Social subsystems are operatively closed, but cognitively open to the environment.[20]

This second interpretation radically changes our interpretation of regulatory change because it not only puts a different cast on the altered character of traditional systems of self-regulation, it also pictures older systems that relied more directly on command law as evolving in a self-regulatory direction. Some of the most convincing studies have come from the regulation of industrial safety, a domain where statute has been established for virtually two centuries. As long ago as 1972, the Robens Report on Safety and Health at Work (which led to the large-scale reconstruction of the whole system with the establishment of the Health and Safety Executive in 1974) attempted to lay down a template for precisely this kind of regulation:

Regulations which lay down precise methods of compliance have an intrinsic rigidity, and their details may be quickly overtaken by new technological developments . . . We believe that wherever practicable, regulations should be confined to statements of broad requirements in terms of the objectives to be achieved . . . We recommend that in future no statutory regulation should be made before detailed consideration has been given to whether the objectives might adequately be met by a non-statutory code of practice or standard.[21]

As we saw in Chapter 2, a good deal of modern regulation of systems of industrial safety—in both Britain and elsewhere—does indeed respond to high levels of social and technological complexity precisely by mandating systems of enforced self-regulation.[22] On these accounts, autopoiesis is creating reflexive regulation: complex sub-systems of society like the law, the economy, and the state have to accommodate each other by cooperative learning and mutual change, thus moving away from the simplicities of either command regulation or regulation through market exchange alone.[23]

We, thus, have two very different accounts of how to understand regulatory change in Britain: as the development of an ever-widening range of state directed control, which has emerged despite the rhetoric of liberalization and deregulation; or as a turn to reflexivity, which is reshaping not only traditional self-regulation, but also systems that were historically more tied to the law.

So, now we turn to what the evidence can tell us about these competing accounts.

MAPPING SELF-REGULATION

The self-regulatory system in Britain is vast. Only a tiny tip of the regulatory iceberg shows up in any systematic listing. The very summit of the tip consists of a small number of consumer-sensitive fields—like funeral services and used car sales—targeted by the Office of Fair Trading in its most recent efforts to give formal support to industry codes with the object of 'putting the "self" back into self-regulation'.[24] Part of the rest of the visible tip can be seen in the Department of Trade and Industry sponsored list of trade associations, which lists 199, most of which have some kind of code of conduct.[25] As a single instance, consider the example of the Public Relations Consultants Association, which has no statutory authority but which has a twenty-seven-point code to which its members must notionally adhere.[26]

That all this is merely the tip of the iceberg is obvious even from casual inspection. The DTI list is itself not comprehensive, and, of course, trade associations are themselves only a small part of the self-regulatory picture. There is the world of regulation represented by organized professions to consider, and beyond this worlds of quasi and aspirant professionalism, of codes administered by charities and learned societies, of sport and leisure associations, and of cultural organizations defined in the widest sense. As just one example of the last, consider the recent transformation of pastoral codes of conduct for Catholic priests developed in the wake of sexual abuse scandals in the Church—a sharp increase in the degree to which one system of self-regulation has been codified and institutionalized.[27]

Drawing a comprehensive map of the self-regulatory system is, therefore, presently impossible. Drawing a map for different periods that would allow us to chart change historically is absolutely impossible, because we could never reclaim enough of the past to allow a defensible comparison over time. And even were we to draw a map we would still be faced with the problem of weighting the significance of change in different regulatory arenas. Changes in the regulation of rugby league—which I discuss later—do not seem intuitively as significant for the wider regulatory system as changes in the regulation of accountants; but it is not at all obvious how to weigh their relative importance to provide an account of the changing general character of the British regulatory system.

I try to solve these problems of mapping in the following ways. What follows is a series of 'thick' case studies of the recent history of self-regulation. The 'thick' case study, like all case study work, involves some difficult intellectual compromises. Selection of the cases demands judgements of a contestable nature. The selection of a number of cases, rather than one, trades off variety for depth: but even this small number of cases cannot be more than a schematic account.

Despite these serious limitations, the practicalities of selection are actually straightforward, involving as they do choice of cases on two broad grounds: selecting examples that help us address the analytic anomalies outlined above; and choosing cases that allow examination of substantively important economic arenas in Britain. Some of the domains, indeed, virtually select themselves, because it makes obvious sense to examine the contemporary fate of the systems of self-regulation whose historical origins were described in Chapter 3. Hence, the recent experience of self-regulation in the two domains of financial regulation and the regulation of professions occupies a large part of what follows. Within the latter, I add a sketch of the recent regulatory history of the legal profession to my account of what has happened to doctors and accountants, principally because the recent regulatory history of lawyers impinges in complex ways on what has been happening in both financial markets and in the market for accountants' professional services.

The linked domains of the regulation of financial and professional services provide the substance of two of the three thick cases studies that follow. When we finally arrive at the third, the regulation of sport, I explain the rationale for the choice more fully. In essence, however, that rationale is the familiar mix of the substantive and the analytical. Historically, sport in Britain was a quintessential example of an activity regulated autonomously in the sphere of civil society. In recent decades, its economic significance has grown greatly and at the same time it has been drawn ever closer into the state's sphere of influence. It transpires that sports—and, as a coda, the arts—provide a fine test of how to view the whole transformation of the system of self-regulation: either as signifying the growth of state command or as the evolution of autopoietic systems into new modes of coregulation. The substantive economic weight of sport as a case study compares well with the other economic domains examined here. Our instinct to view sport and leisure as quintessentially about pleasure should not blind us to its growing industrial significance. It accounts for an estimated £10 billion annually of consumer expenditure, employs 750 000 people, and pays £3.5 billion in tax.[28] And as we shall see, the analytic significance of the change in the regulation of sport for our understanding of the regulatory state is peculiarly important.

TRANSFORMING SELF-REGULATION IN FINANCIAL MARKETS

In Chapter 3, we sketched the special regulatory history of financial services, especially of its most important parts in the City of London. Though there existed some differences of nuance between various markets, the City's regulatory world had a fundamental unity. It provided the paradigmatic case of club regulation both in the general sense used in this book, and also in the more specific sense that many of its institutions were example of Collins's 'club markets': associations of traders grouped for mutual protection whose members agree, as a condition of admission to the club, to be bound by its rules and to honour any undertakings made between members of the group.[29] Some of the most important City examples historically included the Stock Exchange, Lloyd's insurance market, and a network of more specialist 'clubs' like, to take one example, the Baltic Exchange.[30] Some of these had actually grown out of social institutions, in the case of Lloyd's out of a coffee house.[31] There were always important differences between different parts of the City markets, but the major markets—in government stock and equities, in reinsurance, in merchant and to a lesser extent retail banking, in short-term money markets—had by the middle of the twentieth century settled down into a series of clubs. Expulsion was, in principle, a final sanction maintaining regulatory authority; in practice, the rules were upheld by social and cultural solidarity. As we saw in Chapter 3, the historical development of the system in the nineteenth century meant that legal support for the authority of the club was usually unimportant. Relations between the central state and the clubs were distant. External oversight was informally organized by the central bank, which stood apart from the central state bureaucracy. The evidence from separate markets submitted to the Wilson Committee of inquiry into financial institutions in the late 1970s—a comprehensive official inquiry of Royal Commission proportions carried out just at the moment when the system was starting to buckle—showed that both the ideology and the institutions of the club system, though under strain, still largely persisted.[32]

All this has been transformed, mostly during the 1980s and 1990s. That transformation has taken place at distinct levels and these need to be examined separately: regulatory changes in particular sectors (like banking) are first summarized;

the wider changes in the whole architecture of financial regulation are then described. Two features recur. First, the direction of change is in a single consistent direction: towards greater institutionalization, codification, and juridification. Second, the end of the era of club rule had been succeeded by an era of hyper-innovation, often driven by crisis and scandal. This second feature anticipates a wider characteristic of the new regulatory state that will recur in later chapters.

We begin with the banking sector. The case of banking regulation is a good illustration of the difficulties of identifying the bounds between self-regulation and statutory control in Britain. The history of statutory regulation of banks, notably of 'retail' high street banking, actually involves a long accretion of statute.[33] But the most important feature of banking control until the 1970s was the extent to which informal custom and practice rather than statute dominated. Recognition as a bank was largely a matter of discretionary judgement by the Bank of England.[34] As to the exercise of regulatory authority, whenever the Bank wished to issue a regulatory instruction either to the system as a whole or to an individual bank, it did so by informal, often confidential communications. The transmission of regulatory directives relied heavily on communication via trade associations like the Accepting Houses Committee (for the elite merchant banks) and the Committee of London Clearing Bankers (for the high street banks), whose members enjoyed the privileges of central bank sanctioned restrictive practices.[35]

Two periods of prudential crisis destroyed this informal system. The first was produced by the great secondary banking crisis of the 1970s, a crisis that destroyed a whole series of lesser banks and threatened some of the elite.[36] It led to the passage of the Banking Act 1979. The Act, for the first time, attempted to set a statutory definition of a bank, significantly increased the extent to which banking supervision rules were codified, and—precisely as a result of the resort to statute—increased the degree to which supervisory authorities had to report to the central state in Whitehall and to Parliament. In part, the Act gave legal recognition to changes that had already been introduced within the Bank of England as a result of the original secondary banking crisis. Traditionally, the Bank had supervised mostly as a by-product of the market intelligence gathering operations of its Discount Office, an office with nineteenth-century origins that managed the Bank's operations in the short-term money markets. Now a specialist Supervision Division was created, and more onerous formal reporting obligations were imposed on banks.[37] The whole system of regulation, therefore, shifted from one where banking recognition and supervision rested on customary assumptions and discretionary decisions by the Bank of England to one where formal licensing governed entry and formal organization governed supervision.

These changes in institutions and rules only partly displaced the old club culture, as the second great critical episode showed. In 1995, there occurred the collapse of Barings Bank, an elite City institution, following disastrous dealings in currency markets in the Far East by one of its traders.[38] As I show in Chapter 7, this collapse was largely due to the persistence of traits of the old club culture, but the outcome administered that culture its final death blows. The immediate result was once more to ratchet up the degree of formal organization and detailed codification in supervision. The longer-term change has been even more damaging to the old regulatory culture. Following the election of a new Labour government in 1997, the Bank was stripped of its historical responsibility for banking supervision, this being transferred to a new Financial Services Authority.[39] That change not only marked a defining moment in the history of banking regulation, it was also, as we shall see shortly, a key moment in the reconstruction of the wider architecture of financial regulation.

Though banking regulation has been greatly changed, it is actually in a second domain—in the securities markets that trade in instruments like equities, government stock, and futures contracts—where the transformation of club markets in financial services is most obvious, and for an equally obvious reason: this is where the 'clubs' were historically best established.[40] The autonomy of perhaps the greatest of the clubs—the Stock Exchange—virtually disappeared with the passage of the 1986 Financial Services Act, when it was reinvented as a Recognized Investment Exchange under public oversight.[41] That change, as we shall also see in a moment, was part of a wider change in regulatory architecture that brought all the various 'clubs' in the securities markets more closely under public control and subjected them to increasingly elaborately codified rule books.

The transformation of banking and securities regulation is the best-known part of the changed landscape of financial regulation, but less publicly noticed parts of the City have also been transformed in recent decades. At the close of the 1950s, a series of scandalous takeover battles prompted public interest in how the City ran its affairs and threatened to produce some public controls. The episode was particularly dangerous because in the Monopolies and Mergers Commission the state for once already had an institution with responsibility for regulating the substance of takeovers and mergers in the interests of competitiveness.[42] In response to the threat, the City elite managed to establish the principle that regulating the process of takeover and merger was the City's own responsibility. Its first effort at regulation in 1958 was a paradigm of British self-regulation: a short, general, entirely voluntary code of conduct without any formal institutional means of enforcement.[43] But by the 1990s a largely incremental process of adaptation stretching over more than three decades had transformed the code into a complex set of rules policed by a Panel on Take-Overs and Mergers with its own professional staff.[44] It was even increasingly colonized by the law as the result of a court decision extending judicial review to cover the operations of the Panel.[45] Here, then, was a domain where the City had started out with a pure, traditional model of self-regulation only to see it increasingly codified, institutionalized, and juridified. Even more fundamental, and scandal driven, upheaval was experienced by the most historically ancient example of a club market, the insurance market organized by the corporation of Lloyd's. A series of frauds and related scandals in Lloyd's in the 1970s and 1980s initiated an era of regulatory turmoil.[46] First attempts to reorganize the market under closer legal oversight (the Lloyd's Act of 1982) failed to settle the turmoil. By the year 2000, Lloyd's was on its fifth regulatory plan, but by then events had overtaken the attempt to preserve the autonomy of the club:[47] the Financial Services and Markets Act 2000 hands independent oversight of the market to the Financial Services Authority.[48]

Part of the story of regulatory transformation, therefore, is about what has happened to the control of particular City domains, such as securities trading, various forms of banking, and insurance. But, as the references to measures like the 1986 Financial Services Act and the Financial Services and Markets Act of 2000 show, the changes have not just involved piecemeal reform of particular markets and institutions; they have been accompanied by, and in key instances are integrated with, a wholesale reconstruction of the larger architecture of financial regulation. That reconstruction has greatly lessened the regulatory distinctiveness of the City of London, integrating its regulation with the wider framework for the regulation of financial institutions generally. In the process, it has transformed the whole architecture of financial regulation into a more centralized, more state controlled hierarchy. This has taken place in two giant steps. The first occurred in the legislation of 1986, a law that was partly prompted by a series of frauds and collapses among financial investment firms, and partly by pressures from modernizers in the state bureaucracy and the biggest firms who wanted more effective controls to position the City as a key location in the global financial services industry.[49] That legislation is ideologically significant, because it saw a large step in the direction of a hierarchical system of state-backed controls, while nevertheless trying to retain the language, and some of the institutions, of self-regulation. It systematically organized all the main markets into a hierarchy of self-regulatory organizations (SROs). These SROs gained monopoly control over the markets—that is, membership of, and obedience to, their rules was a condition of entry. In turn, their own rules and internal government were subjected to oversight by an overarching SRO, the Securities and Investments Board, which in effect licensed the individual SROs. All this greatly increased the degree to which the self-regulatory system was codified: the SROs of necessity acquired rule books, and these rule books over time became more detailed and more elaborate, and of course acquired legal force. The Securities and Investments Board spoke the language of self-regulation, and as a gesture towards independence was constituted as a corporate body financed by a levy on the industry. But the power it wielded over the SROs was based on statute, its own constitution was prescribed in law, its leading officers were publicly appointed, and it was required to report to Parliament and to the central state in Whitehall.[50]

This remarkable advance in the direction of a corporatist hierarchy in financial self-regulation did not endure. The passage of the 1986 Financial Services Act was followed by more than a decade of instability in financial regulation: periodic regulatory crises and scandals; and internal struggles within the financial services industry, as scandal and failure pushed the regulatory authorities towards more controls, while supporters of traditional light touch self-regulation tried to preserve as much as possible of the old order. That struggle has culminated for the moment in the changes associated with the passage into law of the Financial Services and Markets Act of 2000.[51] The Act completes in a radical way the transformation of self-regulation begun in 1986. Some vestiges of the old forms of self-regulation, admittedly, do still remain: the Financial Services Authority is, for example, a company limited by guarantee financed by a levy on the industry, thus conferring 'ownership' on the regulated themselves. But this is a weak echo of the voice of the old world of self-regulation. The Authority (originally established in advance of the law in 1997, but deriving its powers from the statute of 2000) has some claim to be the most impressively empowered financial services regulator in any leading world financial centre. If, for instance, we compare the system usually taken as the model of tight legal control, the United States of America, we find a striking contrast: all the powers over the full range of markets and institutions concentrated into the hands of the FSA in London are in the case of the USA dispersed among a wide range of regulatory bodies at state and federal levels. The FSA, in effect, licences all institutions and products, and does so by virtue of power conferred by statute. As we saw above, it has finally displaced the Bank of England from any significant role in prudential regulation of markets or institutions. Authorization, standard setting, supervision, and enforcement: all come within its powers.[52] The creation of the Authority amounts to the diffusion into the financial markets of a major recent institutional innovation in the British system, the specialized regulatory agency empowered by law. (In Chapters 5 and 6, we shall see how this innovation has colonized an increasingly wide range of social domains stretching from food production to human reproduction.) As a regulatory agency, the Authority has a radically different relationship with the central state from that enjoyed by the old institutions of City regulation and by the Bank of England. The Treasury appoints its Board, it reports annually to the Treasury and the House of Commons, and it is required to give evidence to the Commons' Treasury Select Committee.[53]

To summarize, in just about 15 years from the middle of the 1980s, self-regulation of financial markets was transformed. There were radical changes along all the three dimensions identified earlier: a sharp increase in state surveillance; a growth in the volume and complexity of rules, including legally prescribed rules; and the development of a comprehensive hierarchy of controls operated by a single, legally empowered regulator. That regulator, in turn, equipped with great legal powers, an increasingly assertive sense of regulatory mission, and subject to powerful popular pressures to respond to cases of regulatory failure, is emerging as a major actor in both the regulatory politics of the markets and the bureaucratic politics of the central state. The changes have a distinctly 'modernist' cast in the sense identified in the opening pages of this book. That is, they take social domains that were largely independent of public control, that were the result of fragmented, gradual historical change, and that relied heavily on informal controls and tacit knowledge, and then transform all this into something recognizably modernist in its workings and ambitions: there has been a radical shift to formality, including legally backed formality, in regulatory relationships; a shift from tacit to explicit knowledge, in the form of more elaborate codification of rules and more elaborate and onerous reporting requirements; and the reorganization of regulated domains into a reshaped set of hierarchically organized institutions subject to systems of close formal reporting and central surveillance.

TRANSFORMING PROFESSIONAL REGULATION

The history of self-regulation in the financial markets might, at the risk of oversimplification, be summarized as the transformation of a structure established in the late nineteenth century under the pressure of late twentieth-century conditions. A similar story can be told about the key professions. The latter decades of the nineteenth century were, as we saw in Chapter 3, the golden age of professional creation.[54] These professions were for the most part founded, as we also saw in Chapter 3, according to a particular template of self-regulation. In one sense, this template made the professions more independent of public power than were the club markets in financial services; in another, less so. They were more independent because the institutions were more scattered and fragmented, and overseen by nothing like as formidable an institution as the Bank of England. They were less so because, in the main, they did indeed come into existence as a result of a founding statute, an explicit contract with the state. 'What produces the privileges of professional status is a profession–state alliance.'[55]

The law was, therefore, more important to the foundation of self-regulatory power in professional markets than in the club markets of financial services. But the actual practice of professional regulation marginalized the state quite as completely as did the City, while self-regulation within professions bore striking similarities to club regulation—informality, reliance on social and cultural solidarity. State oversight was hardly ever exercised. Professional institutions typically had a narrow conception of their controlling role and put few organizational resources into that activity. The most important source of control was assumed to be the internalized codes of professional obligation acquired by the individual professional through occupational socialization. The strength of this model is, paradoxically, particularly well revealed by the history of one occupation that had historically failed to develop the conventional institutional structure that marked out the established professions. Teaching, as Tropp remarks, 'was created by the State, and in the nineteenth century the State was powerful enough to claim almost complete control over the teacher'.[56] Yet, by the 1950s:

many of the aims of professional self-government have been gained independently . . . . at his work the teacher has gained almost complete independence . . . . While there is some talk of administrative interference and petty bureaucracy, the general tendency appears to be towards a lifting of existing restrictions rather than an imposing of new ones.[57]

In the closing decades of the twentieth century, all changed profoundly in the world of professional regulation. In summary: after a long period of quiescence, the central state began to play an increasingly active oversight role; within professions, disputes broke out about the organization of self-regulation, especially about the balance between different groups and interests in the governing structures; and disputes also began to break out about the substance of regulation itself. In the space available here, it is not possible to do more than illustrate some of the changes by reference to three important professions—accountants, doctors, and lawyers. I explain, in turn, why these three are chosen.

Accountants

Accountants merit close attention in any examination of self-regulation because in the twentieth century they emerged as the key profession in the regulation of business life in Britain. Accounting rules and their implementation were the central mechanism of business reporting, and audit as defined by accountants became the key to the accountability of firms.[58] In the classic fashion of professional regulation, two processes were intertwined: the institutional shape of the profession itself and the promulgation of professional standards. As we saw in Chapter 3, accounting as a modern profession is the by-product of state regulation dating back to the middle decades of the nineteenth century. The Companies Acts of 1844 and 1862 created a demand for expertise in auditing, and the administration of company failure, in respect of both bankruptcy and liquidation.[59] The state conferred a monopoly of financial audit business on the professionals, but imposed no reporting requirements on them in return. The interventionist state that emerged early in the twentieth century boosted the profession still further: the transformation of humble account clerks into Cost and Works Accountants with their own Institute in 1919 was, for example, the direct result of the expertise demanded to administer regulations against profiteering in the First World War.[60]

But if the state created the conditions for the foundation of the profession, regulation itself was highly pluralistic. The associations independently controlled accounting standards (and the key related issue of professional training); and the associations, in turn, declined precisely to mandate standards, relying on the discretionary judgement of the individual practitioner.[61]

The decisive changes in the regulation of the substance of accounting practices date from 1990.[62] In 1990, the Financial Reporting Council replaced the Accounting Standards Committee (ASC). The professional associations had independently controlled the latter. The composition of the new Council signified the abandonment of some key features of self-regulation: for instance, the Department of Trade and Industry and the Bank of England now appoint the chair and deputy chair.[63] But the critical change lies in the fact that the Financial Reporting Council has delegated responsibility for standard setting to an Accounting Standards Board (ASB). The ASB, by contrast with its predecessor the ASC, is recognized by statute (in both the 1985 and the 1989 Companies Acts), and the law requires companies (some exemptions for small firms allowed) to state that their accounts are prepared in accord with its standards. The ASB has, in effect, acquired a statutory licence to govern financial reporting.[64]

Just over a decade after the reshaping of the regulation of accounting standards, there took place an equally profound restructuring of the institutions of professional control in accounting, marked by the establishment of the Accountancy Foundation in 2002. The Foundation now has the 'overarching responsibility' for the system of professional regulation.[65] It sits on top of, and appoints members to, boards that govern fields like auditing, ethics, and discipline. Immediately below it sits a Review Board with a full-time staff that is the 'pivot on which the whole new structure turns'.[66] Three features of this new structure should be highlighted. First, its ambition—reflected in both appointment practices and working practices—is to be independent of the regulated professionals: 'it is of the essence of the new system that the Review Board should, to the maximum extent possible, be independent of the accountancy profession.'[67] It, thus, marks a critical departure from one of the central features of professional self-regulation in accounting: the notion that the content and process of regulation should grow directly out of autonomous professional practice. Second, the new structure is the result of a complex bargain with the state: it offers greatly increased formal organization and more elaborate codes in return for independence from direct statutory control. It arises directly out of a review of regulation conducted by the DTI after the return of Labour to office in 1997, which pointedly left open the possibility of incorporating accounting far more closely into the structure of company law, and out of the DTIs acceptance of defensive proposals then produced by the professional associations.[68] One formal mark of independence is the resort to the familiar device—which we have seen widely used in financial market regulation—of constituting the Foundation as a company limited by guarantee, and constituting the boards beneath it as subsidiaries.[69] Third, both the appointment practices that produce membership, and the actual identity of Board members, reveal the creation of a complex interweaving of private and public interests. Official bodies like the Bank of England, the DTI, and the National Audit Office send representatives to Boards, and they sit alongside the great and the good of the financial services industry and non-financial interests. The membership of the Review Board—the pivot of the whole system—nicely illustrates the point: it is chaired by the head of the National Audit Office, while its members include bankers, lawyers, and a representative of the TUC. In this new structure, nobody could possibly work out where the public begins and the private ends.[70] For the profession, this state of affairs is two edged: on the one hand, it serves—like the similarly tortuous arrangements in the City—to obstruct public accountability by creating an impossibly complex set of public/private boundaries; on the other hand, as the presence of a TUC representative shows, it dramatizes how far the regulation of this key profession has now moved out of the direct control of practising accountants, and how this shift has been forced by the need to fend off an interventionist state. But even this painstakingly constructed structure is unstable. At the time of writing, the spillover from US accounting scandals has obliged Ministers in the DTI to form a Working Group to produce proposals for even tighter controls over auditors.[71]

In summary, the changes that came over accounting in the later decades of the twentieth century made its organization more formal, tied it more closely to the oversight of state institutions, and diminished the autonomy of the individual professional in interpreting the rules. But what the bare account of institutional arrangements does not convey is the provisional, unfolding character of institutional arrangements for a profession that for the first three-quarters of the twentieth century was governed by an enclosed, stable regulatory community. An apparently endless spate of auditing scandals has put the regulation of the profession more or less permanently on the political agenda. And, as we shall later, accountants are, alongside other key professions, also under attack from another public regulator, the Office of Fair Trading, this time for their (un)competitive practices.

Doctors

Doctors, like accountants, were the beneficiaries of the nineteenth-century revolution in professional organization, though unlike accountants they could already claim some of the status of an ancient profession: parts of the profession, like some Royal Colleges, had deep historical connections both to the central state and to the elite universities.[72] The critical moment in the profession's regulatory history was, as we saw in Chapter 3, the Medical Act of 1858 that established a General Medical Council.[73] Formally, the Act put the profession under state oversight. In practice, the first century of professional regulation after 1858 was a study in autonomy—both the autonomy of the profession from the state and the autonomy of the individual professional practitioner from the self-regulating body. There was virtually no intervention by either the central state or the legislature in the terms of the regulatory contract with the state, and the little that happened was the result of initiatives from the elite of the profession itself. Within the profession, the institutions crucial to the process of professional education and training, the universities, and the Royal Colleges operated with a high level of autonomy. Meanwhile, the regulation of the individual professional was done with the lightest of touches: it minimized the detail in the rules to be followed and worked with a narrow conception of the range of professional obligations. On the latter, for example, it had a fair amount to say about how doctors should behave towards each other, but little to say about how they should behave towards patients.[74]

All this changed greatly in the closing decades of the twentieth century. The long historical consensus about the shape and structure of self-regulation in the profession came to an end, to be succeeded by open political struggle both for control of the regulatory institutions and about the substance of the rules. The most important signs of this were open revolt by sections of the profession against the authority of the General Medical Council in the late 1960s, followed by the first extensive public enquiry ever—by the Merrison Committee—in the early 1970s.[75] No new consensus capable of returning control of the regulatory institutions to the professional elite has been possible in the intervening years. One reason for this continuing instability is that there have been recurrent scandals about the behaviour of doctors, forcing constant changes in both the content of regulations and the structure of the General Medical Council itself. One of the most striking features of these scandalous cases is the gap they revealed between the conception of professional standards that guided the General Medical Council's own workings and what an increasingly assertive lay public thought were appropriate standards. Thus, a number of highly publicized cases of callousness, incompetence, and neglect were admitted by all, professionals and non-professionals alike, to be quite unacceptable—but could not be deemed unprofessional given the General Medical Council's narrow conception of professional misconduct. Here was a particularly stark instance of the encounter between the nineteenth-century club system and modern democratic society.[76] There has, consequently, been increasing legislative intervention in the regulatory affairs of the profession, including intervention to reshape the composition of the regulatory institution itself.[77]

Behind all this lies the collapse of the compact that doctors successfully negotiated with the state at the foundation of the NHS, a compact memorably summarized in Klein's phrase 'the politics of the double bed': the compact assigned control of the everyday allocation of medical resources to medical professionals, and confined the state to the role of deciding the absolute level of resources to be allocated to the Service.[78] It, thus, 'modernized' the nineteenth-century bargain between the state and profession in such a way so as to defend the profession's autonomy. But after the great economic crisis of the 1970s, and the rise of a state increasingly concerned to squeeze maximum efficiency out of welfare-state professionals, doctors found themselves the object of increasingly detailed public intervention in their working practices.[79] Thus, the specialized turmoil in the regulatory institutions was compounded by a wider breakdown of the political bargain between the profession and the state. As Salter put it in 2001, in the wake of a spate of crises in medical authority: 'Medical regulation, as much as medical self-regulation, is now centre stage in the politics of the National Health Service and the profession can expect to be subject to the full range of devices at the disposal of this particular theatre.'[80]

In summary: at the turn of the millennium the regulation of the medical profession is subjected to unprecedented, and growing, public debate, increasing intervention in the daily professional activities of physicians, and increasing oversight by the central state.

Lawyers

Like doctors, lawyers were an ancient profession who in the nineteenth century reorganized themselves so as to control competition in the new markets opened up by industrialism. What Abel says about the Bar could equally well be said about the profession of solicitors: that it was 'a nineteenth-century amalgam of distinct occupational categories'.[81] Three historical features of professional organization of the law should be highlighted, because they were all central to the turmoil of the closing decades of the twentieth century. First, lawyers mostly sold their services in markets to individual clients. Second, they attempted to control these highly unstable markets by exploiting a mix of statute and the common law to establish monopolies: the conveyancing monopoly, which for two centuries provided about half the income of solicitors, developed from manipulation of taxation law; the Bar's monopoly of audience in court was based on common law and the exercise of customary power by judges. Third, in the late nineteenth and early twentieth centuries, lawyers rebuilt their own governing institutions (the Inns, the Law Society). Analytically, these institutions show remarkable similarities to self-regulatory bodies in medicine. They performed public functions (qualification, training, discipline) with a high degree of autonomy from the state.[82] They also resisted detailed codification in the manner characteristic of the English system of self-regulation: until 1980, for instance, the English Bar had no written rules at all.[83] And just as many of the scandals of the last quarter-century in medical self-regulation arose because the General Medical Council had a highly restrictive conception of what constituted negligence of professional duties, the same was true of the law. The traditional regulation of medical discipline focused more on how doctors treated each other, rather than how they treated patients—and faced increasing patient dissatisfaction as a result.[84] Writing in 1989, Abel arrived at a similar view of the law, both in Britain and elsewhere: 'professional disciplinary bodies typically disclaim jurisdiction over negligence or incompetence . . . . they focus on offences against lawyers rather than clients.'[85]

For over two decades, the traditional self-regulatory settlement in the legal profession summarized here has been in more or less perpetual turmoil, and the proximate causes are profound changes in the profession's economic and political setting. A profession that historically sold its services to private clients had by the late twentieth century come to rely on the welfare state, via legal aid, for a large and growing share of its income—exceeding half in some cases.[86] The parallel with medicine is again uncanny: just as the state's search for efficiencies in medical labour led it increasingly to intervene in the regulation of the medical profession, so through the last two decades of the twentieth century, efforts to control the huge legal aid bill made the Lord Chancellor's department increasingly intrusive in its attentions to working practices. This has presently culminated in the Access to Justice Act 1999, 'the biggest shake-up in legal services for fifty years'. It transforms barristers funded by legal aid into state salaried 'legal defenders'.[87] The regulatory bodies, in turn (notably the Bar Council), now occupy a central role in, effectively, collective bargaining with the state. Wider changes in the market setting of lawyers have further destabilized the self-regulatory settlement. The most important of these has been the growing symbiosis between increasingly powerful firms of commercial lawyers and the globalized financial markets operating in London. In the years of Conservative rule (1979–97), especially under the term in office of the great reforming Lord Chancellor Lord Mackay of Clashfern, this led to immense pressure from both the Lord Chancellor and corporate modernizers in the profession for state-sponsored reform of regulation.[88] Finally, a series of scandalous cases of treatment of individual clients has forced the regulatory bodies (especially those for solicitors) to both codify more elaborately the rules and to invest more heavily in institutional resources to investigate and discipline incompetent lawyers.[89]

The single most revolutionary change occurred in the form of the Courts and Legal Services Act of 1990. The Act moved a decisive step in the direction of state corporatist regulation. The Bar Council and the Law Society were designated authorized bodies in the statute for a wide range of occupational controls (entry, training, maintenance of professional standards) and, in turn, their constitution and functioning were subject to external controls.[90] Once across this constitutional Rubicon, the regulatory bodies for lawyers became entangled in legal controls and central state agencies. Space only allows two examples, one for the Bar and one for solicitors. While under the 1990 legislation the Lord Chancellor can designate the Inns of Court as authorized bodies granting rights of audience in court, in making any order he has been obliged to consult the Office of Fair Trading on any competitive effects of the Order.[91] The Financial Services Authority in respect of their investment business, meanwhile, also now directly regulates solicitors.[92]

This closer integration between self-regulatory bodies and state agencies has in the case of lawyers set up a dynamic that is proving fatal to key components of self-regulation as traditionally practised. The whole self-regulatory order in law rested on a delicate balance of understandings and practices: professionals themselves controlled the key rules governing market entry, forms of competition and forms of business organization. These were then used to impose a wide range of restrictive practices that both helped constitute professional identities and, by using closure to create privileged insiders, to impose discipline and unity. The increasingly determined search by state agencies for market efficiency has destroyed this balance and invaded this self-referential world. By the turn of millennium, the key agency in the process was the Office of Fair Trading. The Office's report on Competition in Professions, though it focused on law, accounting, and architecture, proved particularly challenging for barristers and solicitors, because it demanded changes in the very restrictions that constituted professional identity and provided so many of the privileges of professional closure: for instance, the Bar rule that demanded that client access to a barrister be only through a solicitor, and the rule prohibiting barristers from conducting litigation, thus imposing specialization between barristers and solicitors.[93] When the Office returned to these issues in a follow-up report, it noted that the Bar was preparing to abandon the first of these restrictions, but responded to the Bar's continuing defence of enforced specialization by a promise to pursue the issue further.[94]

The sense that we are witnessing an ambitious state with its own distinctively modernist agenda reshaping hitherto autonomous areas of civil society is even stronger in the domain to which we now turn: the regulation of sport.

TRANSFORMING SPORTING REGULATION

The regulation of sporting activity is itself a complex mosaic, since individual sports have their own special institutional histories. But there is a commonality of experience across a wide range of British sporting arenas, which gives them importance in any discussion of the recent history of self-regulation. This importance is both substantive and analytic.

Sport is of growing substantive importance for some well-documented reasons. For long a major cultural domain of civil society, professional sport, in particular, has in recent decades assumed a growing economic significance, both in the resources that it directly commands and because of its impact on other domains—the shape of competition in the media being an obvious instance.[95] This rise in economic importance, as we shall see in a moment, has been accompanied by major institutional changes: notably, sport has become more formally organized, more concerned with the implementation of increasingly elaborate codes, and more open to the shaping influence of the state and the law.

Analytically, the case of sport takes us to the heart of what sense we are to make of the transformation of self-regulation, and, in particular, how far we can interpret the changes as a process by which autopoietic systems are functionally adapting in the direction of coregulation and enforced self-regulation. This is because sporting activity amounts to a particularly pure test of the theory of autopoiesis in explaining regulatory change. The defining feature of an autopoietic system is that it is self-referential. The most distinguished theorist of autopoiesis, Teubner, has commonly cited the domain of law as an example of an autopoietic system.[96] Legal reasoning does indeed have a powerfully self-referential character, validating itself by its own internally generated modes of argument, for instance, by the conventions that assign power to precedent. It is this engrained character of highly developed subsystems that is held to create the powerful functional pressure for coregulation rather than command.

Viewed thus, sports are an even purer example of a self-referential world, a 'second order autopoietic system'.[97] The rules even of particular sports are *sui generis*. Thus, the codes by which soccer is played, and the standards by which excellence is judged, only make sense on the soccer pitch; they are arbitrary and irrelevant to any non-sporting world, and even to other sports. It is this self-referential character that makes the appeal of sport all-consuming to some, and incomprehensible to others: explaining, for instance, why someone can find soccer sublime and golf 'a good walk spoiled'. But the analytical importance of the self-referential character of sport goes beyond sporting domains, because sport is representative of other spheres in civil society that share this pure self-referential quality. The most obvious examples are in the arts. Many of the most important art forms—notable examples include opera and ballet—resemble sport in deriving their meaning, and their criteria of excellence, from their own internally generated and highly elaborated codes. They, thus, resemble sport in being 'pointless' beyond their coded worlds. That explains why their appeal too is arbitrary: why, for instance, an enthusiast for opera can find the form sublime while viewing ballet as nothing more than a lot of skipping and hopping.

The purity of sporting and artistic self-referential worlds is emphasized when we think of them alongside more conventional instances of autopoietic systems. Domains like law, banking, and medicine have their own self-referential worlds, but fundamentally they exist because they have wider instrumental purposes. It takes an odd personality to practice law, medicine, or banking just for the fun of it. Yet sport and the arts are engaged in precisely just for the 'fun' of the activity. That is what makes them 'pointless' beyond their own self-referential domains, and what gives changes in their regulation such analytic significance. If the changing regulation of sport suggests its growing instrumentalization—its conversion from a pointless self-referential activity to something that serves wider social purposes—then that is an important piece of evidence about the changing character of self-regulation, and thus about the new regulatory state. And, as I now show, the changing institutional organization of sports government, and even more the changing objectives that now guide the government of sport, exactly conform to this process: they are instrumentalizing the activity, undermining its autonomously self-referential character.

Until the 1960s, sport was paradigmatic of the British tradition of self-regulation: 'Sport was almost the quintessential voluntary activity, part of that long tradition of British voluntarism in which people pursued a wide variety of cultural, intellectual and social activities not because the state wanted them to but because they freely chose to.'[98] Government interest was mostly confined to sporadic attempts to use isolated elite sporting events to promote relations with particular states in particular circumstances.[99] It is true that there was an earlier tradition that closely connected sport both to ideologies of imperialism and to projects for channelling and controlling the energies of potentially disruptive parts of the working class.[100] But the organization of the most important sports, as they crystallized in the later decades of the nineteenth century, were characteristically club-like in nature, in exactly the sense used in this book: they involved the domination of individual sports by metropolitan oligarchies often—as in the cases of cricket and horse racing—integrated informally with upper-class gentlemanly cultures.[101]

It is possible to track over the post-war period an incremental growth in both state support for sport and some institutional change: the first British Minister of Sport was appointed in 1964 and a Sports Council, chaired by the Minister, was formed in the same year. The Council, however, still enjoyed only an advisory status.[102] Despite the institutional innovations of the 1960s, therefore, the traditional picture of autonomous self-regulation still survived at the end of the 1980s. The role of the state in sporting regulation had not changed greatly since the golden age of sporting codification in Britain in the closing decades of the nineteenth century.

That pattern of autonomy changed radically in the 1990s. I first summarize the institutional changes. Sport England was established in 1997. It replaced the Great Britain Sports Council. (Separate Sports Councils now exist for the different nations of the UK.) Sport England is a public institution charged with important executive functions in implementing a national strategy for sport. It is accountable to Parliament through the Department for Culture, Media, and Sport, and the Secretary of State appoints its Council. Its primary roles are to develop and maintain the nation's sporting infrastructure. In pursuit of this it allocates substantial moneys, a mix of Exchequer Grant and Lottery funding.[103] UK Sport also came into existence in 1997. It is primarily concerned with enhancing performance in elite sports, and with managing sporting international relations, notably the diplomacy of bidding to host prestige international events like the Olympics and the football World Cup. In its own words, 'the work of UK Sport is targeted towards developing and supporting a system capable of producing a constant flow of world class performers.'[104] One its most important instruments in achieving this is the distribution of a mix of Exchequer funding and Lottery grants to over 40 sports, in return for a commitment by individual sporting governing bodies to achieve agreed performance targets.

Behind these institutional changes lies something more fundamental: radical changes, dating mostly from the 1990s, that have reshaped the hitherto autonomous, self-referential worlds of individual sports. Three connected forces have been at work.

The first is the increasing colonization of sport by the market. This has commonly involved much more than merely selling the activity. It has transformed the way it is organized and even played. Professional Rugby League provides a graphic example. Until the 1990s, it was a code mostly played by part-time professionals in the coalfields on both sides of the Pennines. The contract for television rights agreed with the satellite broadcaster Sky Sports in the 1990s changed almost every aspect of the game: the names and identities of clubs; the calendar of the playing year (from winter to summer); the internal organization of the clubs; their coaching organization; and the player payment system.[105] In soccer too the rules of play on the field, and the rules rewarding victory, have been reshaped in order to improve marketability: thus, the modification of the back pass rule, new rules awarding three points rather than two for a win in league competitions, and the spread of 'golden goals' and penalty shoot-outs to break deadlocks in a draw, are all designed to increase consumer appeal.[106] Thus, is the self-referential world of a sport reshaped by market colonization.

A second powerful force has been the increasing intervention by the state to raise British performance at elite level. The first important public sign of this in the 1990s was the publication in 1995 of *Sport: Raising the Game* by the

Department of National Heritage. This was a response to perceived poor British results in showcase events like the Olympics.[107] *Raising the Game* was the immediate stimulus for the reorganization that created Sport England and UK Sport in 1997, and as the title suggests was mostly concerned with the problem of managing performance in elite sports. Elite sporting success thus achieved significance beyond either sport's internally generated standards of excellence, or beyond the life goals of autonomous individuals; it became an index of national and state achievement. The consequences of *Raising the Game* also anticipate a theme that will be important when we turn to the new worlds of inspection in Chapter 6: the micro-management of service delivery. As a result of *Raising the Game*, the physical education curriculum in schools was changed to place more emphasis on participation in competitive team sports.[108]

By the election of a Labour Government in 1997, therefore, two powerful forces were instrumentalizing the 'pointless' activity of sport: colonization by the external value system of the market and by the values of a state intent on using sporting success as an instrument of national prestige. The new government added a third: a desire to use mass sport as an instrument of social policy, notably as a way of combating social exclusion and promoting public health. These elements all come together in *A Sporting Future for All*, the national strategic plan published in 2000.[109] *A Sporting Future* joins together the two concerns with elite performance and mass participation. It lays down as fundamental principles of policy the objectives of achieving lifelong participation and reducing 'unfairness in access to sport'.[110] It announces that the governing bodies of sports must adopt inclusive policies to widen the range of participation, and expects all major sporting bodies in receipt of significant television revenue to set aside a minimum of 5 per cent of receipts for grassroots participation.[111] But it is in the organization of elite sport that we see most clearly the shift to instrumentalization and integration into a wider national sporting strategy. The strategic plan notes the history of failures in elite sport (cricket, tennis, soccer world cup). It then uses the New Public Management language of target setting and performance achievement to announce a new relationship between sport and the state:

We will be asking the Sports Councils to move to a more open appraisal of the individual performance plans. All the various sports—and the athletes, coaches, and performance directors—must be fully aware of what is required of them . . . The focus will be much more closely on target setting by national governing bodies and on the achievement of targets by individual performers and teams.[112]

The way this works in detail is explained by the description of the World Class Performance Programme, a system of public subsidies for elite athletes:

Awards are made to the governing bodies of sport following their submission of performance plans setting out the future targets for their sports . . . The level of support received by individual athletes is dependent on their individual performance. Competitors are graded according to their ranking or their results in world championships.[113]

How this new instrumentalization works its way down to individual sports can be illustrated by the single example of ice-skating. This is a particularly sensitive case: mass participation depends on the provision of an expensive infrastructure, and thus issues of social exclusion are highly salient; the UK has, unusually, a history of comparative success in international competition at elite level in this sport; and there is powerful potential for colonization by market values because of the crossover between the sport and the lucrative commercial worlds of ice dancing and variety entertainment. The National Ice Skating Association received comparatively modest exchequer funding in 1999/2000 (£80 000), but its mission statement now faithfully reflects the salient features of the new instrumentalization: success at elite level and combating social exclusion.[114] Thus, its objectives and priorities include: 'to be accessible to a broader base of the population; to deliver quality controlled programmes; to establish performance pathways, from beginner to international performer.'[115]

My argument in these passages is that the changed institutional structure of sport regulation since the 1990s cannot be accounted for in terms of the growth of systems of coregulation joining the self-referential world of sport to other systems. The content of the policies associated with institutional reconstruction point to the colonization of these formerly autonomous self-referential worlds by external systems of values. They transform the 'pointless' activity of sport into the instrument for achieving other valued social goals, notably those pursued by state institutions.

There are two other signs that what we are witnessing here is the destruction of hitherto autonomous domains of self-regulation. One has to do with the way entanglement with the European Union is strengthening processes of colonization by both the market and the state. Parrish has documented the effect both of the European Union's competition law and the jurisprudence of the European Court in these processes. Perhaps the best-known example has been the way the 'Bosman ruling' has revolutionized the contractual relationships between professional footballers and their clubs.[116] Less dramatic, but perhaps even more analytically significant, has been the Court's judgement in respect of the selection of pace makers in professional cycling, because it has penetrated the very heart of sport's self-referential system, the rules governing the terms of sporting competition. The Court's judgement lays down the conditions under which national cycling federations can (and cannot) restrict the selection of pace makers in cycling to those of the federation's own nationality. More generally, it establishes that where sport is defined as an economic activity, its conduct is to be governed not by its autonomous rules but by those that govern the wider conduct of economic life in the Union.[117]

The second sign that we are here witnessing the rise of an assertive state is provided by domestic British evidence of intervention in what might be called 'quasi-sports' that hitherto functioned autonomously in civil society. These are organized pursuits that were typically closely integrated with the fabric of particular communities. Various organized forms of hunting with dogs supply the best-known examples in recent years: for foxes, stags, and—in the form of coursing—for hares. The return of a Labour majority in the House of Commons in 1997 saw the beginning of a campaign—not yet successfully concluded—either to ban or closely control these activities.[118] This campaign itself displays a distinctively modernist mentality, in its ambition to control activities and sensibilities—notably to do with human intervention in the natural world—that were hitherto the independent preserve of civil society. But the defensive strategies of the threatened sports have also contributed to instrumentalization, because their case has rested, not on the character of the pursuit itself, but on its alleged instrumental contribution to other aims: for example, pest control or the provision of jobs in local economies in the case of fox hunting; or social control of potentially unruly social elements in the case of another threatened activity, boxing.[119]

The bare institutional details of the changed regulation of sport in Britain are consistent with a variety of interpretations—either that we are witnessing the expansion of the interventionist ambitions of the new regulatory state or the adaptive evolution of a system of coregulation. But the policy content associated with those changes suggests not adaptive coregulation but the destruction of regulatory autonomy and the rise of new modes of social engineering. The best summary way to express this is to say that the changes amount to the instrumentalization of sporting and leisure activity: the transformation of activities that are deliberately 'pointless' into activities justified by their contribution to some external social purpose. Of these, the most important are: fostering sport as an important economic activity; using sport to help achieve wider purposes of social policy, like promoting public health and combating social exclusion; and using sport at elite level as an index of national competitive achievement.

The significance of these shifts in the regulation of sport is reinforced by the way they are reflected in changes in other traditionally autonomous, self-referential social domains. The most obvious parallel concerns the regulation of the arts in Britain, where there is both institutional innovation and a growing instrumentalization of artistic activity. The notion of the arts as a sphere of industrial activity; the notion of high artistic achievement as an index of national success for which the state takes responsibility; and the notion of the arts as an instrument assisting social engineering projects, like combating social exclusion or raising levels of educational achievement: all surface in contemporary efforts to promote and fund artistic activity. Particularly after the return of Labour to office in 1997, the vocabulary of arts policy took a markedly instrumental turn. The setting up of the Creative Industries Task Force in 1997 has inaugurated an era where the arts are assimilated to the wider category of 'creative industries', and where this, in turn, has been followed by the attempt both to develop a strategy for competitive success in these industries and annually to map their economic health.[120] This is also reflected in the account of the arts given by the Arts Council. The Council now speaks of the 'arts economy' as a subset of the creative industries, and adds to it the new concerns with participation and exclusion. Key features include measuring the 'reach' of forms like opera, as indicated by audience participation rates; the stress on the role of the arts in affecting quality of life and decisions about business location; and the use of the arts in revitalizing formerly derelict areas like inner cities.[121]

HIGH MODERNISM AND SELF-REGULATION

The historical boundaries of the system of self-regulation in Britain are hard to describe. The traditionally uncodified and unorganized character of British self-regulation lies at the root of the problem. But this descriptive difficulty is itself highly revealing about self-regulation in Britain. It was precisely the fuzzy boundaries—allowing self-regulation to shade off into civil society at one end, and to shade into the world of quasi-government at the other—that created constitutional ambiguities and silences. That gave self-regulation great ideological power, and facilitated one of the most important functions of regulatory ideology: mystification. The shadow-like nature of self-regulation meant that lines of accountability and responsibility were lost in labyrinths. Watchwords like 'flexibility'—signals of the supposed superiority of self-regulation over more 'rigid' modes—could be invoked to legitimize any one of a large number of different institutional arrangements. This kind of mystification was needed because the dominant parts of the self-regulatory system were by the closing decades of the twentieth century operating in an alien historical environment. Creations of a pre-democratic, nineteenth-century world, they now had to function in the very different world of the late twentieth century.

What was it like trying to live in this new world? It was to experience incessant change from a novel, threatening kind of state.[122] The reconstruction of self-regulatory institutions along more formally organized, more codified, and more state controlled lines was seen everywhere. The history of self-regulation in the last third of the twentieth century exemplifies the age of hyper-innovation. Few important self-regulatory settlements were immune from change, and few of the new settlements 'stuck'. All the institutional arrangements described in these pages are highly provisional in character; if we revisit them in a decade we will almost certainly find that they have been further transformed. These self-regulatory institutions were confronting a new and ambitious kind of state, and this was what so comprehensively undid them. These state ambitions, as the range of diverse examples in the preceding pages show, were shaped, in turn, by a diversity of forces. Schematically, we can identify three.

First, after the great economic crisis of the mid-1970s the state was struggling, especially in the Thatcher years, to reconstruct an economy capable of withstanding the threat of global economic competition. Since huge areas of the self-regulatory system were themselves entangled with an old economy of cartels and restrictive practices, dismantling these restrictive practices entailed dismantling the institutions of self-regulation. This is the single most important reason for the revolutionary reconstruction of regulation in the financial markets, and it is one important reason for the persistent pressures over these decades to reconstruct regulation in the most important 'liberal' professions like law and accounting. By the turn of the millennium, this movement had turned into persistent, nagging pressure by the key state agency concerned with competitiveness—the Office of Fair Trading—on professions either to justify their restrictive practices by some public interest standards, or to abandon them. As the Office of Fair Trading made clear in its investigation of competition in the three domains of law, accounting, and architecture—examined above in connection with lawyers—that investigation was no isolated event. On the Office's own words, it exploited the widening powers of the Office of Fair Trading and was 'a key stage in an ongoing programme of review of competition in professional services in the UK. It built upon past action to highlight remaining restrictions that continued to constrain freedom to compete.'[123] In short, it was a central part of a characteristic project of high modernity: reshaping hitherto autonomous spheres of civil society in the name of a centrally prescribed goal, namely national efficiency.

Second, the state was increasingly entangled in regulatory systems and obligations beyond its borders. In the accounts offered here, these influences are mostly submerged, but when we turn to the examination of globalization and Europeanization in Chapter 7, we will see them made more visible. Even here, however, we can see some obvious effects: the new architecture of financial regulation, erected in two great bursts in the legislation passed in 1986 and 2000, was closely connected to the integration of London's markets into a global system.

Third, the self-regulatory institutions were now operating with a state that was no longer controlled by an oligarchy ruling in a deferential political culture. This explains one of the most persistent features of regulatory change in this era: the colonization of hitherto private regulatory worlds by the institutions and cultures of the public realm—by the law and by central government. The ambitions of the new regulatory state all pointed in one direction: towards the instrumentalization of regulatory systems. A key feature of traditional self-regulation—its ability independently to establish its own regulatory standards—greatly declined. One of the most important signs of the change was the succession of crises, in very different regulatory domains, about standards. There were periodic uproars about the inadequate range and rigour of the professional disciplinary standards applied by leading professions like accountants, doctors, and lawyers. Teachers lost their hard won controls over what went on in the classroom (a process we examine from a different angle in Chapter 6). The City was buffeted by recurrent scandals across a range of financial markets that all had a recurrent theme—they arose from the public exposure and censure of practices that were engrained in the traditional way of doing business. A well-documented example is the old City custom of insider trading that was successively publicized, stigmatized, and finally criminalized.[124] Self-regulation could no longer establish its own terms of reference. If it was to persist it had to justify itself by externally prescribed means and externally prescribed ends: become, in other words, the instrument for achieving wider social purposes, be they the delivery of efficient health care, honest and prudent financial services, competent legal advice, or internationally successful sport.

This instrumentalization is why the example of sport regulation transcends the substantive importance of sport as an economic domain. Sport emerged in its modern codified forms in the later decades of the nineteenth century as the quintessentially 'pointless' activity, governed by its own separate, self-referential codes. Until the 1990s, it remained among the purest examples of self-regulation. The institutional reconstruction of sport regulation that then took place was thus a great historic change. Now sport was increasingly conceived as an instrument for achieving purposes external to the pointless activity itself: national prestige in elite sporting competition or improved public health through mass sport. And, as I have suggested in passing, this instrumentalization has also affected other historically pure areas of self-regulation, like the arts. There is a new regulatory state at work here, but it is hard to reconcile the recent experience of self-regulation with an image of that state as a kind of postmodern exercise in modestly conceived, reflexively executed regulatory ambitions. It looks, to the contrary, like a continuation of the great interventionist projects of Scott's 'high modernism'.[125]

There nevertheless were important areas of economic activity where in the 1980s and 1990s the state in Britain did manifestly give up on an interventionist project: the project that involved large-scale public ownership of key industries and utilities. The regulatory implications of this shift are examined in Chapter 5.

5

Regulating Privatization

PRIVATIZATION IN THE AGE OF HYPER-INNOVATION

Privatization is perhaps the best known, and certainly one of the most thoroughgoing, parts of the revolution in economic policy and institutions that came over Britain in the wake of the economic crises of the 1970s. In both the scale of privatization and the institutional elaboration of a regulatory system for the newly privatized sector, Britain stood out. Among advanced industrial nations, she pioneered routes followed by others, notably in Western Europe. She was in the vanguard in privatizing the key utilities, and in scale of privatization again led the way: for example, among OECD nations, asset sales as a proportion of GDP were exceeded only by New Zealand, and the other nations were well behind these two leaders.[1] The United Kingdom also stood out from her leading partners in the European Union in willingness to create distinct regulatory regimes for the newly privatized sector.[2] In other words, privatization fits our picture of the British as international leaders in institutional innovation in the last couple of decades; and the domestic experience confirms our picture of this period as an epoch of hyper-innovation within Britain.

The privatization programme was, in the most obvious sense, an economic revolution. It overturned commitments to public ownership, which, in many cases, dated back over a century, and it profoundly changed the market setting, the labour relations, and the managerial practices of the privatized industries. But this economic revolution was only half the story; the other half concerns privatization as a political revolution. Graham has crisply identified the most obvious political sense of this change: it was a constitutional revolution.[3] It was a profound disturbance of the prevailing political settlement because it redrew the line drawn separating the public from the private; and it was thus a constitutional upheaval because plainly one function of a constitution is to help draw that boundary.

But there is a deeper, second sense in which privatization was a political revolution, and it is central to this chapter. It epitomized the transformation of the British system into a laboratory of hyper-innovation. Privatization was an unplanned economic and constitutional revolution, but it was not an accident. Powerful pressures pushed the state to privatize, and impelled it to create the regulatory structure analysed in this chapter. In a nutshell: the new regulatory creations reflected the exhaustion of one mode of economic government, which ruled the old system of nationalized industries, and the inadequacy of another, which connected with the traditional mode of regulating business in the private sector.

This argument returns us to themes central to Chapter 4: in particular, to the exhaustion of regulatory settlements originating in conditions very different from those prevailing at the close of the twentieth century. The regulatory settlement created to accommodate privatization did not just result from the exhaustion of traditional modes of public ownership. It also reflected profound problems in traditional modes of regulating the private corporate sector. Privatization has, thus, coincided with—and partly caused—an era of hyper-innovation in business regulation. The privatized regulatory regime has itself proved fragile and unstable, collapsing completely at its first great crisis, in the rail industry. This fragility has also been deeply unsettling for the wider system of business regulation in Britain. The era of hyper-innovation in these twin domains, therefore, is the product of a highly destabilizing mixture: an unstable regulatory regime for privatization itself and a wider, fragile, system of business governance.

The substantive argument dictates the shape of this chapter. Since privatization regulation is an exercise in the regulation of the business enterprise, I begin at the point where privatization entered: with a sketch of what the regulation of the enterprise traditionally looked like. That entails describing, in the next section, both the dominant mode of regulating the private sector and the regulatory mode associated with nationalization. I then examine why the traditional modes were inadequate, show why traditionally established forms for governing the private corporate sector could not be transferred to the government of privatization; and show how the original institutions of privatization regulation were developed as an alternative. This is followed by a description of how that system of privatization regulation became embedded—with all kinds of surprising consequences. The account of rail regulation, which then follows, is of great analytical importance because it is a study of the first great crisis of the regulatory system—and of its failure in that crisis. Finally, I return the chapter full circle to examine wider issues of business regulation, showing how the fragility of this wider system has interacted with the fragile system for governing privatization.

CORPORATE REGULATION AND CLUB GOVERNMENT

Two modes of regulation governed the most important enterprises in the British economy for most of the twentieth century: regulation of privately owned enterprises was done mainly through company law; and many key industries and utilities were governed through various forms of public ownership, of which the nationalized corporation was the most important. Privatization obviously signalled the decline of the latter. In the case of the most important publicly owned industries and utilities, it created large enterprises organized as joint stock companies. In principle, therefore, there was no reason to create a special regulatory regime for the new enterprises, for there already existed an established historic mode of regulation in the form of company law. Indeed, many privatizations were absorbed into that wider system of business regulation: examples from privatizations completed after 1979 include the transfer of publicly owned parts of shipbuilding, oil exploration, aerospace, and air transport.[4] The creation of a network of regulators, notably for what are conventionally called utilities, plainly indicates a belief that the framework provided by company law could not alone do the job of regulating these privatized enterprises.

To understand the problems involved in simply subjecting the privatized utilities to traditional corporate regulation, we need to begin by sketching the established role of company law in the regulation of the corporate enterprise. Company law in the modern market economy has to answer three big questions. The first is: what is the proper relationship between legal owners and those who do the daily job of running corporations? That question arises from the most important structural feature of the modern corporation: the separation of ownership from control, which has since the work of Berle and Means been recognized as a central feature of business life.[5] The second question is: what claims beyond legal ownership give entitlement to a say in governing corporations? In the language that became fashionable in the 1990s, who are the legitimate stakeholders in a firm?[6] How far does stakeholding stretch beyond owners to encompass groups like employees and others such as consumers? It will be obvious that these questions are particularly important in governing big firms because they have elaborate managerial hierarchies and their property entitlements are usually traded on securities markets—and that is exactly the kind of enterprise that was created by the biggest privatizations after 1979. Finally, implicit in all this is the third question, the most fundamental of all: what is the appropriate relationship between the government of the corporation and the institutions of the democratic state? In simple terms: how far can the state intervene to dictate the internal government of the corporation?

It is well established that English company law has given highly distinctive answers to these questions—distinctive by comparison with the regimes of corporate governance that exist in many other advanced capitalist economies.[7] The reason for this distinctiveness lies in experiences that will be familiar from earlier chapters: the particular history of British economic development, notably our role as pioneers of industrialism. Company law, especially company law insofar as it concerned the regulation of the joint stock company, was invented in the critical middle decades of the nineteenth century, mostly to cope with the problems created by the new corporate forms developed, for instance, to finance the great railway building boom.[8] Company law, therefore, evolved in a political and cultural setting with which we are again familiar from our discussion in earlier chapters: in one where the modern interventionist state had yet to be created; in a political system that was pre-democratic; and in a culture where business values, and business power, were hegemonic. This produced powerful biases in favour of autonomous business self-regulation—as we saw in Chapter 4—and similarly powerful biases in the governing assumptions of company law, as we shall now see.

It was the distinctive answers traditionally given by company law to the big questions about corporate governance that stood in the way of merely assimilating all privatized concerns into the prevailing mode of company regulation. Until the beginning of the twentieth century, the traditional legal model treated directors merely as agents of the company. At the start of that century the doctrine was abandoned by the courts in favour of a model that recognized the distinctive role of managers, and treated boards as distinctive organs of companies.[9] That change decisively shifted the initiative, in the wake of the separation of ownership from control, to boards dominated by professional managers. The traditional legal model of the firm, meanwhile, pictured it as the product of a set of contractual agreements between shareholders. The firm was a private entity, and entitlement to a say in its governance was reserved for those with the property rights signified by legal ownership in the form of holdings in equity. In the words of a modern study of company law: 'in Britain the company has traditionally been thought of more as a voluntary association between shareholders than as a creation of the state.'[10] The rise of this model in England also coincided with the waning of what is usually called the 'concessions' model of the company.[11] The concessions model saw the company as a legal creation upon which the state conferred privileges not granted to other economic actors. These included monopoly rights, such as those granted to the great trading companies that were instruments of mercantile capitalism in the early phases of imperialism; rights to infringe the property entitlements of others, such as those necessary to allow railway construction; and, most important of all, the privilege of incorporation with limited liability that allowed the accumulation of large amounts of investment capital from financial markets in the early phases of industrial capitalism.[12]

It will be clear that a concessions model implies a very different relationship between the state and the enterprise than is suggested by one that sees the company as the product of a private contractual arrangement between shareholders. In the concessions model, property rights in the enterprise are conditional entitlements, privileges that depend on performing some public obligations or recognizing some restraints over corporate behaviour in the wider public interest. The conception of the concessions model echoes the argument of Reich's famous paper on property, where some important forms of property are identified as 'largesse'—concessions by public power that entail observing constraints governed by the public interest.[13] To anticipate: the rise of privatization regulation was momentous because it involved the revival of this hitherto anachronistic model of corporate government.

The concessions model had originally declined because the benefits of incorporation—such as limited liability—became widely and more or less automatically available.[14] But other important areas of social and economic life were still treated as the product of state 'largesse'. Some British 'largesse', indeed, exactly resembled Reich's 'new property'. These included rights to private property in agricultural land, whose exercise after the Second World War was conditional on appropriate cultivation: the 1947 Agricultural Act imposed on cultivators a 'duty of good husbandry' and gave to the state the power to sell off the land of those who failed in that duty.[15] Other largesse covered franchises awarded by the state, of which perhaps the best known were the broadcasting franchises granted in commercial television from the middle of the 1950s.[16]

The decline of the concession model, nevertheless, meant that the law operated with a light touch. The central issue created by the separation of ownership from control—the relations between the managers of the firm and its legal owners— was simply not addressed at all. Company law only prescribed that an enterprise had to have directors. It said nothing about the role of non-executive directors, nor about key distributional problems like the way the rewards of directors were to be settled.[17] As we shall see, the privatized industries played an important part in exposing the contentious nature of these distributional issues. An accumulation of economic regulation, true, gave other stakeholders—creditors, employees— some specific entitlements; but these were not entitlements in ownership, only claims against the legal owners. We should also recall from Chapter 4 how the historically prevailing regulatory ideologies, which emphasized the virtues of self-regulation where at all possible, and consensual regulation in those rare instances where the law was needed, buttressed this system of light touch company law. Ideologies of self-regulation, as we saw earlier, placed large areas of economic life beyond the reach of the democratic state.

This abstentionist tradition was reinforced by the dominant post-war style of mergers and monopolies regulation, the one important area of business regulation where the state did establish early a specialized regulatory agency. (The original Monopolies and Restrictive Practices Commission was founded in 1948; it is better known as the Monopolies and Mergers Commission and became the Competition Commission in 1999.) Wilks's history of the MMC demonstrates how far it deferred to business. The Commission surrendered control of the *process* of merger and acquisition control to the City's own self-regulatory institutions—something we have already touched on in Chapter 4.[18] More generally, his summary of the early culture and history of the Commission might serve as a paradigmatic instance of club regulation operating with a distinct business bias. His dominant themes stress:

the avoidance of legal process and the determined retention of room for bargaining implied in ministerial discretion. They emphasise the accommodating approach taken towards industry and the respect for reasonable business behaviour and voluntary compliance with inquiries and recommendations. Additionally they stress the tendency towards 'negotiated legislation' in which the views of business were given considerable weight.[19]

The creation of a nationalized sector dominated by public corporations might have been expected to mark a break with club values in economic regulation, but the reality was to the contrary: the government of the nationalized sector exhibited some of the most pathological features of the club system. The large literature on the nationalized sector paints an extraordinarily consistent picture, whether one looks at the traditional 'commanding heights' like coal and rail, or the more modern forms like the control of the modern technologies of broadcasting. Behind a public language of ownership and accountability, the reality was a sustained history of evasion of public accountability, behind the scenes intervention by Ministers to shape business plans around short-term political pressures, and lack of transparency about institutional arrangements. All this happened inside policy communities that welded together sponsoring departments in the core executive and the elite that ran the industries.[20] The creators of the privatization revolution interpreted these problems as arising from excessive political interference in public enterprise and this, as we shall see, drove them to try to install the privatized industries in a world of depolitcized regulation. But while backstairs political manipulation for partisan purposes was a notorious feature of the nationalized industries, partisan political interference was not the root of the problem. Backstairs arm twisting was made possible because the government of the industries had been absorbed into the club world. Some of this becomes clearer in Chapter 6, when we examine how club government protected policy makers in Whitehall from public accountability and control. Part of the problem was also due to the broader character of constitutional law. Public lawyers like Craig and Prosser have documented the failure to develop in Britain a distinct public service law, and the corresponding failure to develop any explicitly expressed expectations of distinct public service in the nationalized industries.[21] The result was that, in Prosser's words, 'the nationalized industries became notorious for poor customer relations, notably the ineffectiveness of arrangements to protect vulnerable families from disconnection of essential services.'[22] As we shall see later, one unexpected outcome of the development of the privatized regulatory system has been to impose much more stringent public service expectations on the privatized concerns than was imposed on the old publicly owned industries.

This was the institutional world into which privatization was born: one where the prevailing theory of private corporate regulation, and the prevailing practice of public ownership, marginalized public accountability and transparency.

THE THEORY AND PRACTICE OF PRIVATIZATION REGULATION

Stumbling into Privatization

It is well documented that after 1979 the Conservatives more or less stumbled into large-scale privatization. In the words of an insider from Downing Street: 'from the inside we had no coherent policy . . . It came upon us gradually and by accident and by a leap of faith.'[23] There was little by way of public signalling in the 1979 election manifesto: it contained only cautiously worded promises for limited share sales, notably in the National Freight Corporation.[24] It is true that the internal 'Ridley Report' cleared by the Shadow Cabinet before the 1979 general election anticipated some of the early privatizations, but it actually explicitly ruled out what was to become the main feature of the revolution—the privatization of natural monopoly.[25] The combination of the wider British economic crisis and an archaic, incompetent system of economic government had by now, nevertheless, created powerful pressures for radical change.[26] Even before the return of the Conservatives to office in 1979 there were highly critical studies of both the competitiveness and the government of the nationalized sector, notably in a report by the National Economic Development Office in 1976.[27] But, perhaps unsurprisingly, politicians and officials who had grown up in the old world still tried to work the old arrangements. The early years after the return of the Conservatives to office were hence marked by attempts at piecemeal reform of the old nationalized sector.[28] The most obvious public example of this was the extension of the domain of the main competition authority (the Monopolies and Mergers Commission) to cover the nationalized industries in the 1980 Competition Act.[29] That the government did stumble, however reluctantly, into a wider revolution was due to two factors. First, the system for governing public ownership was so unresponsive that the reformist minded were pushed by the pressure of failure into more radical choices. In the words of a key insider writing at the time: the government 'was in a box' and it was 'time to design a better box'.[30] Second—again we have the attestation of an inside observer—the fiscal crisis of the state in the early 1980s was so serious that it drove government to use privatization receipts to try to conceal the fact that an administration committed to rolling back state spending was actually presiding over rising spending.[31] The accounting treatment of privatization receipts helped hide the extent of this failure.

This reluctant stumbling into large-scale privatization had a number of well-documented consequences. An ideology of privatization regulation matching in elaboration the ideology of the old club system was largely developed only after the event, or at least only when it was in full swing.[32] That is hardly surprising given the semi-conscious way the government stumbled into the privatization revolution and the speed with which the revolution, once embarked on, unfolded. More practically, again as insiders testify, the early critical privatizations—notably British Telecom, which was to establish a widely copied regulatory template—happened in an ad hoc fashion under intense pressure of time.[33]

If we step back for a moment from the immediate daily pressures to which decision makers were subject, we can now see that, in principle, they could have chosen one of three modes to govern the newly privatized sector: they could have just assimilated the privatized utilities to the existing regulatory structure provided by corporate law, something already done in some of the more modest earlier privatizations; they could have treated the new industries as a single special sector, subjecting them to their own regulatory regime under one unified regulator; or they could have equipped each of them with their own special regulatory regimes.

We can combine what we now know about the history of corporate regulation with the available insider accounts to understand pretty fully why they hit on the last of these three solutions. The insider accounts of the period show that the first choice was never a serious possibility for the big utilities. Indeed, the whole problem of how to create a special regime for the regulation of monopoly had been the stumbling block that stood in the way of any commitment to this kind of privatization in the internal debates before 1979. That episode showed that, even among the most radical thinkers in the Conservative Party, it was still instinctively assumed that there was something about privatized utilities that made them unsuited to company law regulation alone.[34]

And, indeed, the reasons are fairly obvious. The picture that we painted in the preceding section was of a corporate regulatory culture that assigned a high level of autonomy to individual firms in their corporate governance and market practices. The invention of privatization challenged this model for a simple reason: the special characteristics of the privatized sector meant that it could not be assimilated to this prevailing model of corporate governance in Britain. These special characteristics arose from two features: the unusual product and consumer markets where the privatized industries operated and the way they were privatized. We need to summarize these two to understand why the state was launched on its great period of creativity that produced the new agencies of regulation.

The big corporate privatizations, of course, involved utilities that were part of the core of the economy: telecommunications, 1984; gas supply, 1986; electricity generation and supply, 1989; water, 1991. (For simplicity of chronology, the dates are those of the major regulatory statutes.) There is convincing, and entirely unsurprising, survey evidence that public perceptions place the services they supply as among the essentials of life. Fuel and water, in particular, are ranked by the population right at the top of the necessities of human existence. The goods and services produced by these utilities are also for the most part non-substitutable. There is no realistic alternative for a household in urban Britain to the running water provided by a utility company. Disconnection from that network is thus a disaster for those involved. That observation only highlights the strategic position of the privatized utilities in the wider economy and society: the obvious example is the intimate link that exists between water supply and the infrastructure of urban life, a connection, in turn, vital to public health. Finally, some of these goods and services plainly have the features of classic public goods, notably jointness of consumption and non-excludability.[35]

It is true that goods and services produced and delivered by enterprises historically in the private sector have some of these characteristics. Food, for example, ranks right at the top of any list of the necessities of life when people are surveyed on this matter. And it is indeed striking that this is one area where the state has imposed special limits on property rights: entitlements in farmland have been, as we saw earlier, contingent on proper cultivation.[36] It is also true that neither licences nor franchises are unknown beyond the privatized domain: one has only to think of the regime governing the delivery of terrestrial commercial television. But no significant part of the economy historically in the private sector matches the privatized utilities in the combination of ways summarized above: in perceptions of necessity; non-substitutability; standard public goods features; and dependence on the state for the privileges of licences and franchises.

The circumstances of the privatization programme reinforce the special character of this corporate sector, emphasize its unique legitimation requirements, and show that it amounts to a form of 'new property' in Reich's sense—a manifestation of 'largesse' from the state. The flotations for the most important privatizations had, by the standards of conventional private flotations, an unusual feature. They were deliberately priced at a deep discount, usually offering investors an immediate paper profit when trading opened. The most favourable interpretation of this practice was that it was designed to maximize popular ownership; the least favourable that it was an electoral bribe. Whatever reason is credible, the terms of most privatizations amounted to largesse by the state—transferring public property to private interests at concessionary prices. The value of this largesse was remarkable. All the privatizations registered both short- and long-term gains in share value ahead of the average gain of all traded shares. In some cases, the gains were spectacular: prices in the privatized regional electricity companies grew by more than 120 per cent above the market average over the first four years of privatization, while prices in the water and sewage companies registered a gain of 93 per cent over average market performance.[37]

In short, the newly privatized enterprises revived the old, abandoned conception of the company as the product of concessions by the state. These concessions created a range of privileges: control (often amounting to monopoly) over production and marketing of goods and services perceived by most people as basic necessities of life; transfer of public property to private hands at a discount; and the award of public franchises and licences to many enterprises that had been privatized on these favourable terms.

The combination of these features, thus, ruled out the straightforward choice of just treating the privatized enterprises as corporations that could be governed like any other private enterprise through company law. That realization did indeed drive policy makers direct to the second choice identified above: subjecting the privatized utilities to a special regime, but under a single regulator. Insiders again tell us that this was the first attempted solution: the task was offered to the Director General of the Office of Fair Trading. It is not hard to see why the authors of the revolution would have arrived at this position. The Office was already a well established and successful regulatory agency, so simply endowing it with more regulatory responsibilities would have short-circuited many difficult stages of institutional creation. But that solution was wrecked by bureaucratic politics: the then Director General turned down the offer, on the grounds that he had insufficient resources to do the job.[38] That he felt strong enough to refuse was itself a striking sign of something that was to become more pronounced when the new regulatory institutions became established: the way the creation of a new world of agencies brought into existence new sets of institutions with interests that had to be accommodated in policy making. That now left the third possibility, the one chosen: to create distinct regulatory institutions for each privatized utility.

The heart of my argument thus far is that the British state more or less stumbled unthinkingly into the great constitutional and economic revolution of privatization, in the process entirely redrawing the boundary between the public and the private. The prevailing model of corporate regulation that it possessed, essentially the product of a period of unchallenged business hegemony in the nineteenth century, was entirely unsuited to the regulation of the kind of corporate enterprise created by privatization.[39] Indeed, we saw in Chapter 4 that the model, insofar as it emphasized traditional self-regulation in the corporate sector, was already in crisis from a variety of other forces, ranging from the impact of membership of the European Union to the changing domestic character of the political system. Thus, having stumbled into the privatization revolution, it was necessary to invent a special regulatory framework for this novel sector. The obvious question was: what kind of framework could be created for this new world of specialized agencies? The detailed answers, as we shall see in a moment, were contradictory. They were contradictory because they reflected very different feelings among different groups of key actors. There was disillusionment with what the club system had done to the government of the nationalized industries, especially the way it had fostered a culture of surreptitious arm twisting by Ministers for short-term electoral ends. But in contradiction to this, many of the key decision makers in Whitehall—both civil servants and Ministers—had grown up in the club world and found it hard to let go of its governing assumptions: freedom from public accountability, wide exercise of discretion, and the privileged tacit knowledge of insiders. By contrast again, these very decision makers commissioned an influential account that offered a quite different vision of regulation: of a regulatory world where tightly constrained non-discretionary judgements would maximize the discovery processes of markets. In summary: the new regulatory regime had a contradictory ideological parentage. This contradictory parentage, as we shall now see, was critical to its birth and maturation.

Inventing Privatization Regulation

We have seen that the first, crucial moments of regulatory innovation were in the hurried cobbling together of a regime for the newly privatized British Telecom. Once the hard work of inventing the telecommunications regime was done, it was natural to economize on creativity and work by copying its key features. This gives a special significance to the most considered examination we possess of how to create a regulatory regime for privatization, that produced in the report commissioned by the Department of Industry on the regulation of profitability in privatized telecommunications from Professor Littlechild.

Littlechild's report (and his 1986 report on water privatization) has a threefold significance.[40] The core of his recommended regime—the famous $RPI - X$ price formula—was widely applied across the regulated privatized sector; key insiders like Nigel Lawson and Nicholas Ridley testify that the report had a big impact on official thinking and Littlechild himself became a major figure in the regulated world, as regulator of the privatized electricity supply companies.[41]

Most discussion of Littlechild's report on telecommunications focuses on his famous image of regulation as a kind of transitional period 'holding the fort' until the cavalry in the form of competition arrived.[42] But this was only a contingent image for an industry where Littlechild believed real competitive possibilities existed and could be fostered. His report on water privatization examines the very different world where the sunk costs of local networks created a 'natural monopoly par excellence'.[43] The key to the Littlechild model is not that competition can always be fostered, or that regulation will always wither away. It is that the core of the system, the price regime, should be constructed so as to minimize the discretion given to the regulator—and thus minimize the likelihood of the regime succumbing to regulatory capture by sectional interests. The telecommunications report contains an extended discussion, and rejection, of American style rate of return regulation precisely on these grounds.[44] It is this determination to contain discretion, and therefore the dangers of special interest politics, which explains why the heart of the regime is formulaic. It turns around the $RPI - X$ formula, where RPI is the retail price index, X is a figure determined by the regulator, and the result calculates the allowable industry price increases in an allowable period. The formula, in principle, exercises efficiency pressures on enterprises, while allowing them to benefit from any efficiency gains beyond those mandated by the formula. Even more important, once the regulator has made the (public) determination of X, discretionary intervention in key operational matters is highly circumscribed. In particular, the regulator would not 'make any judgements or calculations with respect to capital, allocations of costs, rates of return, future movements of costs and demand, desirable performance, etc.'.[45]

This is a powerful response to the old diseased club system that had wreaked such havoc in the government of the nationalized industries. It is characteristically modernist, one of the fullest expressions of the democratizing impulse that was now challenging club government: democratic and modern in the way it sought to replace the tacit knowledge of insiders, and informal behind the scenes manipulation, by open systematic calculation and the application of non-discretionary rules. Its scepticism about key features of American style utility regulation struck a powerful chord in the official world that was creating the actual institutional structure. But the official scepticism was focused on very different aspects of American practice, and it actually reflected the continuing powerful hold of the club ideology over the official mind.

Alongside the world of discretionary judgements and the inevitable manipulation by special interests that Littlechild detected, there are two other important features of American economic regulation. Both arise from historically engrained characteristics of the political culture: the influence of democratic doctrines of accountability and the influence of a highly juridified constitutionalism. In the debates about the shape of the regulatory system to be created for the public utilities, these American features were pictured as things to be avoided—as undesirable signs of inflexibility and legalism in the regulatory process. These considerations were largely implicit in the first big utility privatization, of telecommunications, in part, because of the haste with which it was done and, in part, because the very fact of engaging in institutional innovation meant that the designers were feeling their way forward in a half-blind fashion.[46] The privatization of gas was a more self-conscious affair, because this time there was a longer opportunity to lay the ground-work (it was promised in the 1983 election manifesto) and because the regulatory options were much more extensively argued over. The arguments, in part, took place inside Whitehall. The 'sponsoring' Secretary of State and the management of British Gas wanted a privatization that disturbed institutional and market arrange-ments as little as possible, simply privatizing the monopoly. The Treasury and the DTI wanted privatization to go with extensive liberalization. The advocates of the more conservative option won.[47] The view was articulated with particular clarity when the creators of the institutions were faced with arguments that the formality, openness, and accountability of the American system should guide the design of institutions; for instance, when the gas regulation regime was being prepared. The response was a studied avoidance of any process of learning from, still less copying, the American regime. The American system of independent regulatory commis-sions was pictured as prone to 'unduly large bureaucracy'.[48] The actual American experience was pictured as a disastrous experience of over-regulation: 'we discov-ered the terrible mistakes that were made by the American regulatory system and noticed the way they almost destroyed the gas industry in the United States.'[49]

The stress on the importance of flexibility and informality, and willingness to privatize with the minimum of competitive upheaval, show how far the values of the old club world still influenced the official mind. The practical design of the institutions also showed the continuing hold of the club culture. Although there are obvious differences between regulatory agencies, the template fashioned for OFTEL, the telecommunications regulator, was itself borrowed from the Office of Fair Trading, an agency created in the early 1970s. The OFTEL template was then substantially copied in later agency creations. It had three particularly import-ant features. First, in line with the assumption that personal relations rather than formal rules were what really mattered in regulatory design, it assigned a central place to the individual figure of the Director General—a conscious departure, for example, from the standard American pattern of vesting authority in a regulatory board where decisions were taken collectively.[50] Second, it deliberately laid down only a broad framework of powers for the new agencies, seeking to maximize the discretion of the new DGs and to institute a 'light touch' legal regime.[51] Third, it actually sought to weaken mechanisms of democratic accountability, by compar-ison with the old nationalized industry system. While in principle—if not in practice—the sponsoring department of nationalized corporations could be held accountable to Parliament via the Minister, in the new arrangements the Director General was inserted as an extra barrier between Parliament and the industry.[52]

The American regulatory state thus loomed large in the birth of the new regulatory agencies, but it had very different meanings for different groups of influential actors. For Professor Littlechild, the exponent of a modernist theory of regulatory design, what was needed was a regime of maximum transparency and minimum room for behind the scenes manipulation, and what was to be avoided was the scope for discretion and manipulation allowed by American price control regimes. The good regulatory regime minimized regulatory discretion. But for the designers of the regulatory institutions in Whitehall, it was democratic accountability and the American displacement of tacit knowledge by the development of formal rules that was to be avoided—constructed as the rigidity and cumbersomeness of American legalism.[53] This is the sense in which the regime for privatization regulation had a contradictory parentage: one of its parents wanted to minimize discretion and to displace the old club culture; the other wanted to maximize discretion and to preserve as much of the old club culture as possible.

As we shall see, neither was successful.

The Transformed Politics of Price Regulation

The original schemes for privatization regulation reflected different and to some degree contradictory influences: in part, they grew out of a conscious disillusionment with the closed world of club government and what it had done to the nationalized industries; in part, they reflected Littlechild's vision of a regulatory system where discretionary intervention by regulators would be minimized; and, in part, they reflected the continuing influence of the club world. The evolution of the regime, in part, represents the working out of these contradictory legacies, but it also reflects wider processes of decay: the decay of the club system itself; the growing instability of the wider system of business regulation; and the interaction between that wider system and the problems of the privatized sector. In what follows, I examine the mix of these many forces. In particular, I trace the transformation of the heart of the regulatory process—the regulation of price—and then show how this transformation, though connected to some features of the price control regime itself, was part of a wider systemic transformation of the regulatory regime. In a nutshell: the politics of the privatized regulatory system has turned decisively away from both the style of politics that were suggested by the Littlechild model and from the rather different expectations of those who sought to confine it within the old club world. Neither of these visions—of a rule driven, non-discretionary regime, or a regime that retained the informality and closed character of the old price system—has been realized.

At the heart of the Littlechild model was a price regulation regime, and at the heart of that regime was the attempt to create a non-discretionary system that would escape the detailed involvement in operational issues, which, in Littlechild's view, had bedevilled American utility regulation. The heart of the

American system was 'rate of return' regulation. By contrast, as we have seen, Littlechild proposed—and the proposal was accepted—the formula based on RPI − X. This would minimize discretionary intervention in business decisions—and, in so doing, minimize also the incentives for regulated interests to 'capture' the regulator.[54]

But embedded in the RPI − X formula were issues that caused irresistible politicization, in the sense of turning the non-discretionary formula into the object of tugging and hauling by sectional interests. The most important of these was the issue of how 'X' was to be set in the first place—a problem that, admittedly, Littlechild had anticipated as a difficulty for a natural monopoly like water.[55] But the difficulty was not confined to obvious natural monopolies. Here is the account of the first DG OFGAS on his attempt to discover where X might have come from:

The opening price formula was prepared in advance of the formation of OFGAS. When, in 1986, I asked if I could have a set of working papers on the construction of the formula I was told that certain forecasts had been made by industry experts and it had been, in the final analysis, a judgement call. In the circumstances I accepted this, but when I pursued the issue to try to understand the general thrust of the judgement I was slightly disturbed to hear the value of 'X' had been set, 'To get the company off to a good start'.[56]

Thus, there was from the start a fatal contradiction at the heart of the 'non-discretionary' regime: the initial determination of the formula was itself not only the subject of discretionary judgement, but of the kind of off the cuff insider's agreement characteristic of the club system.

A related issue has been closely documented by Graham: it concerns the extent to which, in practice, the operation of the formula has involved powerful tugging and hauling between regulators and industries over its operationalization. It is worth quoting his words because they show how little protection from special interest pleading the formula could, in reality, provide:

the formula has also been adapted to allow for the pass through of what have been considered unavoidable costs, or sometimes socially desirable costs, thus producing an RPI − X + Y formula. This has been the case in relation to gas purchase costs, energy efficiency measures, the costs of electricity generation and the environmental obligations of water companies. This adds an extra dimension to the regulatory task because without monitoring the workings of these pass throughs, which are often the main cost drivers, inefficiencies can be maintained. This is a pointer to a more general issue, namely that price control has become increasingly more complex and that some of the cost drivers are not under the regulators' control.[57]

Gas provides a particularly striking example of the transformed politics of the regulatory regime. The very decision to try to privatize so as to leave as much of the old system as intact as possible set off nearly a decade of regulatory politics in which the economic regime was the subject of reports by the competition authorities and public arguments about price, service quality, and social obligations.[58]

At the back of the struggles over the detail of the price control regime lay a final important issue: what wider consensus existed to support the outturns of privatization? What level of efficiencies and what level of profits could command public support under a supposedly formulaic, non-discretionary price regime? The history of the utilities was bedevilled by arguments about 'excessive' profits, a history that was to culminate in the full-scale politicization of the issue, in the form of partisan argument in the parliamentary and party arena, the appearance of the issue of utility profits as a major issue in the 1997 general election, and the imposition by the new Labour Government of a windfall profits tax on the privatized utilities.[59]

The transformed politics of the price regime—a transformation that pushed it out of the world of the club but also out of the world of non-discretionary rule making advocated by Littlechild—therefore had a great deal to do with linked problems of operationalizing the formula and giving the results legitimacy. But these legitimacy problems were compounded because the struggles over pricing were taking place in a wider system of privatization regulation that was itself changing, and changing in ways that not only undermined the Littlechild system, but also dealt hammer blows to the rather different ambitions to shape regulation around the values of the old club world. Thatcher has nicely summarized the old pre-privatization regime, using the image of a game:

The operation of the regulatory regime in practice was a 'game' largely played between the utility suppliers, large manufacturers firms that depended on utility orders, and ministers and their civil servants. The 'game' was highly closed: occasionally outsiders such as trade unions penetrated it, but even so, mostly on employment-related matters. Users played little role. The decision-making processes were informal and involved discussions and negotiations conducted in private.[60]

Thatcher also nicely benchmarks the extent of the change that had occurred by the middle of the 1990s, after a decade or so of the new regimes:

The closed regulatory game of the pre-privatization era has given way to a more open and public one, with more participants, a higher degree of formalization of decision-making processes, greater public availability of information, more open conflict and complex manoeuvres involving ministers, the DGs, former monopolists, new entrants, consumer bodies and the MMC.[61]

These words, written in 1997, also anticipate a theme which now becomes important in our account. The very character of the structural change described here—the shift to more open, formal systems of politics—after 1997 helped destroy one of the main substantive objects of the privatization regime: the construction of issues in terms of the discourse of efficiency to the exclusion of a range of other considerations, such as social obligation.

The Drivers of Transformation

What drove the system out of the club world into more formal and public arenas? In part, the answer lies in the larger argument of this book: that by the time privatization regulation appeared in the 1980s that club world was itself in decay. But, of course, what was going on involved a complex interaction between these wider processes of decay and the forces shaping the world of privatization more directly. We reduce a complicated story—at the usual risks of over-simplification—to three processes: the enforced creation of an epistemic community of regulators; the increasingly formal organization of the regulatory world, which itself created problems of issue management and contributed to the rise of a wide set of issues to do with the social obligations of the privatized sector; and entanglement with the regulatory regimes of the European Union, which strengthened the already powerful tendencies towards hyper-innovation in the regulatory system. I deal with each in turn.

I use the language of the enforced creation of an epistemic community for the following reasons. As the privatization programme unfolded, and with it was born an increasingly wide range of regulatory institutions, there naturally occurred informal connections between regulators, both at DG level and below.[62] The development of the system deepened and formalized these. The most obvious epistemic effect has been produced in the creation of a formally organized system to examine common problems of regulation. These problems have themselves widened in range and complexity over time, as the price control regime has become increasingly complex and as, since 1997, the social issues involved in regulation have risen in salience. In October 1999, the regulators issued a statement on joint working, with the object of clarifying existing prac-tice. The DGs themselves meet five times yearly, each taking it in turn to chair and provide a secretariat. Regular items on the agenda include updates from each regulator, consideration of government measures on utility regulation—and consideration of a wide range of substantive issues from working parties that operate below DG level. These working parties include: a party on Concurrency issues (the meaning and importance of which I examine in a moment) chaired by the OFT; a working party on Administrative Personnel and Training, a key issue for any regulatory agency since the essence of the job is being on top of the latest details of regulatory regimes; a series of working parties on disseminating best practice standards; a group on the critical issue of regulatory accounting; and one on multi-utilities regulation, also a key issue as structural change trans-forms industries from those where firms specialize in one utility service to those where firms compete across a range of utilities' markets. It is in discussion of the technical detail in these working parties that we can see the emergence of our epistemic community.[63]

Part of the 'enforcement', therefore, is something long observed in the American system of regulation: a kind of inexorable logic by which regulatory intervention breeds an increasingly dense pattern of issues, and also begets the actors equipped with the language to argue these issues out.[64] But the timing of this epistemic creation, coupled with the appearance of concurrency as an issue, also provides another clue to the enforced nature of the change, and it brings us to the second major driver of transformation: those forces that drove regulatory issues out into more open and formally organized arenas, and widened the range of issues that regulators and the industries were obliged to take into account.

After the return of Labour to office in 1997, the main regulatory agencies were obliged to defend their institutional interests, as the new Government attempted to convert its electioneering rhetoric about the regulatory regime into a shakeup of that regime.[65] Labour's initial proposals provided a stimulus to cooperation because it promised major upheavals threatening the institutional interests of the most important regulators.[66] In the event, lobbying by the regulators ensured that only the energy regulators suffered serious upheavals (in the merger of the gas and electricity regulators into the new OFGEM—the Office of Gas and Electricity Markets).[67] The Act passed in 2000 has nevertheless considerably widened the range of privatization regulation beyond the narrow concerns with economic efficiency that were characteristic of the regulatory regime in its first decade. The Act not only established OFGEM but also attempted to shift procedures away from the club-like culture conceived by the original designers of regulation. In design, at least, the OFGEM regulatory regime represents a considerable move away both from the informality of the club system and the 'economism' of the 1980s and early 1990s. It establishes independent gas and electricity consumer councils. It imposes on OFGEM an obligation to have regard in regulation to various socially excluded groups, and to take regard of guidance from the Secretary of State on social and environmental objectives. It gives to the Secretary of State, in turn, new powers to promote energy efficiency and to promote cross-subsidization for the deprived. It imposes new disclosure obligations on both OFGEM and on the industry: on the former, to publish reasons for its key decisions, and to publish and consult on its programme of forward work; on the latter, to disclose the links between directors' pay and customer service standards.[68] It has already led to the publication of OFGEM's first Social Action Plan, at government prompting.[69]

But the Utilities Act, though significant as an expression of partisan political pressure on the regulatory regime, is itself only symptomatic of a movement observable almost from the beginning of the regulatory regimes in the 1980s: the piecemeal but persistent imposition by regulators of an increasingly complex web of public service obligations, covering issues like guarantees of universal service and safeguards against disconnection of services. The result is that, by almost any conceivable indicator of social responsibility, privatization marks a distinct improvement over the old nationalized industries.[70] The return of a new Government after 1997, therefore, speeded up processes of change in the regulatory regime. It led to more formally organized networks of regulators; it widened the range of regulatory issues beyond those of economic efficiency, to encompass more obviously social issues; and, in the institutional reforms of the energy regulation regime, it formalized what had hitherto been an informal drift to the creation of a more transparent and accountable system of rule.

The rise of issues of social accountability in the regulatory system marks a particularly profound change. The original privatization compact, as we have seen, was an attempt to redefine the issues in the government of these industries: in particular, to assert the primacy of economic efficiency and to wipe out issues that had been important in the government of the nationalized sector, such as those to do with the social obligations of the industries. The most comprehens-ive way this process was attempted was by assimilating the newly privatized enterprises in to the wider business sector where the 'normal' disciplines of the market in Anglo-American capitalism operated. As the Department of Energy put it, justifying the original regulatory structure for privatized British Gas: 'Wherever possible, competition provides the best protection for customers and every opportunity has been taken to open avenues to market forces and reinforce competition.'[71] That these words were written about a proposal to, in effect, privatize a natural monopoly shows how hard the official mind had to struggle to appreciate the new corporate animal it had created in privatization. One sym-bolic sign of the triumph of the Anglo-American model of shareholder-driven capitalism in the privatized sector was the virtual disappearance over the years of the instrument of the 'golden share', the mechanism by which government retained a veto in those cases where securities markets, in their pursuit of share-holder value, try to reshape ownership and industrial structure.[72]

This attempt to assimilate the privatized system to the prevailing 'shareholder value' model was undermined by a number of forces. The very rapacity of the wider business system—as we shall see later in this chapter—was itself under-mining the autonomy of business, forcing issues like executive reward, profit, and share appreciation onto the political agenda. In other words, the wider sys-tem of business regulation into which the privatized enterprises were being assimilated was itself becoming unstable. As we saw above, the attempt to 'silence' social questions was itself implicitly in contradiction with the very influ-ences that had led to the setting up of a distinct regulatory system for the privat-ized utilities. The most important privatized enterprises could not simply be assimilated to the wider system of business regulation but required their own special governing systems. These implicit contradictions were made explicit by the workings of the privatized system itself; in particular, by the recurrence of problems over executive pay, enterprise profit, and the scale of shareholder value accruing from stock price appreciation. Executive pay proved a particularly dif-ficult issue to contain, the most politically sensitive episode being the pay pack-age negotiated in 1995 by Cedric Brown, the Chief Executive of British Gas. Many features of this episode are remarkable: it brought executive pay onto the Cabinet's agenda for the first time in decades, and into the arena of the partisan democratic battle on the floor of the House of Commons;[73] it led to acrimonious and highly public grilling of Mr Brown by a Commons Select Committee; and it produced a tumultuous corporate AGM.[74] All these were signs that what had traditionally been conceived as the internal affair of the corporation was now a public concern. But, perhaps, the most remarkable feature of all was that, by the standards of corporate Britain, the behaviour of British Gas was quite restrained: the size of Mr Brown's pay package was modest compared with the pay of executives in similar corporations, while the issue probably only came to light because British Gas practised disclosure rules that were in advance of those for the private sector as a whole.[75] It could only become an issue because privatization had revived the concessions theory of the company—a theory hostile to the notion that corporate government was the internal affair of the corporation and the corporation alone.

The drift of these kinds of changes can also be seen in the rise of concurrency as an issue for the regulatory system to manage. Concurrency is shorthand for those issues of 'turf' and institutional jurisdiction that were from the first built into the very nature of a system of sectoral regulation.[76] In the original regulatory regime, the main line of intersection was with the (former) Monopolies and Mergers Commission, which had an appellate role in issues of competition regulation between the sectoral regulators and regulated firms.[77] The major changes in the 1998 Competition Act made these issues central by giving to the Office of Fair Trading and the sectoral regulators concurrent powers to apply the Act.[78] This has now generated an increasingly formal apparatus to try to settle jurisdictional disputes. An initial set of practical guidelines was created by a Concurrency Working Party made up of each sectoral regulator and the OFT.[79] In 1999, a more elaborate set of Concurrency Regulations was introduced, with the aim of formalizing such matters as information exchange and dispute resolution. As we saw above, concurrency issues are now one of the main concerns of the emerging epistemic community of regulators.[80]

My argument in these passages is not that the policies pursued by the newly privatized utilities necessarily show more social responsiveness than those pursued by their publicly owned predecessors, though there is a powerful case for that view. It is that the history of the privatized system shows that the initial attempt to create an area of silence around these social issues failed, and that the evolution of the system shows a broadening of the range of social issues that have to be addressed in regulation. The changes after 1997—such as the windfall levy and the Utilities Act of 2000—therefore have a significance beyond the comparative modesty of the actual measures they implement. They are a symptom of the fact that the system of privatized regulation could not, despite the ambitions of some of its creators, be run along the lines of club government; and to the fact that it was being inserted into a wider system of business regulation whose traditional procedures and assumptions were also breaking down.

We now have a sketch of two sets of forces that are transforming the politics of privatization regulation, driving it away from both the enclosed, informal world of club government and from the world of transparent non-discretionary decision making envisaged by Littlechild. One set is, broadly, internal to the regulatory regime and involves the growth of an organized epistemic community and increasingly dense networks designed to manage classic issues of bureaucratic politics such as the agency 'turf' problems that lie behind 'concurrency'. A second set of forces are broadly external, and involve a wider system of business regulation that is losing its historical autonomy in classic issues of corporate governance, such as the determination of executive reward and the proper range of the social obligations of enterprises. Finally, we turn to the third major influence on the shaping of the regulatory system since the beginning of the great privatization revolution: entanglement with the European Union. The destabilizing effects of the European Union begin with the very nature of the Union's policy process itself. It is marked by fragmentation; poor coordination; numerous games played in a multilevel system of government; poor public transparency; weak mechanisms of accountability; and shifting and unstable policy networks, especially in Brussels. Each fresh policy episode demands the investment of fresh resources to monitor policy genesis and to shape policy outcomes.[81] It would be hard to imagine anything further from the two competing models of the regulatory process that influenced the British system at its birth in the 1980s: Littlechild's vision of a world where regulation operated under tightly limited discretion; and the 'official' view that tried to shape regulatory institutions so as to preserve the old club system.

This powerful systemic destabilizing force has been strengthened by the complex recent history of EU economic regulation, including utility regulation. The emergence of a significant regulated privatized sector in the United Kingdom in the 1980s coincided closely with the great renewed bursts of policy entrepreneurship in the Community, which at the level of high politics produced the Single Market programme and produced also numerous sectoral incursions, notably by the Commission.[82] The most striking feature of these substantive developments is their variable, and often contradictory, nature. The ideology of the Single Market Programme, for example, pictured it as a turning away from attempts to harmonize competitive practices across Europe towards the 'light touch' regulation of concurrent recognition that was the prevailing legitimizing regulatory ideology of the Programme.[83] Yet the 1980s also saw the reinvigoration of the Community's wider programme of competition regulation, which, utilizing the powers conferred on the Commission by Article 85 of the original Rome Treaty, allowed the Commission directly to intervene in national competition regimes; to become a major influence on the shape of the 1998 Competition Act and in the life of agencies like the OFT and the Competition Commission; and, generally, in Wilks's words, to shape 'the most effective antitrust regime in the world'.[84] Across the network-bound sectors (meaning utilities like electricity, gas, rail, and telecom), the interventions of the European Court of Justice began to develop a complex jurisprudence—precisely the sort of legal entanglement that official designers of the original regulatory system had sought to minimize.[85] Another result of the fragmented nature of the EU policy system has, in turn, magnified the contradictions: it produces very different regulatory outcomes for different regimes. For instance, one part of the system has produced powerful pressures to address an important issue in utility regulation, universal service—thus strengthening the domestic processes that have been undermining the 'economistic' character of the regime that was originally established in the 1980s.[86] By contrast, Prosser has identified another part of the policy production system, which, animated by a liberalizing agenda, has strengthened precisely this economistic tendency: 'the effect of Community law has become so restrictive (in respect of competition law and state aids) as to cause many to question whether it permits any distinctive role for public enterprise.'[87] Finally, perhaps the single most consistent feature of the EU utility regulatory regime over the last two decades—the gradual rolling out of the Union's regulatory ambitions to cover an ever-widening range of services—has interacted with the unfolding of domestic privatization programmes in complex ways. In the case of telecommunications, for instance, the domestic regime has, in general, been in advance of the liberalization programme of the EU.[88] In the case of energy, the impact has been to strengthen the influence of corporate interests over, for example, environmental groups.[89] In the case of railways, the Union's role has been symbolic: the 1991 Directive was appropriated by domestic supporters of privatization as a subsidiary justification for privatizing the rail industry.[90] In the case of a utility which is being disengaged bit by bit from public ownership—the postal service—the 1997 Postal Services Directive required the creation of an independent regulator, now Postcom.[91]

The impact of the EU on the domestic regulatory regimes is thus complex, varied, and constantly changing. Its most important effects on the process of regulation have been to intensify the tendencies towards fragmentation and hyper-innovation. Hunt has caught this well in his summary of the recursive cycles of impact in telecommunications. The effect of the developing EU regulatory system, he writes,

is not the product of any single measure as such, rather it flows from the fact that the rules set down at EU level take a particular form which is fundamentally different to the basis for regulation which previously applied within the domestic British context. The fundamental distinction is that the British regulatory structure is largely founded upon a system of discretionary decision making, where the exercise of discretion is governed by only the broadest legal controls . . . Thus, liberalization and the pro-competitive regulatory measures which have been put in place using the domestic mechanisms, were not strictly speaking a legal requirement, rather they were matters of discretionary judgements. However, the adoption of the EU framework changes this because it establishes a distinct legal framework.[92]

The Crisis of the System

A central argument of the chapter thus far is that the original political settlement governing privatization and the associated system of regulation was fundamentally unstable. It tried to replace a form of economic government that was chronically politicized and showed the features of club government in some of its most pathological forms with a system of ownership, and of regulation, from which this chronic politicization could be removed. As I tried to show in the preceding section, the evolution of the system did indeed displace some of the more pathological features of club government. In particular, it broke open closed policy communities, enforced more transparency in both institutional relationships and in commercial transactions, and forced open argument about a whole series of sensitive issues, notably about the balance between the commercial objectives and social obligations of utilities. By any of the standards by which we might expect to judge economic government in a liberal democracy—accountability, transparency, plurality of representation—it was immensely superior to the way the nationalized sector had been governed. What it emphatically did not do was depoliticize the privatized sector. On the contrary, the history is one of the growth of increasingly complex and dense policy networks, the growth of epistemic communities within those networks, the multiplication of policy issues, and the entanglement of the system of privatized regulation with wider systems of politics, both domestically and in the European Union.

Into this unstable, changing system of economic government dropped the rail crisis of 2001–2. The crisis over Railtrack has an importance well beyond the domain of railway regulation, important though that is. The collapse brought about not only a transformation of the system of rail regulation itself, but also exposed some of the central problems of the whole system of regulation—in the process challenging, and then transforming, the constitutional settlement surrounding privatization regulation far more effectively and comprehensively than any of the considered reviews over the last few years.

We should begin with a straightforward narration of the crisis in the rail industry.[93] There is much debate about its fundamental causes, though most accounts trace it to the forms taken by rail privatization, notably to a combination of a hasty privatization combined with the breakup of the industry into fragmented parts.[94] The immediate sources of the crisis lie in two sets of events. First, there were a number of high-profile disasters, notably two train accidents that resulted in substantial loss of life.[95] How far, again, these can be traced to fundamental flaws in the system, especially the system of rail privatization and regulation, is a matter for dispute.[96] But there undoubtedly rapidly developed a perception that there was a crisis of safety in the system, and this perception led Railtrack (the manager of the network) to institute an emergency programme of repair across the whole network in the wake of the second major crash. For a large part of 2001, there was therefore barely a timetabled rail service across large parts of the UK. Several results followed from the combination of a perception of a safety crisis with a real crisis caused by disruption to services: a great loss of confidence in the industry; falls in passenger volumes after several years of expanding business; and huge demands on Railtrack for compensation for loss of business from the train operating companies.[97]

But this pressure on Railtrack's finances, though unwelcome, turned out to be slight by comparison with a second difficulty. The hugely ambitious and costly programme of investment in the rail infrastructure, notably the upgrading of key inter-city lines like the west coast London to Glasgow line was, it became clear by the summer of 2001, vastly over budget.[98] At the same time, the management of the company was in upheaval following several key resignations in the wake of the debacle over rail safety. When the new management went to the Secretary of State for further financial support in the autumn of 2001, he declined and precipitated events that pushed the company into receivership.[99] It is striking how far all this resembled the kind of relationship that had existed in the old nationalized industries between the industry and sponsoring departments—and, in the accusations and counter-accusations about the exact course of events in the next few days, how like the informality of the old club system these relationships looked.[100]

A great deal of dispute still surrounds these events, and it is unlikely that they will be cleared up in the short term. It is not even certain that a full inquiry with access to the papers could get at the truth because, in another revival of the club system, it is obvious that a great deal of business was done informally by a few individuals operating in the high politics of Whitehall. But for present purposes, fortunately, this reconstruction of behind the scenes bargaining is not necessary. All we need to bear in mind is that, for whatever complex skein of reasons, not only did Railtrack collapse, the regulatory settlement in rail also collapsed. To this we now turn.

Apart from changing the business face of the railway industry, the Secretary of State's decision to force Railtrack into receivership transformed its regulatory face. There were three great regulatory consequences of the crisis of 2001.

It Swept Aside the Regulators

A fundamental premise of the whole system of privatization regulation was that the regulators were the key actors in the industry. And, indeed, this was reflected in real changes in political practice: we have seen that one of the most significant power consequences of privatization was almost universally to displace sponsoring departments and their Ministers by regulators as the most important figures in the lives of the industries. The important political consequence of this change was to ensure that the original attempt to preserve the old club world was doomed. And we have also seen that in the struggles that accompanied the review of the regulatory system set up in 1997, the most powerful regulators emerged unscathed. In the case of rail, the complexity of the privatized structures, coupled with public dissatisfaction with those structures, and the reforms introduced by the new Labour Government after 1997, had left the industry with an elaborate regulatory system. Two figures/institutions were particularly important: the Strategic Rail Authority, and its Chairman; and the head of the Office of the Rail Regulator.[101] Perhaps the most remarkable feature of the way the crisis was tackled in the autumn of 2001 was the extent to which both were left on the sidelines. Although dispute surrounds the actual terms of a critical meeting between the Secretary of State and the Rail Regulator when the Secretary of State had decided to put Railtrack into receivership, what is undisputed is that the Rail Regulator had simply no control over this decision: he was just told of it after the event.[102] The same was true of the Strategic Rail Authority. Indeed, the Head of the Authority believed that the notion of an independent regulator had become a fiction: 'almost every breath we draw has to be cleared by Ministers.'[103]

The plans for the reconstruction of Railtrack have also fundamentally changed the position and role of the Regulators. The new 'not for profit' company will, instead of holding the regulators at 'arms length', incorporate them into its operations: the directors of Network Rail, the not-for-profit successor to Railtrack, will include a representative of the Strategic Rail Authority. Regulators have also been assigned major operational responsibilities of their own. The new company is responsible for day-to-day operation of the track, but major investment projects—such as the modernization of the West Coast line that helped drive Railtrack into bankruptcy—are now the responsibility of the Strategic Rail Authority. Perhaps just as importantly the process of regulatory design has been decisively shifted back into Whitehall.[104]

It Repoliticized Regulation

A fundamental aim of the original structure of privatization regulation was to 'depoliticize' the privatized industries. It sought to replace the club government of the old nationalized sector, which had allowed central departments and their political heads to play a dominant role, with a very different system of regulatory politics: a low politics of technical argument insulated from partisan political debate, and a low politics of extensive regulator discretion. At least in railways the crisis of 2001 swept all that away. The very mode of operation by the Secretary of State itself indicated the extent of politicization, since as we have seen the regulators were only told of decisions after the event. But this had further consequences, notably doing precisely what the whole elaborate institutional structure of privatization was designed to prevent: it shifted the arena of debates about the control of the industry back to the world of 'high politics' and the partisan politics of argument in Parliament and outside.[105] If the fundamental purpose of privatization could be said to have been to create a new constitutional settlement concerning the government of key parts of the economy—the newly privatized parts—the events of autumn 2001 effectively destroyed this purpose.

It Put Corporate Form and Purpose Back on the Open Political Agenda

One of the most striking features of the whole privatization regime was the extent to which it represented the triumph of a particular corporate form—a form that was heavily influenced by the dominant culture of Anglo-Saxon capitalism and by the institutional domination of stock markets, the publicly traded company, and the assumption that shareholder value should be the key consideration in making corporate policies. Even before the rail crisis, it was possible to see cracks in this structure. The Utilities Act, which resulted from the 1997 review of regulation, included, as we saw earlier, a modest strengthening of the social priorities of the regulated sector as one of the functions of regulators. In the water industry, there was taking place a campaign to reinstate a form of mutualization in place of the corporate forms established at privatization, in essence because the companies had realized that the scale of investment needed in the water delivery infrastructure, coupled with the price regime of privatization, meant that it was impossible to extract significant shareholder value from the industry.[106] And even before the collapse of Railtrack in the autumn of 2001, it was possible to see the signs of extreme tension between the demands of the corporate form adopted and assumptions about what should be the fundamental purpose of business organization in the industry. Thus, the decision by the Railtrack Board in 2001 to declare a dividend for shareholders was greeted with widespread criticism.[107] Yet, if the logic of a stock market driven corporate form was accepted, the dividend was not only perfectly normal but also indeed necessary to maintain the confidence of capital markets. This latter argument was precisely the justification offered by the Board in defence of the dividend declaration. The criticism it provoked was a sign of the draining away of support for the shareholder value corporate model in this key part of the privatized sector, for criticism only made sense if one had in mind a very different model of corporate organization. And, indeed, a very different model both of corporate organization and regulation appeared in the successor to Railtrack: a not-for-profit institution in which regulatory authorities served as Board members.[108]

The system of privatization regulation developed after 1979 proved highly resilient, particularly given the intense partisan argument that surrounded both the privatization programme itself and the shaping of the regulatory regime. The system was created more or less off the cuff in the early 1980s when the government first realized the scale of the economic revolution into which it had stumbled. The original solution devised in this way for telecommunications was then widely diffused throughout the privatized sector—and, indeed, even into other sectors: the regulatory agency was adopted both for parts of the public sector that had not been fully privatized—like the Post Office—and for the licencing of new enterprises, like the National Lottery.[109] It all amounted to a major, and highly successful, institutional innovation. During the 1980s and 1990s, the Labour Party moved from outright hostility to privatization to a point where, when it assumed office in 1997, it was actually proposing further privatizations and only marginal changes to the form and purposes of privatization regulation.[110] The rail crisis was the first major setback for the great economic and institutional innovation of privatization, for while there had been great public conflicts over the practice of privatization earlier (such as those caused by the problems of the water companies at various stages in the 1980s and 1990s), none of these had actually endangered the very structure of the system.[111]

REGULATING BUSINESS AND REGULATING PRIVATIZATION

The argument of the preceding pages has been that the original privatization 'settlement' has been undermined. That settlement created a special regulatory regime, and this had a paradoxical function: though plainly a political settlement, its primary purpose was to depoliticize the government of these formerly publicly owned utilities. But the modes of regulation adopted at birth involved two more or less contradictory solutions to the problem of creating this depoliticized world: a distinctly modernist attempt by Littlechild to create an open, transparent world of non-discretionary regulatory decision guided by fixed rules; and the very different attempt by the official creators in Whitehall to replicate as much as possible of the old discretionary and informal world that had privileged insiders in the club system. Neither of these models has survived. The new settlement was, I have argued in the preceding pages, undermined by two forces: in part, by evolutionary changes in the system (a mixture of market-induced changes in structures and changes in the political setting of regulatory institutions); and by periodic 'crises', spanning crises over competence in delivery of services, shareholder entitlements, executive reward, and finally the great crisis of Railtrack in 2001, which condensed most of the earlier sources of crisis into a single case.

The periodic crises of the privatized sector arose, in part, from the special circumstances of that sector—circumstances that were a mixture of the markets in which it operated, the goods and services provided, and the contingent circumstances of privatization itself. But the crises did not happen in isolation. They were occurring in a wider business culture that exhibited some odd features. The destabilized world of privatization regulation and the wider destabilized world of corporate regulation have interacted with each other to magnify the single most important systemic feature we have noted throughout this book: hyper-innovation in the institutional system.

The wider fate of corporate regulation is full of paradoxes and puzzles. The best way to understand these is to begin by considering what has happened to the political environment of business in the era of hyper-innovation. Viewed from some vantage points, the decades since the 1970s have been golden years for the political fortunes of business. For over two decades, governments in Britain have been committed to strengthening private enterprise. Since the return of Mrs Thatcher's first Administration in 1979, public policy has been biased towards fostering free markets, widening managerial authority, and increasing the rewards to those successful in private enterprise. These policies are well documented, and indeed they include many of the changes that form the focus of this book, such as changes in financial markets and in utility markets. But they also extend to well-documented changes in law and policy on labour markets that were designed to strengthen the hands of managers and property owners at the expense of workers;[112] and to changes in taxation regimes designed significantly to cut the tax burden on the best paid in business.[113] The return of a Labour Government in 1997 did not greatly alter these priorities: Labour's recreation of itself after the electoral disasters of the 1980s was designed to remake itself as a business friendly party.[114]

The results of this persistent bias in public policy are obvious. At the turn of the millennium, business in Britain enjoyed a stronger position than at any time in living memory. All the major political parties now believed that free markets and private enterprise were the keys to a successful economy. Critics of the market—whether of the left or the traditionalist right—had been marginalized in the Labour and Conservative parties. A combination of changes in employment law, reforms in trade union law, and structural changes in markets meant that British labour markets were now highly 'flexible' by the standards of our major European competitors—which is to say that managers had much greater freedom in Britain to hire, deploy, and fire labour.[115] And the combination of changes in tax regimes and the rewards to the successful accruing from freer markets meant that those successful in business now enjoyed fabulous rewards.

In short, business values looked uniquely hegemonic. But this appearance was illusory, as two pieces of evidence show. First, there is convincing survey evidence of widespread disapproval of business as a system of power—and evidence too that this disapproval actually grew in the years when public policy favoured business. The relevant polling data must be interpreted with care, since public responses can vary greatly depending on the moment of a particular survey or even the phrasing of a particular question. But the weight of evidence that there has been a long-term decline in support for, and approval of, business is consistent enough to override these cautions.[116] In short, as the political elite moved in favour of business, popular attitudes moved against it.

These changed public attitudes are plainly, in part, a response to public policy—the result of a feeling that the pendulum of policy had swung too strongly in the direction of business power and economic inequality. But that really only restates the puzzle, for it just tells us that the normal mechanisms for the legitimation of business power began to break down, despite sustained support across the political elite.[117] This brings us to the second piece of evidence that business, for all the support it now enjoys from party elites, is encountering serious difficulties in defending its privileges. This is provided by the mass of evidence about the changing regulatory environment of business, for one other paradoxical feature of the political environment of business since the 1970s is that, as the political elite moved in its favour, business encountered persistent problems in defending many of its historically entrenched regulatory privileges. That was precisely the lesson of the fate of self-regulation discussed in Chapter 4—reflected in the increased difficulty of defending the settlements in business self-regulation that originated before the rise of the formal democracy. In part, then, the story of the legitimation crisis of business entitlements is a story of secular change in British politics and society. But it is also a story about what might be called the 'spillover' effect of the problems of privatization regulation.

All systems of property need legitimation if they are not to be seen merely as the exercise of power and greed, but in a democratic political system the need to legitimize business property is especially pressing. Corporate property (and the entitlements to power and wealth that it brings) is unequally distributed—and indeed has become more unequally distributed in recent decades. On the other hand, the democratic political system is premised on rules of citizenship—on rules attaching equal rights and obligations to all. Some way has to be found of establishing a stable relationship between the egalitarian citizenship presumptions of democratic politics and the inequalities represented in business power.

Legitimizing corporate property entitlements is, thus, about legitimizing the unequal distribution of power and economic rewards. As we saw at the start of this chapter, legitimation was traditionally done by legal doctrines that pictured the company as a private association only marginally subject to public power, and by regulatory ideologies that pictured corporate regulation as the independent job of the business community. These linked doctrines, as we have seen, were badly damaged in the 1980s and 1990s: what had seemed part of the natural order of things ceased to be so. In these very decades, however, the inequalities generated by corporate activity became even more marked. As profits and the rewards to senior executives grew, the need for legitimation became more pressing at the very moment when the traditional legitimation mechanisms were being weakened. In this conjunction lies the continuing struggle by the business community to establish some morally defensible basis for corporate power.

The problems of legitimation in the 1990s crystallized around the linked issues of the profits achieved by many of the newly privatized utilities and the rewards received by their senior managers, as we saw in our discussion of corporate reward in the regulated privatized sector. But these were symptomatic of a more general problem in exercising corporate entitlements. Throughout the 1990s, a succession of committees and working parties, set up by business institutions and chaired by the great and the good of the business community, tried to reconstruct codes of business behaviour: they involved enquries chaired, in turn, by Sir Adrian Cadbury, Sir Richard Greenbury, and Sir Ronnie Hampel.[118] The history of these groups is illuminating: they betray a fatal widening of the terms of regulatory debate into spheres of once unchallenged corporate prerogative. For instance, the primary concerns of Cadbury were traditional: how to protect the interests of shareholders and creditors against fraudulent executives. (This was the age of swindlers like Maxwell and Nadir.) Greenbury's report was about the very much less traditional issue of corporate pay, and not confined to the privatized sector. The fact that it was set up with the encouragement of the deputy Prime Minister, and that Greenbury reacted with hostility and bafflement to the rough treatment he received at the hands of the press and Parliament, only shows how far issues that were supposed to be non-political were now being battled over in a more public, partisan world.[119] Hampel's report spanned the widest issues of corporate governance, and was intended to lead to a 'supercode', a self-regulatory code prepared by the Stock Exchange, which would still once and for all continuing public interest in issues of corporate governance.[120] By 1995, the issue of director and executive remuneration had passed into the sphere of partisan parliamentary politics: in that year the Commons' Select Committee on Employment was advocating an end to what it called 'self-regulation' and the incorporation of rules for determining pay into the Companies Act.[121] At the time of writing, government's continuing interest both in the structure of utility regulation and the wider regulation of companies shows that this effort has failed. There is no settled framework for corporate governance. The Government's White Paper on the reform of company law, published in the summer of 2002, promises a wide-ranging reform of the existing regulatory framework.[122] There has been no reconstruction of a lost legitimacy.

The central argument of this chapter has been that the system of privatization regulation is a reflection of the age of hyper-innovation in British government, and the onset of hyper-innovation has a great deal to do with the collapse of a club world that had pre-democratic origins. Looking back over Chapters 3 and 4, we can set the privatized regulatory system into this wider collapse, and the way it has interacted with the wider problems of business regulation in Britain. Despite the fact that we live in an age when public policy has systematically shifted both power and reward in the direction of those who manage and own corporations, the evidence of these chapters shows a system of business regulation that is fragile and unstable. The instability is revealed in three particularly important forms: the collapse of self-regulation in the most important heartlands of the economy, most obviously in the financial markets; the failure of the attempt to create a privatized regulatory world which would escape democratic political intervention and contestation; and the way the problems of privatization regulation, and the wider regulation of corporate form, have fed on each other. As we shall now see, the theme of hyper-innovation is if anything more important when we turn to the wider regulation of the public sphere, the subject of Chapter 6.

6

Regulating and Colonizing Public Worlds

HYPER-INNOVATION AND HYPER-POLITICIZATION

We now turn to what could be considered the heart of the regulatory state: the organization and regulation of the governing machine itself. But employing that image of a 'machine' to define the boundaries of the subject covered in this chapter immediately causes problems, though problems of an illuminating kind. Speaking of the machinery of government implies the existence of a set of institutional mechanisms that we can identify with government and definitively separate from spheres of civil society. Yet, as we might have guessed from the recent history of self-regulation described in Chapter 4, no such sharp delineation of a separate public sphere is possible. The single most important feature of regulation in Britain has been precisely the lack of any clear boundaries between the institutions of the state and the institutions of civil society. Reregulating the public sphere in the last couple of decades, therefore, has involved more than changing what is conventionally called government. The reorganization indeed covers four major domains and their examination is the task of this chapter.

The first, indeed, covers the reorganization of the central machinery of the state, the world of the metropolitan elite, and especially the world of the metropolitan administrative elite. Precisely because reorganization here affects the interests of those at the very core of the club system, the subject is both important and contentious. It amounts to the most serious frontal assault on the institutions and culture of club government in the whole development of the new regulatory state. The second domain examined is the reorganization of institutions of inspection. As we saw in Chapter 3, these institutions, indeed, also became embedded in the metropolitan machine but, with their 'field' organization, they ramified into the wider civil society. Change here is best thought of as the reorganization of some of the great inspectorates inherited from the Victorians. Examining this domain, therefore, provides us with a particularly striking instance of something that recurs constantly in the creation of the new regulatory state: the reshaping of the Victorian, pre-democratic regulatory inheritance.

The third domain examined extends deeper still into civil society. It covers the world of quasi-government. This labyrinthine world was where the state intersected with the wider civil society and with the world of self-regulation. Quasi-government—the world of the quango—provided vital support for the club system, for it reinforced some of its defining features: lack of transparency; insulation of interests inside cohesive policy communities; complex, hard to understand lines of accountability. In this way, it allowed powerful interests to feed off the formally democratic state while minimizing democratic accountability. The changes in quasi-government in recent decades, therefore, involve both a major institutional reorganization and a great change in the whole character of democratic politics. Finally, a fourth domain brings us directly to a key feature of the new regulatory state: what for shorthand I call the colonization by the state of new worlds of regulation. I show by three very different examples how this colonization has reshaped all three institutional domains discussed earlier in the chapter: the world of inspectorates; the world of quasi-government; and the governing world of the metropolitan elite—regulation of the constitutional conventions which it observes and the standards of conduct by which it is bound.

The above is a summary of the substance of the chapter, but a broader theme runs throughout. Much that is described in the following pages overlaps with what is summarily called the New Public Management. The British have been notable innovators here, prepared to push reforms further than most other advanced capitalist democracies.[1] Thus, we confront again the transformation of Britain from a regime of stagnation to a regime of hyper-innovation, but this time with an added twist: hyper-innovation has been closely associated with what I call hyper-politicization. The old world of stagnation was the product of a historically successful strategy to cope with the threat of democratic politics. That strategy involved depoliticization of key domains, in the sense of removing them from the spheres of partisan, electorally influenced politics and replacing these potentially democratic forces with the routines of low politics.[2] In this way, governing issues were converted into grist for the mill of specialized elites. The exhaustion of that strategy has produced hyper-politicization. The breakdown of the old mechanisms protecting interests from democratic accountability has also exposed these domains to the full force of partisan adversarial politics. By the end of the chapter, we will, thus, confront an apparent paradox: the new regulatory state, so often identified with the rise of neutral, non-majoritarian decision making, has actually exposed hitherto 'non-political' domains to the power of elected politicians. It is precisely this new exposure that has prompted such hostility to the new regulatory state from some of the old governing elites who benefited from the club system.

REREGULATING THE METROPOLITAN MACHINE

At the heart of the club system lay what I have at several points in this book for shorthand called the metropolitan machine: that set of institutions and practices whose natural home was Whitehall. Its full modern emergence coincided exactly, appropriately, with the onset of formal democracy at the end of the First World

War. That moment also saw the appointment (in 1919) of Warren Fisher as first Head of the Civil Service. Fisher's 20-year reign shaped definitively the unified culture of the Whitehall mandarin elite.[3] The year before Fisher's appointment had seen another key statement of constitutional doctrine: the publication of the Haldane Report, whose response to the problem of how to settle the power relations between the administrative elite and elected government prescribed a model of informal uncodified partnership between the civil servant and the Minister. The importance of Haldane lay not in its novel proposals, for instance, to reorganize government departments along functional lines, for these never came to anything.[4] Haldane's significance lay in its conservatism, for it affirmed an entirely traditional model of internal departmental relations based on theories of ministerial responsibility.[5] In this it also reaffirmed a key feature of the pre-democratic nineteenth-century constitution: a model of informal uncodified partnership between Minister and civil servants that originally crystallized in the 50 years before 1830.[6] It, thus, bequeathed to the age of formal democracy a set of constitutional doctrines developed in an age of oligarchy.[7] Two critical pieces of constitutional doctrine—the anonymity of civil servants and the notion of the minister/civil servant relationship as a personal, uncodified partnership—date from that oligarchic era.[8] As we will see later in this chapter, the breakdown of the Haldane partnership model caused major constitutional disturbance at the turn of the present millennium.

The twilight of this world of metropolitan club government was famously described in Heclo and Wildavsky's picture, derived from work done in the mid-1970s, of the 'Whitehall Village'.[9] In the more formal language of regulation, Hood et al. identify 'mutuality' as the model by which this elite traditionally regulated itself: a model that produced 'soft', negotiated standards, information gathering as much through professional exchange as through formal requisitioning, and 'behaviour modification by clublike persuasion rather than formal graded sanctions'.[10] That is exactly what we might expect, since the metropolitan elite in Whitehall—especially the civil service—were the very heart of club government; it is hardly surprising that the values and practices of the club were, therefore, distilled to their very essence in this world. Equally unsurprisingly, the history of this part of the governing system in the last couple of decades is dominated by a constant battle between the defenders of the club world and the advance of a world that exactly matches Scott's characterization of high modernism: 'standardization, central control and synoptic legibility to the center.'[11] A crude but effective summary of what has been going on is that the great changes in organization and practice at the centre amount to regrouping by traditional elites to try to recreate the club world—but a regrouping that is failing.

Here, I summarize the changes under a set of crudely differentiated headings: changes in formal organization; changes in managerial practices; and changes in constitutional understandings.

The changes in formal organization are best known and documented, and are central to most accounts of the British face of the New Public Management. At their heart, in turn, lies the great programme of Agency creation arising from the implementation of the 'Next Steps' programme originally outlined in the 'Ibbs' Report.[12] The 'Ibbs' vision is congruent with the image of the new regulatory state as an exercise in decentralization. Here is its version of how government would work when the agencies were operational:

The main strategic control must lie with the Minister and Permanent Secretary. But once the policy objectives and budgets within the framework are set, the management of the agency should then have as much independence as possible in deciding how these objectives are met. *A crucial element in the relationship would be a formal understanding with Ministers about the handling of sensitive issues and lines of accountability in a crisis.* The presumption must be that, provided management is operating within the strategic direction set by Ministers it must be left as free as possible to manage within that framework.[13]

The scale and diversity of the Next Steps programme makes generalization of its impact on regulatory relationships difficult. By the end of the 1990s, over one hundred agencies had been created. Even in their study of a sample of twenty agencies, Hogwod and colleagues found immense variation, arising from a number of unsurprising factors: the size of the agency; its history; the partisan sensitivity of its functions.[14] Nevertheless, a number of effects have inexorably pushed the regulation of these systemic relationships in a more codified, formal, and explicit direction—in other words, away from a world where informality and tacit knowledge give special privileges to insiders.

The first effect is on the side of agencies themselves, in the creation of a more contractualized set of relationships with the centre. This is shown most obviously in the explicit embodiment of the agency/department relationship in a founding framework document. The accumulation of evidence from the separate studies of the agencies is here unmistakable: there has been a long-term growth in this kind of formality and explicitness.[15]

The second effect is on the side of the central departments. As Hood and colleagues document, the effect here was to transform into a formal system of oversight what had in the past been a product of mutuality. They report as follows: 'One of the biggest items of regulatory growth within central government was the development of oversight units in the "parent departments" of Next Steps executive agencies, as what were once notionally direct line-of-command relationships were replaced by more regulatory arrangements.'[16]

The third effect is what might be called a resource effect. Regulation of relationships within the administrative elite in the old club world hardly involved any separate investment in the activity of regulation; the 'mutuality' model meant that regulation happened as a kind of by-product of other relationships. But this has now been replaced by a massive and increasing investment in resources explicitly allocated to inspection and control. Hood and colleagues have again documented this huge increase in spending by government for the purpose of regulating itself—so great an increase, indeed, that in the new regulatory state these resources now outweigh those directly devoted to the regulation of business.[17]

So much for changes in the organization of the new regulatory state. But there is an obvious link between these and our second broad set of changes, labelled for convenience 'managerial': institutional changes have been accompanied by an emphasis on performance management, the development of performance indicators, both at individual and institutional level, and the stress on the acquisition of operational and managerial skills.[18] This new world of the agencies is one of the most striking cases of the extent to which the core of the governing machine is being transformed by new modernizing values, for it involves a concerted attempt to shift to a world where explicit knowledge is superior to tacit knowledge. The shifts are so pervasive and so far reaching that it is difficult to do more than give a summary account of their impact in the space available. Three instances have to suffice.

First, there is the perception of change from those inside the machine. This is how a key insider (the then Cabinet Secretary) characterized the changes in 1999:

> If you entered the civil service in, say, the 1960s (as I did) the literature would have told you that senior civil servants were policy makers. They were not expected to know the cost of the resources that they controlled or the staff who worked for them. They would not have had budgets. They would not have described themselves as managers.
>
> By contrast: 'We now require people in public service to be good managers and good leaders of their organizations and to know how to achieve results through the people who are working for them and through the application of project management skills.'[19]

The second example is provided by the way the process of agency creation in the Next Steps programme was accompanied by another movement: by the rise of performance indicators and evaluation processes, especially in policy delivery. The spread of the 'Charter' craze after 1991, which swamped the concurrent process of agency creation, is a kind of shorthand for the rising importance of measurable quality in the delivery of services.[20] Following the publication of the original Citizens Charter, with its mantra of performance targets, charters spread like wildfire: by the end of the Conservatives' long reign in 1997, there were forty-one national charters and over 10 000 local ones.[21]

And the third illustration of the managerial face of change is how far this mix of changes has translated, in the daily work routines of the new agencies, into an increasing control over individual work practices and performance. This was particularly marked when agency creation had been accompanied or succeeded by policies like market testing, compulsory competitive tendering, and other species of privatization. Within the agencies, the pressures of performance management, far from 'decentring' authority and developing 'soft' bureaucracy, have led to more emphasis on hierarchical controls and the micro-management of individuals.[22] The last thing the labour process looks like in the 'new model civil service'[23] is a post-modern 'soft' bureaucracy. On the contrary, it looks like the quintessence of modernism: a hierarchically controlled, closely disciplined workforce subjected to the most minute surveillance and effort measurement. What is this but the attempted realization of one of the first great manifestations of modernism in organization theory: the Taylorist vision of a work organization in which minute control is exercised over the labour process?[24]

We have now examined two broad ways in which the new regulatory state has imprinted itself upon the metropolitan governing elite: in formal organization and daily managerial practices. There is a striking absentee so far from this discussion: the politicians (Ministers, especially Cabinet Ministers) who are also central actors in that elite. Now, in discussion of the third imprint—the constitutional—they occupy centre stage, for these changes affect a key relationship in the old system: that between the elite of the appointed civil service and elected partisan figures. It is striking how insistent have been the most established of insiders—like the Head of the Civil Service—in denying that reforms like the creation of agencies have anything to do with constitutional change: 'The reform is a management reform, not a constitutional change.'[25] Yet the form of management at the centre was critical to the most delicate constitutional relationship at the heart of the old club world: that between elected Ministers and permanent officials. The terms of the relationship for most of the twentieth century were, as we have seen, laid down at the birth of formal democracy in the Haldane Report's prescription for an informal and uncodified partnership between the mandarin and the elected politician. The partnership model institutionalized a range of constitutional understandings that had originally developed in pre-democratic Britain.[26] It was now to govern relationships in conditions where politicians had to fight elections under universal suffrage, and where there had appeared the threatening spectre of a Labour Party that used a newly radical rhetoric of socialism. Thus, the specification of a partnership model at the end of the First World War is not a coincidence; it was functionally necessary to domesticate the new democracy.

This domestication worked in a variety of ways. While there is a huge volume of work that attests to the fusion of roles right at the top of the policy-making machine, the traditional organization of the club was protected by a number of features: by a doctrine of individual Ministerial responsibility that meant that only the elected politician had to answer in public for policy, civil servants remaining anonymous and, therefore, protected; by the lack of any explicitly documented line of division between the roles of civil servants and politicians, a critical feature of the partnership doctrine; and by the fact that dominant control of the running of the administrative machine itself lay in the hands of the elite of the civil service.[27]

Critics of the way the new agencies were created have often noted the disjunction between the theory in the 'Ibbs' Report and the actual institutional world created by the Next Steps reforms. In the theory there is revived what Foster and Plowden call a 'Wilsonian' notion of the separation of policy making from its execution.[28] Not only is this distinction discredited in the policy literature, but the multiplication of agencies has created a fantastic kaleidoscope of institutions incapable of being fitted to the general formula, ranging from tiny bodies lodged in operational backwaters to those enmeshed in the most high

profile, politically sensitive issues. Of course, the pre-agency constitutional doctrines were also based on fantasies, but fantasies with a purpose: they protected
the confidentiality of the governing process inside departments from public and
democratic scrutiny, and in this they joined Ministers and civil servants by a
powerful common interest. The world of the New Public Management (of which
the New Agencies were an important part) was itself a sign of the declining hold
of such traditional understandings, as both politicians and Ministers throughout
the 1980s responded to the feeling that the centre of the machine was overloaded
and needed an infusion of very different theories of management from private
business to raise operational efficiency.[29] The Next Steps Agencies were, therefore, created when the constitutional ideology of club government at the centre
was already fragile.

The hopelessness of actually working a formal arrangement where policy objectives were set, and operational independence was devolved, damaged the original
constitutional consensus still further. The most revealing crisis was in the management of the Prison Service Agency. The crisis was most acute here, but it cannot be dismissed as marginal, or as a single-case aberration: the Agency was one
the largest produced by 'hiving off'. The Learmont Report into the crisis
(prompted by escapes from Parkhurst that Learmont traced to operational errors
and incompetence) led eventually to the dismissal of the Agency's Chief
Executive.[30] That dismissal also produced the Chief Executive's self-serving memoirs, with their revelations of the deep involvement of the Home Secretary in
operational matters.[31] But Learmont itself, and the related revelations about
operational practices, made clear that the problems of the division of labour in the
crisis were engrained in the very working of the system, for neither 'side' could
observe the 'policy framework/operational matters' distinction. Learmont
documented the way Ministers were deeply involved in operational matters; correspondingly, the Agency was itself deeply involved in policy advice. For instance:

In order to gauge the extent of involvement with the Home Office, the Inquiry asked
Prison Service headquarters to produce copies of all correspondence with Ministers in the
previous four months, from October 1994 to January 1995, comprising 83 working days.
Just over 1,000 documents had been submitted, relating to life sentence prisoners,
appointment of members of Boards of Visitors, parliamentary questions, ministerial cases,
briefing on incidents, reports on media stories with 'lines to take', briefing for visits and
meetings and briefing on specific prisoners or prisons. *One hundred and thirty-seven were
'full submissions', containing substantive advice about policy or operational matters.*[32]

The problem was systemic, and was not due, as his public vilification sometimes suggested, to the managerial personality of the particular Home Secretary,
Michael Howard. The contractual relations were simply swept away when issues
of sufficient political sensitivity appeared. When the Home Secretary made his
famous interventions in the operational detail of the management of individual
prisons, the Agency was actually meetings its agreed targets on cutting the
rate of prison escapes.[33] The political sensitivity of a few high-profile breakouts

rendered this achievement irrelevant. The very public nature of the crisis, notably the recriminations following the dismissal of the Chief Executive, was in many ways the most revealing feature of all.[34] The old 'partnership' model of the relationship between Ministers and the civil servants had left plenty of room for tense and difficult relationships. But these relationships, expressed largely in non-codified understandings within a culturally well-integrated elite, did not usually spill out into public argument. Prisons policy is, of course, a highly charged field subject to enormous pressures of politicization. But the breakdown of the relationship here was only the most extreme example of a wider tension in the Next Steps experience: between traditional constitutional Haldane-like conventions about ministerial responsibility, and the attempt to impose a more codified, standardized division of responsibilities.[35] The 'Ibbs' Report, we can recall, prescribed that: 'a crucial element in the relationship would be a formal understanding with Ministers about the handling of sensitive issues and lines of accountability in a crisis.'[36] Yet when the crisis appeared, the understanding produced the nightmare that club regulation was supposed to prevent: acrimonious public exposure of tensions within the metropolitan elite.

As we shall see later, this particular crisis is only part of a wider breakdown in constitutional understandings within that elite—tensions that were to become explosively public under the Labour Government after 1997.

REREGULATING THE INSPECTORATES

Inspection, as we saw in Chapter 3, was one of the great Victorian institutional innovations, the heart of the regulatory state that the Victorians created. The specialized inspectorate was the characteristic mode by which government sought to discharge its responsibilities to regulate the social and economic problems created by industrialism. But it also developed as the characteristic mode by which government sought to regulate itself: to monitor the areas where government emerged as a large-scale service provider—for instance, in incarceration and education.[37] Inspection was shaped by, as it helped to shape, the characteristic practices of club government: it operated cooperatively; it operated in a business friendly fashion when business was the object of control; it operated informally, which is also to say that it privileged insiders; and it worked in worlds where insiders were typically organized into small cohesive policy communities.

Almost all the major inspectorates saw great changes in the age of hyper-innovation.[38] The most obvious public sign was, precisely, the major symptom of hyper-innovation: the ubiquity of institutional reorganization. Barely an inspectorate, whether concerned with the regulation of civil society or with the regulation of the public sector itself, escaped some reorganization in this period. But the process was not even across the inspectorates: in some, change was fundamental; in others, marginal. That is only to recognize the obvious: that the

ability of different constellations of interests to resist change varied. More interesting is why the variation exists. I explore this in what follows by taking four
cases. Two involve traditional areas of inspection of business: environment, in
the form of regulating air pollution, and health and safety at work. Two involve
cases of 'inspection of itself' by government: one concerns the particular domain
of school education, the other what is generally summarized as the 'supreme
audit' function. Of these four cases, the regulation of health and safety is the
most analytically interesting. This is because it is the one domain where institutional upheaval and moves to more hierarchical surveillance and control have
been successfully resisted. It, thus, potentially throws important light on the
nature of change in this part of the new regulatory state, and of the limits to
realizing the state's ambitions.

Smith, and O'Riordan and Weale, together document the upheaval in the UK
air pollution regime—a regime that, as we saw in Chapter 3, had exemplified the
Victorian face of club government in inspection.[39] In the 1970s, new institutional
actors (such as the Royal Commission on Environmental Pollution) and new
policy entrepreneurs promoting 'green' issues entered the policy domain. A reform
network developed to challenge what Smith characterizes as the 'cosy relationship'
in the air pollution regulation community—a cosy relationship that was essentially
a replication of the values of the original Victorian system.[40] The crystallization of
that challenge was expressed in the Fifth Report of the Royal Commission on
Environmental Pollution of 1976, a characteristically 'modernist' document in its
stress on the importance of transparency in procedures and integration of administrative practices in the name of better implementation and control.[41] Smith has
shown how the entrenched interests—both of business and of bureaucrats in
Whitehall—obstructed institutional change for over a decade.[42] Nevertheless, his
comparison of the 1970s system with the new air pollution control regime introduced by a unified pollution inspectorate in 1987 shows clear change along a number of important dimensions: there was a shift towards a new principle (Best
Practice Environmental Option) advocated by the Royal Commission; there was an
increase in the formal requirements to consult publicly in setting standards; there
was a shift to writing regulatory standards into a formal consent; and there was an
increase in rights of public access to information at the disposal of regulators.[43] As
we might have predicted in the age of hyper-innovation, the institutional upheaval
at the end of the 1980s was not the end of the matter. In 1996, the Environment
Agency was created, bringing together in England and Wales Her Majesty's
Inspectorate of Pollution and the National Rivers Authority, the latter itself a by-
product, in 1989, of the institutional upheaval associated with water privatization.[44] Alongside these new arrangements there continues the Royal Commission
on Environmental Pollution, originally established in the 1970s. The Commission
is an institutionalized source of independent scientific advice, which, by the turn of
the millennium, had produced nineteen reports on a wide range of pollution-
related subjects.[45] In effect, therefore, the separate air pollution regime was now
integrated into a larger, more open world of pollution regulation generally.

If we compare the institutional world of pollution inspection at the turn of the millennium with that existing even two decades earlier, we, therefore, see some striking changes: a decline in the extent to which regulatory regimes were informally controlled; a decline in the cohesiveness of the pollution policy community; a significant increase in the range of institutional actors and in the formality and openness of the system; and a determined attempt to apply systematic coordination of different regulatory arms within a single coordinated institution. Small wonder that Weale invoked an image of club government under pressure to describe the trajectory of change.[46] (When we turn to the colonization of new regulatory worlds later in this chapter, we shall find that another characteristic Victorian inspection system—for food safety—was at the end of the 1990s entirely transformed in a similar direction, but in a more radical fashion: not only were the characteristic modes reorganized out of existence, but entirely fresh responsibilities accompanied this fundamental institutional reconstruction.)

A second major inspection system that saw upheaval was school inspection. This is both substantively and analytically an important case. It is substantively important because education provision was a major and pioneering part of the modern interventionist state: the state sector has long accounted for about 90 per cent of primary and secondary education.[47] It is analytically important because it was a domain where several different parts of the state—a partially autonomous profession, layers of government below the level of the metropolitan central state itself—inhabited a 'secret garden' of regulation.[48] This was a world where the 'British' style of informal, cooperative regulation was deeply embedded, and where the scrutinizing gaze of the state had all but disappeared: the Secretary of State at the beginning of the present upheavals that have transformed this system once estimated that under the old system it would take central inspectors 200 years to complete inspection of all schools.[49] As we saw in Chapter 3, it was also a domain where, despite the fact that the teachers were a client profession of the state, they had won an operational autonomy that compared well with the autonomy of traditionally 'self-regulated' liberal professions.

Much of this was turned upside down in the 1990s, following the passage of the Education Reform Act (1988) and the Education (Schools) Act of 1992. The formation of OFSTED in 1992 heralded a significantly different regulatory approach.[50] It created an institution that in culture and working practice was far removed from the main interests that had supported the old cooperative system. At the same time, there was a marked increase in the formal organization and institutional density of the regulatory system. In place of the fairly simple, small regulatory community that had joined an educational elite and a mandarin elite, there now developed a large, overlapping, and often competing range of regulatory bodies. By the late 1990s, in addition to OFSTED, there also existed: individual local authorities, the kingpins of the historically displaced system, who still nevertheless retained significant roles; a Funding Agency for Schools; a Schools Curriculum and Assessments Authority; and several others, including 'all purpose' regulators like the Audit Commission and the National Audit Office who intervened unpredictably in the regulatory system.[51] At the same time, there developed a marked shift in regulatory style, especially after the appointment of a new Chief Inspector in 1995, towards a more adversarial and judgemental system. This was, in turn, associated with a move to more explicit, quantitatively expressed regulatory standards, notably in the use of standardized attainment tests and targets, and a policy of 'naming and shaming' those who failed to meet targets.[52] The return of a new Administration in 1997, though it ultimately displaced some individuals, changed little. The Labour Government was convinced both that educational standards were an electorally sensitive issue, and that fostering human capital and the skill base were the keys to international competitiveness. Thus, the pressure to achieve targets was if anything intensified.[53]

In summary: in the space of less than a decade a cooperative, enclosed, oligarchic world had been broken open. Micro-management of the school system from the centre was now so great that Ministers were forming views even on such detail as particular methods of teaching.[54] In the course of the 1990s, the country acquired one of the most ambitious schemes of school inspection in the world. Wilcox and Gray's summary catches the ambitions of all this:

the system of inspection inaugurated by the 1992 Act represented an unprecedented attempt to apply a universal model of inspection of ambitious frequency and comprehensiveness, carried out by independent inspectors drawn from a wide range of backgrounds and operating on a competitive commercial basis. We doubt if any more ambitious programme of school-by-school evaluation and review has ever been mounted anywhere in the world.[55]

In its form and ambitions this new inspection system looks anything but a turn to reflexive regulation and soft bureaucracy; on the contrary, it looks to be one of the clearest cases of the new regulatory state in Britain as the incarnation of an ideology of high modernism. Its origins can be traced right back to one of the main sources of change in the modern British state—the great economic crisis of the 1970s and the consequent first appearance of a 'great debate' on education, a debate that was stimulated by the belief that the malaise of the economy was, in part, traceable to a malfunctioning school system.[56]

In government's own 'inspection of itself' through what is usually called the 'supreme audit function', the institutional reorganization was, if anything, even greater.[57] In the 1980s and 1990s, 'audit' was greatly altered in both purpose and scope. Audit of government's own activities was another characteristic Victorian invention. It had led to the creation of a general audit institution, the Exchequer and Audit Department headed by the Comptroller and Auditor General.[58] In the 1980s and 1990s, this general audit function was transformed. The Victorian institution itself was reorganized into the National Audit Office, an institution which soon developed as a kind of all purpose evaluator of policy delivery across the range of government: in its own words, 'helping the nation spend wisely.'[59] The creation of the new Office was closely accompanied by the creation of an Audit

Commission with a similar mission for local government and parts of the Health Service.[60] Writing in the mid-1960s, Normanton remarked that 'the state audit bodies have mostly been silent services';[61] from the 1980s, they found an insistent voice. The foundation of the National Audit Office also coincided with a transformation of the meaning of audit, from a characteristic Victorian concern with economy in a narrow sense, and with ensuring that spending could be accounted for, to a wider concern with the dominant themes of the new public management, such as efficiency and effectiveness.[62] The change in meaning has been so radical that some observers argue that the language of audit has lost its meaning and is merely being appropriated to give weight to wider modes of performance evaluation.[63] Pollitt and colleagues, in their comparative study of supreme audit institutions, have nicely caught the exact character of the change: it involves a shift from the attestation of financial accountability to the substantive evaluation (by various criteria) of programme or institutional success. In their longitudinal study, this is reflected in the marked shift in the activities of the National Audit Office to substantive as distinct from procedural audit.[64] These changes within public audit institutions have been accompanied by a complex interchange between the public and private sector. The process is a central theme of Power's classic study *The Audit Society*.[65] Audit, we know from previous chapters, historically had a central role in the regulation of business life. We also know that in the 1980s and 1990s a series of business scandals and failures forced a transformation in both the institutions of business audit and its purposes. Audit in business was, thus, also transformed from a mechanism of narrow financial attestation into a much more wide-ranging mechanism of managerial accountability.[66] This transformed conception of audit then spilled over into the public sector. It showed itself in the attempted subjection of institutions to the new conceptual apparatuses of business audit, involving the spread of audit practices into activities like medical care.[67] And it also showed itself in the widespread resort to corporate accounting firms as providers of managerial audit in the public sector.

Much of the inherited Victorian inspection system—whether it was concerned with government's own inspection of itself or with the inspection of business—was, therefore, turned upside down in the 1980s and 1990s. This makes the stability of the system for inspecting health and safety at work all the more remarkable. It is true that particular parts of the system do show change, and in the 'expected' direction. Thus, Hutter's study of the Railway Inspectorate, the body historically concerned with rail safety inspection, shows striking changes even in the period around rail privatization: there was an increase in the formality of the relations between regulators and regulated; an increasing tendency to codify both substance and procedures; and a decline in the cooperative character of relations, a new adversarialism showing itself in a willingness to threaten, and use, legal sanctions.[68] But there are larger, 'unexpected' features in the system. The overall institutional architecture that had been created in the wake of the Robens Report (in the Health and Safety at Work Act 1974) has survived: contrast the blizzard of institutional innovation in environmental regulation.

Nor can this be traced to a record of remarkable success. On the contrary: in the late 1980s, at the very moment when other systems of inspection were most under the pressure of change, there occurred a series of disasters causing massive loss of life. The Piper Alpha disaster in the North Sea oil industry, the King's Cross Underground fire, the Clapham Junction Railway Accident: all showed scandalous elementary failures of the safety system. Nothing matching these scandalous disasters could be found in domains that were radically reconstructed, like environmental regulation. Piper Alpha is a particularly compelling case. The disaster was a fire and explosion on an oil exploration rig in the North Sea in 1988 that claimed 167 lives. The official inquiry revealed scandalous and elementary failings of safety control by both corporate and official agencies. For instance, the key inspections, whose shortcomings were part of the root of the disaster, were 'superficial to the point of being little use as a test of safety'. Moreover, 'the inspectors were and are inadequately trained, guided and led.'[69] But the institutional consequences were a world away from the fundamental reforms that came over environmental regulation: in the wake of the inquiry, responsibility for North Sea oil safety, which had been separately administered, was simply incorporated into the domain of the Health and Safety Executive.[70] In other words, by contrast with other regulatory domains—of which environment is a well-documented instance—the health and safety regime seems to have been largely immune from damage by scandalous and horrifying regulatory failure—the magnitude of which was expressed graphically even in the restrained language of the report of the Cullen inquiry into the Piper Alpha disaster. There is also evidence that in this period the regulatory regime actually moved in a direction opposite to the one documented here for other inspection systems: towards a lighter touch and towards more mandated self-regulation. Health and safety is the core case used by Gunningham and Johnstone in their analysis of the growth of 'smart' reflexive regulation. They also show how an important contingent feature that has helped reshape environmental regulation—the influence of the European regulatory state—has been heavily muted in the case of health and safety at work, directives being incorporated so as to produce minimum disturbance both to regulatory substance and to the existing legal framework.[71]

How do we explain the contrasting fortunes of these different inspection systems? Two competing hypotheses are immediately evident: the first is that the health and safety regulatory system was already congruent with high modernism; the other that it was captured by powerful interests. The first hypothesis is supported by the observation that the system of health and safety regulation was one important part of the Victorian legacy that had already been reformed and modernized before the twin crises of policy failure and institutional upheaval swept over the club system, as they did with greatest force in the 1980s and 1990s. Fundamental institutional reorganization took place in the wake of the publication of the Robens Report in 1972. The Report itself was a landmark document both in its scrutiny of the system of health and safety inspection and in its critical analysis of the wider Victorian regulatory legacy.[72] The Robens model—especially its picture of the ideal system as one that is inclusive of the widest range of interests in the workplace, and its insistence that in the end the most effective systems of regulation have to be based on self-inspection and self-regulation—is recognized to have been influential in other jurisdictions, notably Australia.[73] Innovation in this domain is one of the few exceptions, therefore, to our opening picture of the British system as stagnant before the age of hyper-innovation.

Yet the implicit hypothesis here—that in contrast with other inspection systems that for regulating health and safety at work was better functionally adapted because of the reforms arising out of Robens—is hard to reconcile with the regulatory history, especially with the occurrence of disasters like Piper Alpha, catastrophes that in other regulatory domains would surely have created huge pressure for fundamental institutional change. The admittedly extreme case of safety in the offshore oil exploration and extraction industry suggests a second competing hypothesis: that we are here observing a domain where regulatory capture is complete. From Carson's observations of the 'political economy of speed' in the 1970s, to the state of affairs revealed by the Cullen report into the causes of the Alpha Piper tragedy, a consistent picture emerges: state agencies and multinational oil companies have been united in a common interest—the extraction of oil from offshore sites with maximum speed and maximum efficiency.[74] There is, thus, a well-documented history of 'light touch' regulation that allowed the cutting of corners on safety. Smith's study of safety and self-regulation devastatingly catalogues safety failures in another industry, chemicals, supposedly the quintessential example of effective reflexive regulation.[75] In the 1970s and 1980s, the colonization of the inspection system by regulated interests in the domain of pollution was, as we have seen, challenged by the invasion of that domain by newly organized interests and institutions: alternative sources of expertise channelled by the Royal Commission; alternative interest constellations organized by environmental pressure groups. No such institutional changes have come over health and safety. The most important sources of opposition to business colonization in the workplace were the trade unions. But the decades in question were years when union influence in the workplace in the United Kingdom suffered a well-documented decline. That the key variable in health and safety in resisting business colonization is union strength is supported by James's study of the operation of the system of health and safety representatives in the workplace, where the extent to which regulations were applied was found to be a close function of density of union membership and effectiveness of trade union organization.[76]

Environmental and workplace safety inspection make an instructive comparison because historically in Britain the inspected business interests colonized both. The key to the transformation of the inspection system has lain in how far this colonization has been successfully challenged. This hypothesis is given further support by what we can see of the actual implementation of environmental regulation after the institutional upheavals summarized above. Smith's study of the implementation of the system of integrated pollution control shows a reassertion of some traditional features of the inspection system: a renewed emphasis on the importance of negotiated compliance and of avoiding confrontation with inspected enterprises. The sources of this are also familiar: they have to do with the imbalance in resources between inspectors and inspected and the consequent need to carry the inspected along voluntarily. In other words, while new actors like environmental pressure groups have been able to invade the world of high policy and to influence the larger architecture of the regulatory system, their influence weakens when work place implementation is attempted.[77]

REREGULATING QUASI-GOVERNMENT

The changing regulation of quasi-government is simultaneously among the most puzzling and most revealing aspects of the new regulatory state. It is puzzling and difficult to sort out because it is both a labyrinthine part of the state and the part that is hardest to disentangle from other domains. We have already seen that much of the discussion we had in Chapter 4 of self-regulation, such as the description of the changing regulation of sport and the arts, might as easily have occurred under the heading of quasi-government. As was shown in studies of the world of quangos in the 1970s and 1980s, the decades when quasi-government first achieved political salience, it was almost impossible to set clear boundaries to the quango system.[78] But this, of course, was of its essence: it was the lack of clear boundaries, and the lack of clear lines of accountability, which were an important part of constitutional mystification, protecting powerful interests from democratic accountability. Correspondingly, the upheavals of the last couple of decades have involved attempts to reorganize and control this world, and to subject it to closer accountability.

The serpentine-like nature of the world of quangos, thus, creates one problem of exposition that we have solved by the crude device of allocating part of the material to the chapter on the system of self-regulation. But it creates two other difficulties in exposition, which also need to be flagged. First, as we will see later in this chapter, part of the colonization of new regulatory spheres—especially as a result of the activities of the Committee on Standards in Public Life—has had important consequences for the regulation of quangos, and I simply relegate the discussion to the moment when we come to the Committee. Second, we have examined, at length, perhaps the single most important upheaval in the world of quangos, in Chapter 5.

Publicly owned enterprises, and especially public utilities organized either in public corporations or in other kinds of boards, are among the most important parts of the quango world, if only because they represent such a large concentration of economic resources. We, therefore, need briefly to recall what we found about the way the regulation of that domain has developed. The picture was as follows. The reconstruction of the regulatory regime after privatization initially sought to retain those elements of club government that had provided protection against open decision making and accountability. Institutionally, the new system was designed to maximize discretion and minimize legal control. Ideologically, regulatory issues were constructed as belonging to the domain of technicalities and of the market. These stratagems failed. This part of the quango world was drawn inexorably into an increasingly open, partisan, and juridified world. The process culminated in the collapse of the regulatory system at its first great crisis, in rail regulation.

In the following passages, I take three more domains of quasi-government and examine their recent history: the world of the national health service; the linked worlds of higher education and research funding; and the world of broadcasting regulation. The substantive and analytical reasons for this selection are given in turn, but an important part of their interest lies in the way they illustrate the different fates of different domains of quasi-government in the age of the regulatory state. In summary: health care shows a domain marked by a sharp increase in central control coupled with what I call hyper-politicization; higher education is a domain where there has been wholesale institutional reconstruction with the aim of securing central control, but one where the new institutions have suffered regulatory capture by the old elite; broadcasting is a domain where the break-up of a club system has left a legacy of fragmented pluralism, hyper-innovation, and a rearguard action by the interests most closely connected to the old club system.

By the 1970s, the National Health Service was, alongside the system of school education, the most important institution of service delivery (as distinct from income transfer) in the British welfare state. The Service was formally organized along command lines, dominated by public funding, public ownership of the health infrastructure, and public employment of health personnel. It looked like a paradigm of centralized control. The reality was very different: like other important parts of the welfare state it was ruled by an uneasy mixture of professionalism and bureaucracy, with the former mostly in the ascendant. As the numerous studies of the Service in the first 40 years of its life make clear, it was a service operating a dual system of politics.[79] Setting the overall level of resource for the Service was a matter of high politics at the metropolitan centre—going right up to the level of expenditure battles in Cabinet. By contrast, operational matters were decided by a shifting alliance of medical professionals and health service managers, with the professionals—especially doctors—in the saddle for most of the history of the Service. The regional structure of the NHS, and the weakness of the centre in operational matters, symbolized this state of affairs.[80] The system persisted for a well-documented reason: it obscured lines of accountability and responsibility. The Service was historically seriously underfunded in relation to its formal promise of extending health care as an entitlement of citizenship. That entitlement could only be met by a system of health care rationing—in effect, extending very modest entitlements as a way of realizing the promise of free health care for all. Health care rationing was a politically explosive issue from which the metropolitan elite, sensibly, shied away.[81] The rationing was, therefore, done on the ground, notably by general practitioners acting as gatekeepers to the hospital system.[82] The entitlement in the NHS, thus, only amounted to, except in cases of emergency, an entitlement to register with, and consult, a general practitioner, whose decisions then determined whether a patient could immediately consume resources, or be referred on into the hospital system for the further consumption of resources. Within the hospitals, in turn, consultants in the name of clinical necessity took the key rationing decisions.[83]

The governing world of the old NHS, therefore, bound together professional elites, a spatially dispersed set of institutions, and the metropolitan governing elite in a world where it was imperative to obscure lines of responsibility. In return, the metropolitan elite was freed from difficult operational matters and politically explosive choices; professional elites and managers got to control public resources and the fate of patients.

Many factors led to the breakdown of this world, and they can only be summarily described here. Some recall themes that have cropped up earlier in the book in our account of the sources of the crisis of club government: the draining away of the traditional authority of professional elites; the decline of popular acquiescence in the choices made by elites, and, therefore, the increased difficulty of operating rationing in a non-political, implicit fashion; the great economic crisis of the 1970s, and way this impelled the metropolitan elite to breach the terms of the historical contract with the professional elites, leading them to intervene increasingly to try to wring more efficiency and effectiveness out of the Service.[84] Throughout the 1980s, there were incremental incursions into professional autonomy, and incremental politicization, coupled with an attempt to incorporate medical practice into more effective managerial hierarchies.[85] The first big breach came with the publication of the White Paper *Working for Patients* in 1989. This inauguration of a sustained attempt to introduce an internal market into the Service was expressed, in the dominant discourse of the time, as an attempt to introduce neo-liberal disciplines into a command system.[86] But the practical organization of the NHS since the beginning of the age of institutional reform at the end of the 1980s has moved in a very different direction: in the direction of more hierarchical, central controls and in the colonization of formerly 'non-political' worlds. In the immediate aftermath of *Working for Patients*, there was institutional reorganization to subject the Service to more formally organized central control.[87] There has also occurred the imposition of an elaborate, intensive regime of evaluation and performance standards, covering both the management of individual doctors (through the spread of devices like medical audit) and the management of the performance of individual institutions, like hospitals.[88] These have over time been integrated into larger schemes designed to manage the health condition of the population at large, for example, in the White Paper on a 'healthier nation' published in 1999 and the consequent creation of a Health Development Agency to implement a national health strategy.[89] All the changes summarized here point in the direction of a system matching the project of high modernism: they involve both an extension of controls over formerly autonomous spheres, like the sphere of clinical judgement, and the investment of resources into assembling a detailed, centrally created map of the performance of all parts of the health world.

But it is important not to picture what has been happening in overly rational terms. Another consequence of the breakdown of the old system has been the chaotic invasion of the operational world of health by the values and incentive systems of partisan competitive politics. The breakdown of the old doctor-dominated systems of control, and the translation of rationing issues into increasingly open political argument, has heightened the partisan political salience of operational issues. As operational issues have been politicized, the metropolitan elite has intervened increasingly in the micro-management of the system. This has shown itself in both a blizzard of centrally prompted initiatives, driven by the short-term pressures of issue management to which elected politicians are subject, and by the manipulation of key performance indicators that are the subject of partisan political argument, of which treatment waiting lists and 'league tables' of performance are the two most obvious examples.[90]

The decay of an autonomous world of quasi-government dominated by professionals; the creation of a centralized, hierarchical system of administration that is attempting to drive the system in the direction of achieving nationally mandated targets derived from a synoptic overview of the domain; the chaos ensuing from short-term attempts at micro-management in a domain invaded by partisan politics: analytically, the new world of the NHS looks very like the picture we assembled of the new world of school inspection.

The story of the changed regulation of higher education and research funding in some respects echoes the history of the transformed quasi-government of the NHS: there is a similar draining away of professional authority, the invasion of enclosed policy communities by the central state, and a new institutional architecture designed to achieve greater central control. But in this domain the response of the regulated has been to capture the new regulatory world. It is this experience of regulatory capture that makes the case of higher education funding and research illuminating. An additional substantive importance is that higher education is one of the few parts of the welfare state that saw serious expansion in scale in the 1980s and 1990s.

The institutional history of the regulation of higher education is well known and need only be summarized briefly. The first sign of significant state funding at the end of the First World War was accompanied by a familiar institutional move: the creation of a quasi-public body, the University Grants Committee, in 1919. This was controlled by the university elite, and it both disbursed public funds and managed the system.[91] Halsey and Trow express exactly how the new threat of democracy impelled an alliance of a mandarin and an academic elite to create this quango: looking back over more than 50 years of the UGC they detected 'an historical continuity, within the framework of a recently completed parliamentary democracy of de facto control of élitist institutions by likeminded members of the élite.'[92] The world typified club government, and was not seriously disturbed by the changes in funding that accompanied either the passage of the 1944 Education Act or the creation of the 1960s generation of 'Robbins' universities.

Paradoxically, one of the acts that did administer it a serious blow was a gambit designed to preserve the club world of the old elitist universities: the initial concentration of expansion in the polytechnics, whose history offered a very different, and more public, world of government.[93] The polytechnics were the first part of higher education to be colonized by the central state, in the creation of the original Polytechnics and Colleges Funding Council, but were soon followed by the old universities in the institutional upheavals associated with the creation of unified higher education funding councils in 1992. By then there was already well established a system of research quality evaluation, which over the decade acquired increasing 'bite' in its influence over the allocation of resources. In the effort to gain an overview of the regulated world, the inspecting gaze in the research evaluation exercise has shown an increasingly impressive capacity to inspect and judge individuals—something rarely achieved in other parts of the new regulatory state. In the 1990s, this was supplemented by a system for assessing teaching that involved an increasingly elaborate mode of measurement and the assignment of grades to individual units.[94] Since the typical university department is a small unit, this evaluation is also impressive in its ability to descend to the level of micromanagement. The picture that emerges from a decade of change, therefore, is twofold: reorganization of the institutional architecture of the system designed to integrate the funding bodies more closely into the machinery of the central state and to diminish professional (academic) power over their policies; and the development of a system of research evaluation enabling central scrutiny of performance right down to the level of individuals, and a system of teaching evaluation enabling central scrutiny down to the level of individual academic departments.

These developments have undoubtedly had radical consequences within institutions. They have unleashed fierce struggles between different interests both within and between classes of institutions, and have greatly increased levels of formal measurement and hierarchical control within universities. The future of higher education in an 'evaluative state' foretold at the beginning of the era of reform by Neave has been proved extraordinarily prescient.[95] The ferocity of these struggles means that the era of hyper-innovation continues, typified by the continuing instability of key parts of the evaluative regime. The teaching quality regulatory regime has been marked by rapid evolution, especially since the consolidation of assessment responsibilities into a single Quality Assurance Agency in 1997. At the time of writing, yet another new framework of national assessment is about to be introduced.[96] In 2002, following the results of the 2001 Research Assessment Exercise, the Funding Council commissioned a root and branch review of the exercise with a view to fundamentally changing the rules of the assessment game.[97]

This search for new rules arises from a key feature of the regulatory regime in higher education: from its almost total capture by the traditional academic elite. The working of the most highly developed part of the new regulatory system—the Research Assessment Exercises—provides a striking illustration. The system has from the beginning been dominated by the principles of peer review.[98] This assertion of the primacy of core 'scholarly' values has proved the key to capture, for it has created one of the critical conditions always needed for regulatory capture: the expertise to make regulatory judgements being controlled by the regulated. The primacy of the principle of peer review has meant that the panels performing the evaluations have been dominated not only by academics, but by academics drawn from the 'old' universities; the detailed criteria, in turn, have been specified by these peer-dominated panels; and the outcomes, unsurprisingly, have then overwhelmingly favoured units from the old universities. The outcome of the 2001 Research Assessment Exercise shows the processes by which capture works. In RAE panels the role of chair is critical. In the 2001 exercise, only five chairs of panels were from 'new' (ex-Polytechnic) institutions and only two were non-academic 'users'.[99] The panels, in turn, dominated by academics, had substantial autonomy in drawing up their own rules of engagement. This inevitably gave the process a recursive quality. The rules privileged scholarly work, and the outcome was unsurprising: complete domination of the top rankings by the institutions of the old elite. Although construction of institutional league tables from RAE results is recognized to be a black art, it is impossible by any formula to construct a league that gets any of the 'new' universities into the top twenty, and most measures of the top five in the 2001 exercise showed them to be institutions drawn from the magic triangle of elite universities in southern England: Cambridge, LSE, Oxford, Imperial College London, and Warwick.[100] The ratings also show striking consistency over time, an unsurprising outcome again given the structural capture of the process.

A coda can be added about the changing government of research funding because this related policy domain replicates the wider story of higher education. As was the case with the wider university system, the state emerged early in the twentieth century as a significant funder of research, and (in the first instance for medical research) established the pattern of 'arms length' public funding, involving the creation of a quango controlled by the research elite to distribute public money.[101] This pattern was then widened into other research domains, even reaching the social sciences in the creation of the Social Science Research Council in the 1960s. It was an arrangement that replicated in important ways the system governing the funding regime for the universities—an unsurprising fact since there was obviously a large overlap between the two communities. It involved colonization by an elite community of academic users, the insulation of the community from the open world of democratic politics, and a light touch regulatory regime in which recipients receiving funding had neither to compete hard for resources (if they were in the club) nor to give an elaborate account of how the resources had been used. In the 1980s and 1990s, the research funding community experienced parallel pressures to those experienced by the wider funding and control regime for the universities. The research councils were reorganized so as to integrate them more closely with the central machinery of the state; there was an increasing emphasis on transparency and open competition in the funding regime itself; there occurred a partial displacement of the academic elite at the top of the regime by users, especially users from the business community; and, at the end of the 1990s, there was an attempt, in official documents like *Realising Our Potential*, and in exercises like the Foresight programmes, to shape research policy around one of the characteristic projects of high modernity: maximizing the competitive efficiency of the national economy.[102]

Although these changes broke up the old academic elite and its world, they did not produce centrally controlled systems of research funding. They let loose destabilizing forces and created a (still continuing) struggle for control of resources. As in the case of the wider university-funding regime, they led to a more formally organized world with far less emphasis on tacit knowledge. But as the flow of funding resources showed, the traditionally dominant institutions, if anything, strengthened their hold over resources. Data from the big research councils illustrates the point. Since the flow of resources changes little from year to year, the data from the most recent annual reports can make the point. The top five recipients of research funds from the Engineering and Physical Sciences Research Council (EPSRC) map closely onto the top five in the 2001 Research Assessment Exercise: Cambridge, Imperial, Oxford, Southampton, and Nottingham.[103] The top five for research and capital grants for the Biotechnology and Biological Sciences Research Council are York, Cambridge, Manchester, Imperial, and Oxford.[104] And the top five for the Economic and Social Research Council are LSE, Essex, Manchester, Cambridge, and Oxford.[105] The consistent appearance of the two great universities at the heart of the old club world—Oxford and Cambridge—is particularly striking.

This assertion of control over both processes and outcomes is not the result of any improper mode of capture. It is essentially the result of a successful strategy of ideological construction by traditional academic elites. The critical move has been to establish the primacy of traditional scholarly values in the various evaluation processes. It is striking how feeble have been the efforts by carriers of alternative evaluative ideologies, such as business interests and the managers of the economy in the core executive, in asserting alternatives, like the contribution of research to national economic efficiency or business profitability. The analytical significance of the higher education case is that it shows capture to depend critically on fashioning and defending a regulatory ideology alternative to that of high modernism.

Capture is hard to sustain in the modern regulatory state. The breakup of the old club world has consistently opened up hitherto enclosed domains to a wide range of competing interests, so capture is continually open to potential challenge. The capture of the new regulatory processes by the academic elites has indeed strengthened the tendency towards hyper-innovation, as competing interests struggle for new ways to shape the regulatory game to their advantage. In the regulation of teaching, it has taken a decade of constant change to try to create a settled system of teaching regulation in order to accommodate the struggling interests, and there is no sign that the system has reached a point of stable equilibrium. The review of the fundamentals of the research assessment exercise is also a response by the funding council to the outcomes of the 2001 exercise—outcomes that reflected the almost total capture of the processes by the academics. Hence, the victory of the academic elite may turn out to be Pyrrhic, as other interests—for instance, those who wish to shape higher education around the needs of industrial users—regroup to make fresh attempts at control.[106]

Health and higher education, therefore, show two very different fates for domains of quasi-government in the face of the ambitions of the new regulatory state: on the one hand, hierarchical control and hyper-politicization producing micro-management by the metropolitan elite; on the other, the capture by traditional elites of institutions and processes that were designed to secure tighter central managerial control over those very elites. Our third example—broadcasting—shows yet another pattern: a kind of pluralist fragmentation and institutional instability. The historical regulation of broadcasting is exceptionally revealing analytically. Broadcasting is, of course, a twentieth-century technology, and the issue of its regulation did not arise in any serious way until after the onset of formal democracy in Britain. (The two key early official reports on its structure date from the 1920s.[107]) The system of regulation that was then adopted was, however, almost a caricature of traditional club government. A state monopoly was rapidly created in the hands of the BBC.[108] The apparently arcane device of establishing the BBC by Royal Charter ensured that, unlike public broadcasters in other parts of western Europe, it functioned outside normal domains of constitutional responsibility.[109] Location, organizational culture, and working practices rapidly integrated the Corporation into the closed informal world of the metropolitan elite. Indeed, the Corporation played an important part in strengthening the grip of that elite and creating a 'national', metropolitan centred identity.[110] Its great founding Director General, John Reith, left a cultural imprint that reflected the values of the metropolitan mandarin elite: commitment to public service; suspicion of the world of partisan political debate; a bias favouring the dissemination of conventionally defined 'high' and 'middle-brow' over popular culture; even, at a symbolic level, the dissemination of the accent of the metropolitan elite as the 'standard' form of official pronunciation.[111]

The story of the decline of this regulatory world has been richly documented, both as a British story and as part of the wider story of the decline of the hegemony of the 'public service' broadcasting model across Western Europe.[112] The mix of the cocktail of change varies from state to state, but the ingredients of the cocktail are pretty similar. For Britain they include: the impact of technological innovation, which has both reshaped broadcasting markets to a global scale and blurred the boundaries between broadcasting and other media markets; the mobilization of competing interests to challenge those entrenched by the original public monopoly, the most obvious examples being the creation of first a commercial television sector and then, two decades later, a commercial radio sector; the impact of market competition, which has continually reshaped the institutional identity of key players in markets, creating new alliances of interests and destroying old ones; and long-term changes in popular culture, and in elite perceptions of popular culture, which have made the crucial areas of programme content and standards areas of public contestation over the last couple of decades.

The consequences of this state of affairs can be seen by comparing the regulatory history of the first three decades of broadcasting with the last three decades. After the entrenchment of the 'BBC model' in the 1920s, the system was stable in both institutional form and practice for three decades: it was an exemplary product of the age of stagnation. The last three decades, by contrast, exemplify the story of the British system as a regime of hyper-innovation: the multiplication of regulatory authorities to try to control the new technologies of communication (e.g. the short-lived Cable Authority, the Radiocommunications Agency); the ensuing struggle to cope with the fragmentation produced by these innovations, resulting in the reshaping of the 'peak' institutions of regulation (the foundation of the Independent Television Commission and the Radio Authority in 1990); the shift from informal and secretive modes of decision (for instance, in the earliest allocations of broadcasting franchises) to more transparent, formal, and even juridifed modes; the entry into broadcasting regulation of a wide range of regulatory institutions (established regulatory agencies like OFTEL, the courts, self-regulatory bodies from the world of sport, to name only three) not traditionally associated with broadcasting.[113] In short: the destruction of the world of the club and its replacement by a world of increasing transparency, partisan contestation, and formality, and the integration of broadcasting regulation in a wider world of regulatory politics. These developments have now culminated in a step change in institutional structure: the 2002 White Paper on communications regulation (and the succeeding Communications Bill) are intended to create a unified regulatory agency, the Office of Communications (OFCOM). It will absorb the existing functions of the Broadcasting Standards Commission, OFTEL, the Independent Television Commission, the Radio Authority, and the Radiocommunications Agency. It continues, in other words, the trend towards the creation of regulatory agencies designed to provide synoptic overviews of wide social domains.[114]

THE COLONIZATION OF NEW REGULATORY SPHERES

Thus far we have been describing the way the existing institutions of the state—in the inspectorates and in quasi-government—have been reshaped in the era of the regulatory state. We now turn to what is in many ways the most novel and striking change of recent decades: the expansion of the state's regulatory domain into new social spheres.

Three caveats are necessary at the start of this discussion. The first is, as we shall see, that no simple separation can be made between this experience of colonization of new social worlds and the intensification of existing systems of inspection and control. As we saw in, for example, our discussion of the upheavals in the school inspection system, the changed regime went beyond a new style of scrutiny: it encompassed the specification of new performance targets and a great expansion in the range of controls over the daily activity of teachers in classrooms. Nevertheless, it did work on the foundations of a historically established system of inspection, which is why it was discussed earlier. The second caveat is related to this. The examination in Chapter 4 of the changed world of self-regulation overlaps with the description here, for much of what I argued then—for example, about the changed regulation of sport and the transformation of financial services regulation—amounts to a species of colonization of formerly autonomous spheres of civil society. Nevertheless, though there have been dramatic changes in the regulation of sport it has not (yet) been incorporated into the formal apparatus of the regulatory state, which is why I discussed it in a chapter on self-regulation. The third caveat is that we should acknowledge that the process of colonization described here has been accompanied by some very well known cases of 'decolonization': notable examples include the sphere of sexuality, and many competitive practices in markets. Even here, however, the story is mixed. For instance, as the state has renounced control over some domains of intimate personal relations (e.g. regulation of same gender sexual relations), it has increasingly intervened, often using the law, in related domains of intimate privacy: for example, it now more closely regulates the treatment of children in families, and the kinds of physical coercion which legal spouses and other partners can exert on each other.

In this section, I illustrate the scale and nature of the new colonization by taking three spheres: the development of regulatory capacities to control human intervention in the natural world; the reconstruction of the regulation of key markets under newly created state regulatory agencies; and the increasing turn to formal regulation of public life itself, covering standards of conduct and modes of appointment to public bodies.

The regulation of human, especially scientific, intervention in the natural world is from one point of view an obvious and characteristic manifestation of modernism, since it deals with attempts to subject nature to systematic observation and control. The attempt to manipulate nature is, however, hardly a product of the last generation, or even of the last century. But until recently, there was a well-established process by which this activity was regulated in Britain, well documented in the history of the regulation of scientific research: it essentially involved self-regulation by the elite of the scientific community, allied often with corporate interests in the world of applied research. I take the regulation of human reproduction as an example, for the obvious reason that it touches on some of the most delicate areas of public control. Until recently, the history of the regulation of new technologies (for instance, for the direct control of female fertility, or for treatment of some of its aspects like morning sickness in pregnancy) was a characteristically British story: light touch, peer controlled, of insiders by insiders. It took some striking regulatory failures (the Thalidomide tragedy inflicted by a drug to control morning sickness, worries over the long-term health effects of the contraceptive pill) to reshape this system in a more open, formally organized way.[115] The creation of the Human Fertilisation and Embryology Authority (HFEA) in 1991, although it addressed a narrow range of the most advanced technologies for the manipulation of fertility, now marks an analytically highly significant advance in the domain of the regulation of reproductive technology. It shows that what is for Britain a comparatively novel institutional innovation—the specialized regulatory agency—has become an established part of the repertoire of responses to policy problems. It also reinforces our picture of the British as pioneers: the Agency claims to be the first statutory body of its kind in the world for this regulatory domain.[116] The HFEA regulates all facilities that offer *in vitro* fertilization, or donor insemination, or storage of eggs, sperm, or embryos, and it also licenses all human embryo research in the UK. These responsibilities have drawn the Agency into attempts to detail the most intimate of personal decisions: witness the detailed guidance in the Authority's *Code of Conduct* covering the age at which women may have access to treatment, and the regulation of the age and other characteristics of sperm donors.[117] The very act of constituting the Authority has also obliged a shift from the implicit to the explicit in consideration of a whole range of important issues. These issues are partly substantive (the adjudications made by the Authority in particular cases) and are partly procedural (how membership of the Authority is constituted, what its powers are, and the way it gives a public account of its decisions). The shift is shown in mundane but important ways: the Authority administers written codes and even publishes Internet versions of the minutes of its hearings.[118] One sign of the shift is the way the Authority's decisions have been challenged in the courts, in the process forcing the regulatory system further down the road of making explicit the grounds of its rule making: for instance, the licensing of cell nuclear replacement research was subjected to judicial review following a legal challenge from the (anti-abortion) Pro-Life Alliance.[119] Another is the invasion of the policy domain by 'non-experts' from the world of competitive democratic politics. Thus, the Authority has fought a losing battle to protect issues to do with the regulation of stem cell research from the pro- and anti-abortion lobbies, and has likewise tried unsuccessfully to persuade Members of Parliament not to take an interest in this part of its domain.[120]

In a modern economy, of course, there is no simple line to be drawn marking the divide between the regulation of technological innovation and the regulation of market practices. The second important illustration of regulatory colonization, though it involves the control of market practices, was indeed, in part, prompted by a catastrophic failure of control over a defective and dangerous technology. It concerns the upheaval in the food safety regime at the end of the twentieth century. I use the example of food safety because the scale of change has been so great, and the regulatory innovation so significant. But this area of market regulation also shows how uncertain is the divide between a discussion of colonization and reconstruction: there is a case for treating the great changes in financial regulation surrounding the creation of the Financial Services Authority, which we discussed in Chapter 4, as a species of regulatory colonization very like the story we are about to tell for food.

We saw in Chapter 3 that the early history of food safety regulation was virtually paradigmatic of the development of the British regulatory style. The law appeared comparatively early in response to food adulteration scandals, but implementation was dispersed, was low key, and involved the familiar construction of regulatory offences as technical and economic, rather than criminal, in character.[121] The great modern event that transformed the debates about food safety in the 1990s was the BSE disaster. The report of the Inquiry into that animal and human tragedy paints a graphic picture of a particularly diseased form of club government, in which those responsible for food safety were bound together with powerful economic interests in a closed collusive world.[122] As the earlier work of Smith demonstrates, this was only a particularly extreme form of a wider system of club government in post-war agriculture and food processing, a system that privileged the interests of producers over consumers.[123]

The BSE Inquiry and the report itself was an important part of the process by which this particularly pathological form of club government was broken open and subjected to public scrutiny. But the Inquiry, and the crisis of confidence in the old club world that it represented, was only part of a larger crisis of confidence in the food safety regime that had produced periodic 'food scares' for at least a decade. One consequence of this was the entry into debates about food safety of actors who had no established connections with the club. In March 1997, the Rowntree Trust (a foundation with a reputation for commissioning policy-relevant research of a reforming kind) commissioned an independent report on the structure and functions of a proposed official Food Standards Agency. That Report was presented to the Prime Minister in May of the same year, was sent out immediately for consultation, and was followed in January 1998 by a White Paper. A Bill to establish an agency was published exactly a year later and became the Food Standards Act in November 1999. The new Agency became operational under the Act in April 2000.[124]

Food safety control is an area historically dominated by powerful corporate actors with key allies in part of the state machine. We still have comparatively little experience of the actual workings of the new Agency, and, therefore, cannot be at all certain that it will escape capture by these powerful interests, as has happened, as we saw above, in the case of the new world of higher education. But we can be certain that capture, if it takes place, will occur on very different terrain from that occupied by the old system of club government in this domain. The very act of establishing the Agency drew huge numbers of new institutional actors into the field: the public consultation on the original Rowntree commissioned report produced over 600 responses and drew in, additional to the usual industrial suspects, representatives of consumers, public health medicine, veterinary services, and scientific research.[125] This looks analytically very like the way the old pollution regulation community was invaded by new groups and interests a couple of decades earlier. The Agency's formal mandate is wide: to 'protect public health from risks which may arise in connection with the consumption of food, and otherwise to protect the interests of consumers in relation to food.'[126] It has rapidly developed an elaborate array both of scientific committees and specialized working groups, and has widened out to cover a broad range of subjects: the scientific advisory committees include groups on toxicity, on animal feedstuffs, on nutrition, on novel foods and processes, on vitamins and minerals, and on the microbiological safety of food.[127] One of the signs that the FSA is a manifestation of the regulatory state as a project involving modernization, standardization, surveillance, and control are the connections being forged between the activities of the Agency and similar projects elsewhere in government. Thus, in partnership with the health departments of the different devolved administrations, the Agency has created a national Nutrition Strategic Framework to monitor the national diet, to create an evidential basis for a healthy diet, and to promote the adoption of a healthy diet among the population at large. Thus, the mandate of regulating food safety (ambitious in itself) is supplemented by the ambition to monitor and guide the eating habits of the whole population.[128]

One reason capture, if it is to take place, will have to take place in a very different world from that of the old club system, is connected to the third face of colonization, to which we now turn: what in summary I call the colonization of the regulation of the conduct of public life itself. In retrospect, it now seems astonishing (and a testimony to the resilience of the old pre-democratic governing culture) that the appearance of formal democracy after the First World War had such a small impact on the regulation of the conduct of public life. Three examples show the resilience of the old world. First, the political parties, the key institutions in the new democratic system, continued to be treated as largely unregulated actors in the sphere of civil society—a treatment that, as we shall see in a moment, has been significantly modified by the passage in 2000 of the Political Parties, Elections and Referendums Act, and the establishment of the Electoral Commission in the same year.[129] Second, the regulation of corruption—a major concern of the First Report of the Committee on Standards in Public Life—has been governed by statutes all dating from before the era of formal democracy: the Public Bodies Corrupt Practices Act (1889), the Prevention of Corruption Act (1906), and the Prevention of Corruption Act (1916).[130] Indeed, for the most part, the regulation of corruption has rested on reforms from a single great period of innovation in the later decades of the nineteenth century.[131] Third, the regulation of relations right at the heart of the club system was done almost entirely informally. As we saw earlier, the Haldane Report was a successful pre-emptive strike, establishing doctrines of informal partnership as the norm in governing relations between elected politicians and civil servants. The regulation of both Houses of Parliament—in respect of such key issues as the connection between parliamentarians and powerful outside interests—was also treated almost entirely as a matter of self-regulation. Indeed, until the 1970s, it was both self-regulated and uncodified: it was only in that decade that the innovation of a written, publicly available register of members' interests was introduced.

All these club-like domains came under intense pressure in the 1990s. Some are presently in the process of being subjected to entirely new, and more formal, regulatory regimes. A central actor in this process—both a symptom of long-term cultural change and an important independent agent for change—has been the Committee on Standards on Public Life, originally established under the chairmanship of Lord Nolan in 1994 and presently on its third chairman.[132] The shift to a more formally regulated world, and the struggles with traditional interests aroused by the shift, can be economically traced through the fate of the seven major reports that the Committee has so far produced. The Committee's First Report ranged across the whole sphere of public life: it codified principles of conduct that had hitherto been tacit (in its seven principles of public life); led to the widespread adoption of Codes of Conduct by public bodies incorporating those principles; led to a review of the statutes governing corruption; and led both to increased explicit regulation of Parliamentary behaviour and the establishment of a Parliamentary Commissioner for Standards to police the new regulations.[133] This last was a defensive response by Parliamentarians to the threat of more formal, and externally controlled, regulation. The Seventh Report—which recommended more rigorous and more codified standards to govern disclosure of interests by members of the House of Lords—produced an even more defensive response, as one might expect from an institution that, though enjoying little power, was the symbolic incarnation of club government.[134] The Second, Third, and Fourth Reports led to further rules covering disclosure of interests, and more transparent and formally stated rules governing appointment, in public bodies, in local government, and across the whole quango system.[135] The Fifth Report, responding to scandals in party financing, led to a sharp increase in formal regulation in this domain: a codification of the rules governing large donations; an increase in the transparency requirements governing the publication of the financial accounts of parties; wider controls on non-party spending during election campaigns; a ban on foreign donations; and the creation of an independent Electoral Commission to administer the newly codified system.[136]

The new regime for parties is governed by the Political Parties, Elections and Referendums Act 2000. It for the first time incorporates parties into their own special regulated domain. It codifies rules, many of which have statutory force, to govern the entity called a political party; registration with the Commission is virtually a condition of eligibility to fight elections as a party; registration, in turn, is conditional on approval of schemes regulating a party's financial affairs; registered parties must file an annual statement of accounts, and quarterly donation reports (weekly in election campaigns).[137] The Act also creates a permanent Electoral Commission to implement the legislation. The title Commission hides the fact that we are seeing here the further diffusion of a characteristic innovation of the regulatory state: the use of a specialized agency to control newly colonized domains. The Commission's own rhetoric is also in tune with the ideology of modernism. In the words of its first chairman, introducing its rolling

5-year corporate plan: 'the Commission's key responsibilities are as a regulator . . . as a moderniser . . . and as an educator.'[138]

The activities of the Committee on Standards in Public Life have become a kind of litmus test for the instability of the old club-based system of standards regulation: the appearance of the Committee with a proposal to investigate an area is an infallible sign of the breakdown of traditional controls, and the aftermath of the Committee's investigations has led everywhere to increased regulation, and to instability in regulatory arrangements as the endangered traditional interests have tried to undermine the new regulatory world. The fate of the reforms in the funding of parties and the regulation of standards of disclosure in the House of Commons illustrates this process. The reforms from the Fifth Report have turned out to be only the first instalment: a further series of scandals arising from suspicious connections between policy outcomes and donations to the Labour Party reignited the issue at the start of 2002 and have led to calls from Cabinet Members for more state funding for political parties.[139] At the time of writing, there are numerous newspaper leaks indicating a debate inside government precisely about this possibility.[140] In the House of Commons, bitter struggles over the role of the first Parliamentary Commissioner, and the appointment of her successor, have destabilized the attempt by the House to resist full external regulation. Following the bitter infighting at the end of 2001, the Committee on Standards announced in December of that year a new inquiry into the arrangements for the regulation of standards in the Commons.[141]

Although it is possible find evidence of incremental change in the two regulatory spheres examined here before the 1990s (some changes in both party funding and in disclosure of interests in the Commons go back to the 1970s), the 1990s was the decade when the whole concept of autonomous self-regulation of public standards experienced profound crisis and change. With hindsight it is also possible to trace the roots of the final area examined here—the regulation of relationships within the upper reaches of the Executive—back before the 1990s. 'Irregulars'—special advisers chosen for their partisan connections and separated from the civil service—first appeared in significant numbers with the return of the Labour Party to power after its long period in opposition in 1964. The return of the Conservatives to office with radical reforming ambitions in 1979 placed immense strain on relations with the civil service and led to frequent accusations throughout the 1980s that Mrs Thatcher as Prime Minister was 'politicizing' the upper reaches of the civil service—which is to say, was violating the terms of the partnership which assigned control over top appointments to the civil service elite.[142] As we saw earlier in this chapter, the Next Steps reforms further destabilized the partnership, leading to the major constitutional crisis in the government of prisons in 1995. There are two connected patterns here: the first is the long-term decay of a constitutional ideology formulated in the face of the onset of formal democracy at the end of the First World War; the second is the special disturbance to the understanding arising from the return to office of parties either after long periods outside government (Labour in 1964) or after a traumatic period in opposition when new radical reforms were formulated (Conservatives in 1979). The pattern was repeated in 1997 with the return of Labour to office after an 18-year break. There was a sharp increase in the numbers of special advisers, the creation of a range of special units around the Prime Minister and Cabinet Office designed to increase partisan control over policy implementation, and a turn (for instance, in the White Paper on *Modernising Government*) to a rhetoric of modernization in the name of more effective coordination.[143]

The tensions that these developments created in the established partnership model exploded in the autumn of 2001 and early in 2002 in a ferocious struggle within the Department of Transport, Local Government, and the Regions. They included the leaking of an incriminating email by one of the Minister's special advisers, the notorious email sent on 11 September 2001 recommending the release of any bad news in the belief that it would be buried under coverage of the terrorist attack on the World Trade Centre in New York; competitive briefing of journalists by civil servants and supporters of the politicians; the resignation of a senior special adviser; and a bitter public row over the dismissal of a senior civil servant in the Department.[144] This was followed by the now unmistakable sign that the system was in crisis: the announcement by the Committee on Standards in Public Life in March 2002 that it was to conduct an enquiry on defining the boundaries within the Executive between Ministers, civil servants, and special advisers, with a report promised for the end of the year.[145] An extended debate has now begun about the desirability of codifying understandings in a new Civil Service Act—in short, about abandoning one of the key practices of the old club world.[146]

To summarize, my contention in these passages is that in numerous arenas we can witness in a powerful form the dominant teleology of the new regulatory state: the drive to try to subject areas of life not previously formally controlled to formal regulation with the aim of more synoptic legibility. This is partly happening through the adoption of an imported social innovation—the specialized regulatory agency—to scrutinize areas formerly conceived either to be in the domain of civil society or to be properly the subject of informal regulation by club insiders. It is partly being enforced by the state's need to re-examine the regulation of relationships that lay at the very heart of the old club system, both within the Executive and within Parliament.

SYNOPTIC LEGIBILITY IN THE NEW REGULATORY STATE

In Chapter 7, I examine some of the origins of the teleology of the regulatory state described in these pages, notably its uneasy relationship with some of the characteristic contemporary forces of modernism, such as globalization in the name of market capitalism. Here, I simply re-emphasize the single most important recurrent feature of the changes documented. This is the incessant drive towards synoptic legibility: installing systems of comprehensive reporting and surveillance over numerous social spheres; the consequential pressure to standardize and to codify, which is to make explicit what had hitherto been tacit; and the creation of new institutions (mainly the specialized regulatory agency) to help enforce all this. These changes have been bitterly resisted and, in part, subverted, because they threaten powerful traditional interests—including, as we saw near the end of the chapter, interests at the very heart of the club system. The consequences for the British state have been highly variable. There have been extensions of the state's domains and a growing transparency and accountability. But we have also entered an age of hyper-innovation, hyper-politicization, and policy chaos. Large parts of the traditionally administered welfare state (represented in this chapter by school-level education and the health service) are experiencing all these varying outcomes: the invasion of worlds hitherto dominated by an alliance of professionals and mandarins has produced micro-management from the centre, often driven by the short-term horizons of politicians enmeshed in the partisan political struggle. This experience of hyper-politicization has been avoided in other arenas by the device of regulatory capture, where traditional elites have successfully regrouped to control the new world of regulation—the essence of the story I have argued for higher education and research funding. In some instances, we see the collapse of traditional understandings and the unfolding attempts at their replacement, punctuated by vicious infighting with the traditional club interests—the story I have argued in respect of the regulation of relations within Parliament and the Executive. The new regulatory state is, therefore, creating worlds of chaos, policy fiascos, and bitter struggles between old and new interests.

Chaos and fiasco, as we shall see, also figure largely in Chapter 7.

7

From Stagnation to Fiasco: the Age of the Regulatory State

THE TELEOLOGY OF THE REGULATORY STATE

The single most important feature of the British regulatory state emerges when we consider it comparatively and historically: a governing system that was uniquely stable among the other great capitalist nations for the half-century after 1918 has been uniquely pioneering during the 1970s to the 1990s. This has driven reform in two directions: towards hyper-innovation and towards synoptic surveillance, central control, and the colonization by state regulatory agencies of once independent spheres of civil society. There are irrationalities, perversities, and contradictions in this process, and at the root of all these lies the teleology of the new regulatory state.

To speak of the teleology of the state is not a mere metaphysical flourish. Historical fate is being worked out—or, rather, a series of fates, and because they are multiple fates outcomes are not foreclosed and room is left for the influence of human agency. Fate and agency are at work because in the 1970s three great, linked, historical enterprises reached exhaustion. By the start of that decade, imperialism was a totally spent force: thus ended the project that had been a rich source of symbolic capital for domestic elites, offering a vision of a hierarchical society and polity, and a providential historical mission. In the same decade, the legacy of Britain's pioneering role in industrialism was finally exhausted. The end of the long boom revealed the deep competitive problems of the economy and, more immediately, pitched economic management into crisis. Finally, in part because of the exhaustion of imperialism and of the legacy of pioneering industrialism, club government likewise reached exhaustion; and thus ended what had been a highly successful strategy to equip Britain with a system of government that could protect elites from formal democracy, and from the social and cultural forces that lay behind that democracy.

What succeeded all this—notably in its fullest and most self-conscious expression, Thatcherism—now gave to the teleology of the state a profoundly modernizing cast. Substantively, the state turned to the reconstruction of institutions and economic practices, with the aim of raising competitiveness against global competition. Thus, finally developed the full germination of the 'national efficiency' movement whose original seed was sown in the first debates about national decline over a century ago.[1] This substantive modernization—the attack on social forces that were held to stand in the way of efficiency in global markets—was allied to, indeed required, a more procedural modernization: the transformation of government from the club model to one where transparency, synoptic surveillance, and central control were possible. Put thus, the modernizing teleology looks comparatively ordered and controlled. But, as the preceeding pages show, the actual institutional reality has been anything but ordered and controlled. Much of the chaos has been what one might call chronic: that is, it arises from the crises that produced pressure for change, the various coping strategies that emerged, and the ambitions pursued under the new regulatory arrangements. But there are three important recurring forces that should better be considered contingent: that is, they amount to a set of extraneous forces that have nevertheless shaped the recent history of the regulatory state. Labelling them contingent does not make them unimportant; on the contrary, as we shall now see, they have contributed greatly to fiasco and hyper-innovation. They are each examined in the three main succeeding sections of this chapter.

The era of institutional change described in this book neatly coincides with greater epochal developments. From the early 1970s, there were radical changes in the character of the global economy, signalled in an immediate way by the collapse of the Bretton Woods system, and more fundamentally by a renewed burst of globalization. Some of the most important consequences for the British regulatory state are examined in the next section. But, of course, the decades examined in these pages also coincide almost exactly with the United Kingdom's membership of the European Union. Entry into the original European Economic Community at the start of 1973 was an obvious recognition that the historical enterprise of empire was exhausted, and amounted to the beginnings of a search for an alternative historical fate.[2] What is usually summarily called 'Europeanization' is, therefore, obviously central to the changing character of the regulatory state. It forms the substance of the following section.

To some degree Europeanization and globalization offer alternative historical fates to the regulatory state, and therein lies much of their importance for the themes of this book. But the penultimate section of the chapter is in an analytical sense the most important of all. The great changes that succeeded the collapse of club government were justified on all sides in a rationalizing language of policy competence and effectiveness—as one naturally would expect of a quintessentially modernist enterprise. Yet the age of the new regulatory state has also been the age of policy fiasco. Fiasco is, as we shall see, both a reflection of hyper-innovation and a force driving the state into even greater frenzies of hyper-innovation. The conjunction of a governing ideology that puts immense faith in achievement with a history of policy disaster is, to put it mildly, inconvenient; this penultimate section of the chapter, therefore, examines the extent to which policy fiasco is indeed inscribed in the character of the new regulatory state.

THE AGE OF GLOBALIZATION

Globalization is simultaneously one of the most fashionable and most contested concepts in modern social science.[3] Here I only emphasize three themes, because they all provide links to the history of the British regulatory state. They are: the special historical and contemporary place of the UK in the global system; the special links between globalization and modernity—a key theme, obviously, of our account of the rise of the regulatory state in Britain since the early 1970s; and the special institutional reconfigurations, both at the global level and at the level of nation states, associated with the changes that have come over the global economy in the last 30 years.

One great global shift coincided with the collapse of club government in Britain. The club system was irrevocably bound to the social hierarchies of imperial Britain—and with the collapse of empires between the 1940s and the 1960s there collapsed also the social and cultural foundations for hierarchy provided by the imperial system. Some of the key themes emerge in Cannadine's study of the hierarchies of Empire—a study that is, as he himself stresses, as much about the hierarchy at the metropolitan centre as about its imperial outposts.[4] And summing up her history of nation building and the consolidation of elite authority in Britain, Colley stresses the centrality of imperial mission to both the creation of a public language of providentialism and the consolidation of hierarchy:

For most Victorians, the massive overseas empire which was the fruit of so much successful warfare represented final and conclusive proof of Great Britain's providential destiny. God had entrusted Britons with empire, they believed, so as to further the world-wide spread of the Gospel and as a testimony to their status as the Protestant Israel. And this complacency proved persistent. Well into the twentieth century, contact with and dominion over manifestly alien peoples nourished Britons' sense of superior difference. They could contrast their law, their treatment of women, their wealth, power, political stability and religion with societies they only imperfectly understood, but usually per-ceived as inferior. Empire corroborated Britain's blessings, as well as what the Scottish Socialist Keir Hardie called 'the indomitable pluck and energy of the British people.'[5]

Critical moments of consolidation and dissolution of the club system coincide with critical moments in the history of imperial cultural creations. Perhaps the single most important few years in the consolidation of the club system were those around the end of the First World War, when there was a need to domesticate formal democracy and the even more frightening spectre of a wave of revolutionary socialism emanating from the European mainland.[6] As we have seen in earlier chapters, these were also years when key institutional innovations were made at both the centre of the machine and in quasi-government. Virtually the same moment (1917) also saw an important cultural innovation, the creation of the Most Excellent Order of the British Empire (from GBE to MBE), an order designed to unify the hierarchical cultures of domestic society and its imperial domains. It rapidly emerged as the centrepiece of the domestic honours system, 'the order of Britain's democracy'.[7] The external collapse could not but affect the domestic system. The history is full of striking coincidences, both large and small: the grand coincidences of the end of empire in the two decades after the close of the Second World War, followed in the 1960s by the collapse of deference and then the wider collapse of club hierarchies across British government and society;[8] the smaller coincidence of the liquidation at the end of the 1990s of the last significant relic of Empire—Hong Kong—and the virtually simultaneous liquidation of a domestic institutional relic of the pre-democratic system, the hereditary House of Lords.[9] It is also full of ironies. The single movement that did most to destroy club government and create the new regulatory state—Thatcherism—also fought in the Falklands a war over a relic of empire; and the stunning electoral victory of 1983, which did so much to empower Thatcherism's most radical instincts, may also have been due, in part, to that military victory.[10]

This link with imperialism is but a special example of a more general feature: Britain's unique historical role in, and exposure to, the development of the global system. However one measures globalization—whether by the rise of global trading systems, by the accelerated diffusion of technologies of global communication, or by the advance of a more refined global division of labour—the period between 1870 and 1914 was a critical period in the process. Britain, as the leading international industrial power, as the leading imperial power, and as the leading financial power, was probably the single most important national agent in shaping the global system in that era. And as we saw in Chapters 3 and 4, some of the prototypical institutions of club government—notably in the City of London—were fashioned in that period, partly as a result of this burst of globalization. This history laid the foundations for British economic uniqueness, a uniqueness neatly summarized in Hirst and Thompson's phrase 'Globalization in one country': the development of an economy which was uniquely integrated with the global system and therefore uniquely sensitive, in its institutional arrangements, to the changing pressures created by that system.[11] In short, the combination of her imperial and economic history makes Britain special in the globalization process and, therefore, we must expect something as revolutionary as the great domestic institutional transformation of recent years to be intimately linked to what has been happening to the wider global system.

The point is hammered home by the more recent history of that global system. The great burst of global change that began about 1870 was arrested by the outbreak of the First World War and by the destruction of many of the institutions—notably the Gold Standard—that were vital to that spate of globalization. But a great new wave of global change has been rolling since the early 1970s and it shows no signs of abating. It has the familiar marks: rapid innovation in the technologies of global communication; the continuing spread of globalized markets and globalized brands; an increasingly refined global division of labour; a finance-market-led drive to create a unified global trading system; and the incipient development, both in individual sectors and at the system level in forms like the World Trade Organisation, of global regulatory institutions. The timing of all this, of course, coincides almost exactly with the great domestic revolution in British government that fills the pages of this book, and for some of the most straightforward of reasons. The most straightforward of all is that the great structural changes that compelled a reshaped global order in the early 1970s also reshaped the domestic governing order by the brutal agency of economic crisis.

This brings us to the second theme identified at the start of this section: the special connections between globalization and modernism—and, thus, to the heart of the analytical argument of this book. I have maintained throughout that the new regulatory state in Britain is essentially a further unfolding of the cultures and institutions of high modernism. I have sought to make this argument partly negatively, by showing that the great changes of the last 30 years involved the destruction of a wide range of traditional institutions and understandings in Britain. They were traditional in the sense that they were a mixture of pre-democratic survivals, and the adaptations of those pre-democratic survivals to preserve the autonomy of traditional elites from the institutions of formal democracy that developed up to 1918, and from the growth of a modern democratic political culture. But I have also argued a more positive case: that what has replaced these arrangements has been quintessentially modern in the sense identified by writers like Porter and Scott.[12] It has involved the attempt to make transparent what was occluded; to make explicit, and if at all possible measurable, what was implicit and judgemental; and, above all, to equip the state with the capacity to have a synoptic, standardized view of regulated domains and to use that synoptic view to pursue a wide range of projects of social control.

The rise of this modernist system domestically has been congruent with, and further stimulated by, 'globalization in one country'. We can observe this in at least three ways: in rhetoric, in culture, and in the concrete institutional reforms of recent years.

The rhetorical history of 'globalization' in recent political debate in Britain is entwined with the policy revolution that destroyed club government. Invoking the imperatives of global competition has been central to attempts by reforming elites to create the symbolic capital needed to legitimize radical policy and institutional change.[13] That rhetoric has partly filled the vacuum left by the disappearance of an earlier potent symbolic resource, the sense of imperial providentialism that permeated the language of public life and popular culture well into the twentieth century.[14] Indeed, the earliest appearance of the national efficiency movement over a century ago 'set' the search for efficiency into the demands of the imperial mission, not into the imperatives of global competition: in the words of Roseberry's manifesto for the Liberal Imperialists, the aim was 'a condition of national fitness equal to the demands of our Empire.'[15] Thus, at the end of the nineteenth century domestic reform was legitimized in a public language that stressed the imperatives of the imperial mission; at the end of the twentieth by a public language that stressed the imperatives of globalization. And the history of the globalization rhetoric mirrors that of empire in other striking ways. For elites, shaping policy around empire and globalization were both versions of Britain's providential mission: Mrs Thatcher's and Mr Blair's lectures to foreigners on the need to adapt to global markets reflected the belief that Britain, once marked out as an imperial civilizer, now had the providential mission of leading into the new world of globalization.[16] Domestically, dissent within elites now turned on how to cope with the demands of the global system, as in an earlier epoch it had turned on how to cope with empire. And just as radical dissent a century ago was expressed in the language of anti-imperialism, so a century later it was expressed in the language of anti-globalization.[17]

This level of rhetoric is, to express it crudely, about how policy actors 'constructed' globalization and then tried to use it as a source of symbolic capital to help legitimize reforms. But there are more concrete connections with the decades of hyper-innovation, and one of the most important is the existence of what, in summary, might be called a cultural congruence between the globalization process and the culture of high modernism that is reshaping governing institutions in Britain. To put it simply: globalization too is a modernizing project in a number of very obvious ways. It involves standardization and the obliteration of local variation: it reshapes local markets in labour, goods, and services; it standardizes hard and soft technologies, the latter varying from language to software; it produces more uniform consumption modes, in forms like the spread of global brands and the spread of more uniform kinds of cultural consumption; it standardizes regulatory regimes themselves, both at the grand level of rules of trade in the global system, and in the greatly extended development of systems of global regulation at both the meso- and the micro-levels.[18]

Understanding the cultural congruence between the new regulatory state and the developing world of globalization involves teasing out complex, highly mediated connections. By contrast, the stimulating effect of globalization on domestic institutional reform has been much more direct and historically concrete. It can be seen at virtually every level of the destruction of the club system over the last 30 years. Plainly, the onset of the very crisis that led to our three decades of hyper-innovation was directly connected to the history of the global system, for it was the end of one epoch in the history of the global economy—the close of the '30 glorious years'—that caused the economic crisis in Britain in the mid-1970s, and, thus, led us to our present condition. Many of the reforms that involved dismantling particular domains of club government are, in turn, directly traceable to the effort to respond to the competitive pressures of the global system, and to the felt need to respond to the demands of powerful interests generated by that system. Some of the most important instances formed a large part of the substance of Chapter 4. The recent history of the decay of club government in the City of London, perhaps the single most emblematic change in the system of self-regulation, is inexplicable without understanding what has been happening to the global organization of financial markets. The case of the most important moment of change—the 'big bang' of 1986 and the associated passage of the Financial Services Act in the same year—makes the point. After it, strenuous efforts were still made to preserve key parts of the club world, and, in particular, to construct the new regulatory systems in a self-regulatory mode, so as to defend markets against democratic control. But both at the level of economic institutions—the organization of firms and markets—and at the level of regulatory practices, 1986 administered a death blow to club government in the City. The death blow was partly the product of the influence of great global actors in London: multinational global financial services firms, Japanese, American, German, and even some British allies. It was partly the result of a strategic decision by state actors, notably those in the core executive and in the Bank of England, to reposition London so as more effectively to promote the City as a leading centre in the global finance system—a strategic decision that the subsequent economic history of the City (and of the wider South-East economy) has triumphantly vindicated.[19]

This single, though emblematic, example also illustrates a more general connection between the changing shape of the global system and what I have been calling the teleology of the regulatory state. Globalization and its pressures hold the key to one of the most far-reaching, indeed utopian, of this new state's ambitions. The strategic decision to force City interests to reorganize in tune with the global world of financial markets was one part of a more general upheaval in British economy and society designed to improve national competitiveness. Indeed, it is precisely because the reorganization of the City was not an isolated event that it is emblematic. The drive to produce institutions—in the economy, in the welfare state, and in the heart of the state machine itself—that contribute more effectively than hitherto to national success in a world of global competition is the single most important policy objective that binds together both the numerous institutional reforms discussed in this book, and the numerous policy actors from nominally different parts of the ideological spectrum who have contributed to the reforms. This drive for competitive advantage is what has given substantive form to so many of the changes, and explains why in speaking of the regulatory state's teleology we are referring to concretely observable social processes.[20]

Put in this form, the impact of globalization on the new regulatory state looks unproblematic, or at least consistent in its direction. The developmental state whose absence was lamented by Marquand at the end of the 1980s might now be thought to have arrived.[21] The reality is more chaotic. In a later section, I sum up the domestic sources of this chaos, and show that the state is impaled on the horns of a dilemma: neither its present incomplete, nor a full, reconciliation with modernism can create effective policy instruments. But not only is the capacity of the regulatory state subject to all the domestic limitations and inconsistencies that have recurred throughout these pages, the impact of the global system is also itself problematic in its effect on the state's capacities to realize its modernist ambitions. At one and the same time, it is fuelling the ambitions of the British regulatory state and depleting the resources, symbolic and material, that would allow those ambitions to be realized. Three particularly important sources of depletion should be highlighted.

The first intersects with one of the most distinctive features of the new British regulatory state: the development of more ambitious state controlled systems of business regulation, notably to displace much of the traditional club-based system of business self-regulation. Braithwaite and Drahos's monumental study of global business regulation shows that much of business regulation has not only now migrated to the global level, but has in many cases reconstituted itself there in a self-regulatory mode. Global business regulation, thus, has a 'recursive quality'.[22] That is, it turns not on the exercise of authority by a traditional hegemon like a state, but on modelling and learning in dispersed webs of actors. These webs incorporate international business regulatory organizations, international institutions of trade diplomacy, large firms, and states themselves. In this global world, the state remains a critically important actor, but its importance lies less in traditional command than in the contingent ability to operate in globally constituted networks. The regulatory process is recursive because standard-setting is now at its heart, and standards are set in global webs marked by modelling and mutual learning: 'Modelling achieves globalization of regulation by observational learning with a symbolic content, learning based on conceptions of action with cognitive content that makes modelling more than mere imitation.'[23]

The focus of this book has been the domestic face of the regulatory state in Britain, but the clear consequence of the kind of institutional developments charted by Braithwaite and Drahos is that a full picture could only be obtained by a complementary book, one that provided a close study of the British state as an actor in the developing global system. Some of the most important sectoral self-regulatory institutions described by Braithwaite and Drahos—such as in maritime communications—are actually headquartered in London, but the networks they coordinate and the processes by which they develop rules owe much more to the world of self-steering networks disconnected from state power, than to the new systems of hierarchical control that have developed domestically in the new regulatory state. Their case study of sea transport is a particularly instructive example, because the British state and British business institutions have historically been embedded in this bit of the global regulatory process, and because maritime regulation is one of the most historically ancient examples of original club government in Britain.[24] Summing up the history, they resort to Giddens' images of structuration:

the practices of individuals like Lloyd and his shipowning customers structured an insurance market, which in turn reconstituted Lloyd's from a coffee-house to a gentlemen's club and institutionalized information exchange for shippers, then to a Register Book Society and reinsurance auction and brokerage house. Edward Lloyd, doubly institutionalized as reinsurance exchange and classification society, then acted to constitute the British maritime regulatory state, which in turn acted to reconstitute the Lloyd's institutions and the people who reproduce them. This structurates the embedded but constantly adjusting state-market ordering of maritime capitalism.[25]

A crude summary of the implications of this account for the British regulatory state that has been built during the 1970s to the 1990s is, therefore, as follows: a huge gap is opening up between the recursive world of global business regulation and the command-like ambitions of the new domestic regulatory state.

A different kind of gap, but equally daunting, is opened up by the impact of global pressures on the institutional configuration of key policy domains. This brings us to the second source of depletion. At the heart of the global reconfiguration is central banking, the institution that in the age of globalized financial markets is critical to economic policy. There has occurred an international rise in the independence of central bankers from democratic control.[26] Jayasuriya sums up both the cross-national institutional trends and the forces shaping them:

independent central banks have become a major focus in the internal restructuring of the state because of the inherent complexities of a global political economy such as those resulting from highly mobile capital requiring a high level of credibility, and the commitment to the pursuit of 'hard money' policies.[27]

The complexities of the resulting interactions are illustrated by the history of the central bank in Britain in the 1990s, especially since 1997 when the new Labour Government stripped the Bank of traditional responsibilities for prudential supervision and, via the creation of a newly constituted Monetary Policy Committee, strengthened its independent grip over short-term interest rates.[28] The latter is well known to have been calculated to reassure the financial markets; but the new independence is surrounded by characteristic requirements of the new regulatory state, including formal requirements for transparency in reporting and the shaping of operational issues around achieving targets.[29] The reforms are, thus, inscribed with the contradictory influences transmitted by domestic and wider global forces: they simultaneously shift central banking further away from democratic control while continuing the destruction of club government in banking.

A third source of depletion bears on some of the most important ambitions of the regulatory state—notably the ambition to equip itself with accurate synoptic intelligence about key social domains and to acquire the resources to convert that intelligence into control. We have seen in these pages some striking instances of the realization of these ambitions. Yet globalization also provides striking instances of their frustration—and, indeed, of decline even in traditional areas of surveillance and control. One of the most important and best documented concerns taxation, a domain where the state traditionally invested a great deal of effort in gathering accurate intelligence and in using power to extract resources.[30] The modern story of tax planning by large corporations and the super-rich tells a well-documented story—indeed, is the standard source for some classic explorations of creative compliance with regulation. That creativity constantly robs tax regulatory regimes of meaning and effectiveness, by developing elaborate modes of legally circumventing regulations—the basis of the modern service industry dominated by global accounting firms that provide tax planning for large corporations and the very rich.[31] It also constantly obstructs, and is designed to obstruct, one of the central ambitions of the regulatory state: to assemble accurate synoptic pictures of regulated domains. The elaborate maze of shelters and havens, and the elaborate chains of ownership that run through them, are designed precisely to do the very reverse of one of the main ambitions of modernism—in short, to reduce transparency to the very minimum compatible with the letter of the law. Finally, the consequence of all this has been, successfully, to deplete the state's capacity to exercise control in the entirely traditional field of resource raising via taxation.[32] A similar story—once more involving big multinational accounting firms as key actors—can be told about the creative manipulation of corporate accounts to hide the true state of company financial conditions. That story lay behind the series of accounting scandals that appeared on both sides of the Atlantic in 2002, and led in both the USA and the UK to a further attempt to subject the accountants and their corporate clients to even closer state regulatory control.[33]

In short, globalization has had ambiguous and contradictory consequences for the new regulatory state. It has provided a public language allowing elites to equip themselves with a new source of symbolic capital after the disappearance of empire; it has provided powerful cultural support for the modernizing, standardizing impulses in the new state; and it has stimulated institutional reforms contributing to the destruction of some of the bastions of club government. But it has also robbed the regulatory state of some of the critical resources needed to realize its ambitions: by the migration of regulatory responsibilities to the global level; by creating pressure to depoliticize key regulatory activities like central banking; and by the highly sophisticated creative compliance of global corporate actors designed to rob states of resources like taxation and to evade national accounting controls.

THE AGE OF EUROPEANIZATION

The 'coincidence' of Britain's entry into what was then the European Economic Community with the onset of the great economic crisis, and the onset of the full blown crisis of club government, is, of course, not an accidental conjuncture. The turn to Europe was a self-conscious choice by governing elites faced with the historical depletions that lie at the heart of this book—notably the end of the imperial 'mission' and the exhaustion of the country's legacy as the pioneer of industrialism.[34] In the intervening three decades, membership of what is now the Union has transformed everything from the high politics of great strategic national choices to the most routine areas of low administration. The broad outlines of the substantive policy consequences and the institutional reconfigurations that can be traced to our membership of the Union are now well documented.[35] They show the EU increasingly embedded in the domestic governing system, and the UK embedded in EU institutions. The image of 'embeddedness' conveys the complex intertwining where conventional divisions between the domestic and the European are losing meaning. Many devices, ranging from simple images to elaborate analytical frameworks, are employed to convey the change. Thus, 'Europeanization' is commonly used as a kind of counterpoint to 'globalization'; but it turns out to be an image that is almost as slippery in meaning.[36] At the other end of a spectrum of analytical elaboration lies the increasingly influential model of multi-level governance, in which the governing process is modelled as a game played by institutional actors criss-crossing numerous levels in their search to realize strategic objectives.[37]

The EU policy process—whether measured through the production of its characteristic authoritative policy documents like Directives, through the policy entrepreneurship of key institutions like the Commission, or through the creative jurisprudence of the European Court of Justice—is a major source of substantive policy innovation. Its importance is summarized in the often-cited statistic that the Union is responsible for 80 per cent of all rules governing the production, distribution, and exchange of goods, services, capital, and labour in the European market.[38] This rise of the EU as a major source of substantive innovation has been accompanied by some obvious and well-documented institutional adaptations. We can see them in summary if we glance quickly back through the main areas covered in earlier chapters. In the heart of the old club system—the overlapping worlds of the core executive and the metropolitan civil service elite in Whitehall—there has been substantial reconfiguration of both institutional structures and the procedures for processing business, to try to take account of the significance of the EU at all stages of the policy process.[39] The world of privatization regulation has also been profoundly shaped by the coincidence between the rise of privatization as a major policy innovation in Britain and the revitalization in almost exactly the same period—since the early 1980s—of EU competition regimes.[40] The reshaping of self-regulation, notably in the direction of more juridically regulated regimes, has likewise been heavily influenced by the rising importance of self-regulatory bodies in the implementation of EU-derived policy innovations.[41] Most of these developments validate one of the central insights of Majone's account of the consequences of the rise of the EU as a regulatory state: the Union has both restructured, and empowered, domestic institutions in its search for implementing agencies—and in the process has powerfully contributed to the reshaping of the old club system.[42]

We will examine in a moment the actual consequences of this 'European' reshaping, but it is also worth noting in passing some striking parallels in the impact of Europeanization and globalization on the public language of high politics over the last thirty years. Some of the most obvious parallels include: the way invocations of a European destiny have, like invocations of globalization, filled the gap in public language left by the disappearance of the language of empire; the way providentialism has reappeared amongst almost all shades of elite opinion—whether in the account that Britain has a special role in Europe as a sceptical participant with global connections and ambitions, or as a pioneer of a less regulated, more free market oriented Community; the way political dissent has organized itself intellectually around attitudes to Europe in the same way that it also now organizes itself intellectually around attitudes to globalization, and once organized itself around attitudes to empire.

This connects to the one of the most profound links between membership of the European Union and the rise of the regulatory state in Britain: the way the European connection both reinforces and reflects the new regulatory state as a modernist, and a modernizing, phenomenon. The effect is clear in three forms.

The first we have already summarized above: the turn to Europe was a conscious final abandonment of empire, and all that empire stood for culturally—notably the hierarchical political culture that had underpinned the oligarchical institutions of club government. It, thus, marked a turn to modernity in exactly the sense identified by Therborn as a quintessential trait of the modern: it was a shift from an orientation with the past (empire) to the future (the developing European system).[43] Of course, as we shall see, new oligarchies were also being created in the EU—but as we shall also see these oligarchies rested on very different foundations from the hierarchies of deference that had underpinned the club system.

The second destructive impact on the club system was much more concretely institutional and concerned the process of policy making itself. The club image conveys many things, but one of the most important is an image of (small) scale. Club worlds were small worlds that could function as they did (informally, putting a premium on tacit knowledge), in part, because their small size allowed high levels of social and cultural integration. In more formal language, they were policy communities rather than policy networks. The European policy world is very different: we summarized it in Chapter 2 as a shift from the 'village' of Heclo and Wildavsky's picture of Whitehall to the image of the 'government of strangers' drawn from Heclo's portrait of executive politics in Washington.[44] A large body of research about the European policy process, whether it concerns the comitology of Brussels and the European Parliament, the bureaucratic politics of the Commission, or the high politics of the Council, paints a consistent picture. Analytically, this is summarized in the literature as heterarchical, or even, in Caporaso's language, as a kind of 'post-modernism', a contrast with the traditional Westphalian state: 'abstract, disjointed, increasingly fragmented, not based on stable or coherent coalitions.'[45] It is a world of intensely complex policy debate where there is a premium on success in monitoring, and contributing to, the details of policy initiatives from their very earliest stages. Policy networks are dispersed and heterogeneous, in part, because of the diversity of national and sectoral interests involved. Consequently, heavy investment of institutional resources is needed to monitor the policy process, to maintain a presence at all stages of the process, and to manage the fate of policy as it is transmitted throughout these complex networks.[46] A large premium is, therefore, placed on specialized expertise and on the commitment of time and money to close policy monitoring. The premium on expertise is increased because the single most important policy actor—the Commission—has few resources of its own and, via the comitology procedure, relies heavily on sectoral expertise, notably on business and the professional expertise which business has the money to buy.[47] Policy worlds themselves are very fragmented, so that high levels of investment again are needed to gain entry in a wide range of different domains, and even into different policy episodes in the same domain. The demand for the investment of organizational resources is ratcheted up still further by the juridified character of the process created by the prominent role of the European Court of Justice as an important source of policy creation and adjudication: monitoring, exploiting, and, where necessary, challenging the Court's jurisprudence is no job for amateurs or part-timers.

These features will all sound familiar to anyone with knowledge of regulatory politics in Washington. Indeed, there are even some more direct links: as in Washington, the complex and juridical nature of the policy process has meant that big law firms are among the most important lobbyists; in some instances, the same multinational firms are active in the two centres, Brussels and Washington, and, indeed, across all the major world centres of regulatory decision making.[48] As is the case in Washington, EU regulatory politics mobilizes its own distinctive biases and empowers its own distinctive oligarchies. The premium put on close monitoring of the process of policy creation, combined with the Commission's own heavy reliance on outside specialist expertise, creates powerful biases similar to those in US regulatory politics, in favour of interests with the resources to make the investments in policy monitoring and the hiring of expertise—in short, in favour of business, especially big business.[49] In this way, many of the biases of the old club system in the UK are recreated, notably the privileging of business interests in the regulatory process. The world of EU policy making, therefore, has offered elites a potential solution to one of the big problems created by the demise of club government domestically: the way the passing of the club system removed a key means of insulating elites from the institutions of majoritarian democracy. The process by which this happens in Europe, however, is usually very different from the characteristic modes of club government where, through customary integration, powerful interests could dominate the policy process without the expenditure of any significant organizational resources. And partly because the process of exercising power is different, the regulatory outcomes of the process are also different. This is the third destructive impact on club government, to which I now turn.

If any single sign could sum up the changes that have come over British government in the last 30 years, it would be the shift from the tacit to the explicit—from a world of broad informal understandings to one where arrangements became more precisely codified. This seemingly small shift was associated with great developments, notably the destruction of the oligarchical club system and, in its fullest culmination, with the rise of systematic surveillance and reporting that has marked the new regulatory state. The substantive impact of the European Union has been to magnify this shift from the tacit to the explicit and, thus, to reinforce the displacement of the traditional by the modern. It has done this in the most obvious, straightforward ways, by pressing domestic institutions in the direction of more explicit codification of their practices. This effect can be seen at every level, from that of the highest of high politics to the most mundane routines of low administration. Thus, in the transformation of the regulation of the public sphere—the major theme of Chapter 6—the incorporation of the European Convention of Human Rights into domestic law via the Human Rights Act 1998 amounts to a fundamental codification of the relations between public bodies, self-regulatory agencies, and individual citizens; and as Graham shows it even has the potential to penetrate the lowest routines of the administration of the privatized utilities.[50] The widespread juridification of self-regulation has been heavily influenced by one of the characteristic features of Majone's European regulatory state: the extent to which it has turned to domestic self-regulatory institutions endowed with powers to implement its directives. It is reshaping regulatory domains even where the UK's regulatory regime was the pioneer in privatization and liberalization—a process we noted and documented in Chapter 5 in the case of telecommunications.

In three ways, therefore, 'Europeanization' has contributed to the systematic destruction of club government: in encouraging the definitive abandonment of old historical enterprises, notably empire, that provided a supporting culture of deference; in helping transform the informal, enclosed club world of policy making into something more extended and unstable; and in pushing the substance of regulation into more codification, more formal organization, and more juridified administration. Estimating the independent contribution of entanglement with Europe to the overall transformation would involve a complex and probably inconclusive thought experiment. It could be nothing but a thought experiment because the timing of entanglement with Europe is itself hopelessly entangled with the domestic crisis of club government. Weale and colleagues, however, nicely catch the complexity of these effects in the account of environmental regulation. What they write of the UK in this domain could stand for a wide range of other domains:

Perhaps the greatest challenge to the system of administrative discretion has arisen from the impact of EU legislation. The setting of emission standards for urban wastewater treatment plants, quantitatively prescribed reductions in sulphur dioxide emission levels, and changes in procedures of environmental impact assessments are merely examples where a more formal style of regulation has become part of British practice. But the pressure from the EU has combined with other new developments on the UK scene. The rather closed and specialist character of British policy style has undergone some change. A growing public concern about environmental questions has played a part in opening up the standard-setting system to scrutiny.[51]

This judgement is corroborated by the similar picture in Knill's policy history of the development and impact of three key Directives on air pollution, drinking water purity, and public access to information about pollution control.[52]

But here we now come to another striking parallel with the experience of globalization. For just as globalization had ambiguous and contradictory effects—simultaneously 'modernizing' policy and robbing the state of its capacity to realize modernist ambitions—so the impact of Europeanization has been contradictory. All the effects summarized above have pushed the state in the direction of the modern. But some other effects have had very different consequences. These we now summarize.

Writing in the mid-1980s, and reporting work that was influenced by observations made in the era of the club system, Vogel offered a convincing generalization about regulatory patterns: to wit, that in different regulatory domains they showed remarkable national uniformity.[53] Thus, when we discovered regulatory patterns in a domain like environmental regulation—to take one of Vogel's main cases—we would be in a position to predict pretty accurately regulatory patterns in a whole series of other domains within the same nation. It is extremely doubtful that we could now make such an economical 'reading off' in Britain. In part, that is because of the domestic era of crisis we have lived through: an age of hyper-innovation that produced an often chaotic opening up of once enclosed communities to a huge range of competing interests, and an age that saw the destruction of the homogeneous elite culture that bound together so many of the institutions of the club system. But this fragmentation has been reinforced by the impact of the EU, notably by the diversity of its substantive impacts on domestic regulatory arenas. This diversity arises from a variety of sources: from variations in regulatory domains; from the varying timing of 'European' interventions; and from variations in how the policy process looks at different stages. I examine each in turn.

In regulatory domains, one key field is a conspicuous 'outlier', very different from that which might be predicted from the theory of the 'European' regulatory state. It concerns competition policy. This is a field where the EU has manifestly not followed a 'light touch' strategy of simply delegating responsibility to national regulatory bodies. Here we can see a direct relationship between the reshaping of important parts of the British regulatory state and policy innovation from Brussels. Competition policy is one policy domain where, unusually, two linked conditions exist: important member states of the European Union, notably the United Kingdom and the Federal Republic of Germany, have well-established competition regimes (in the case of the United Kingdom, dating back at least to the foundation of the MMC in 1948); and the Union itself has acquired power to intervene directly in competition issues. This latter unique direct EU competence derives from Articles 85 and 86 of the Treaty of Rome (81 and 82 of the Treaty of Amsterdam) and Council Regulation 17 of 1962. In the words of Wilks and Bartle: 'Regulation 17 gives the Commission a superior role over the national competition authorities by giving it a monopoly over the operation of the crucial article 81(3) which grants exemptions from the prohibition on agreements which restrict competition.'[54]

These powers remained dormant for a quarter-century after the initial empowering regulation. The situation then changed radically at the end of the 1980s when DGIV, the competent DG, began actively to use its powers to intervene directly to enforce competition regulations, often through highly publicized American style regulatory 'raids' on firms and by the imposition of large fines. The result created Wilks's 'most effective anti-trust regime in the world'.[55] The change is traceable to several developments: political entrepreneurship in the shape of two highly capable and 'activist' Commissioners, Leon Brittan and Peter Sutherland; generational change within the Commission, notably the rise of a new cohort of lawyers influenced by anti-trust regulatory ideology; and a rise in the activism of the European Court of Justice, which thereby created a powerful supporting jurisprudence.[56] This activism not only produced direct intervention in competition regulation, including the extension of Union competence to ever wider domains like utility regulation. It also helped reshape the domestic structure of competition regulation in Britain, in the form of the new Competition Act of 1998.[57] Wilks's own summary of the way the 1998 Act compared with the predecessor founding legislation of 1948 stands also as a summary of the joint effects of the domestic transformation of club government and this area of unusually direct EU impact:

> the 1948 Act catered to the voluntarism, the self-regulation and the accommodative arm's-length relationship between government and industry which permeated the political economy of the 1940s. The 1998 Act creates a more formal and legally objective framework for industry. It provides didactic guidance rather than the co-operative exploration which underlay its 1948 predecessor.[58]

The history of EU competition policy also hints at the second source of variation in the impact of the EU on the development of the regulatory state: the variable timing of policy development. Here there is a hugely variegated patchwork. Although there is a striking coincidence between the great age of institutional reform domestically and the revival of the EU as an agent for competitive change from the early 1980s, the timing and incidence of EU impacts is still remarkably diverse. Take the example of a single industry that we have already encountered: telecommunications. As we saw in Chapter 5, the impact of the EU has been to 'lock in' independently generated domestic competitive reforms by the subsequent development of a juridified EU regulatory regime.[59] Or consider the broadly related world of network-bound industrial sectors (from telecommunications to rail) that depend on a fixed network and, therefore, raise issues about natural monopoly. The recent regulatory picture even for these linked domains is of high variability in both the extent of EU and national presence in regulation, and of the speed and timing of regulatory change. Consider only the contrast between the regulatory worlds of telecommunications, where the Union is a powerful actor, and the railways, where it is marginal.[60] Within a single industry, the effect of the EU can be to take the industry on a regulatory roller coaster ride: a well-documented instance is airline regulation, which has rapidly gone through national deregulation and liberalization, and then EU level re-regulation.[61]

Finally, perhaps the most important source of variation in impact is provided by inspection of different stages of the policy process. A domain where the EU has had a substantial impact, environmental regulation, provides one of the best documented instances of this source of variation. At the level of policy formation, the effects are all in the 'expected' direction. That is to say, there has been a transformation of policy-making worlds away from the small-scale, integrated world of the club to extended, multinationally organized networks; and a substantive policy shift towards more codification of regulatory rules. But Smith's study of policy implementation, which we encountered in Chapter 6, shows that at 'street level' implementation many of the understandings and power relationships that were characteristic of the old club world have once more been reasserted.[62]

The case of the implementation of environmental policy shows graphically how much scope still exists in the new 'Europeanized' world for the reassertion of oligarchical practices and privileged business interests. Nor is this just a matter of what happens in the low politics of regulatory implementation. It permeates the high politics of the EU itself. Verdun's study of the comitology of monetary policy that led to the establishment of EMU tells a story that might have been about British central banking in the 1930s rather than Europe in the 1980s and 1990s: the workings of the committees were 'purposefully secretive'; no written record was taken; there was a great reluctance to speak to the press; even committee membership was confidential; 'secrecy was the dominant attitude'; and the culture was that of an old boys' club.[63] Nor is the final phrase a mere figure of speech: this really was a collection of elderly gentlemen determining the economic future of the continent. It is hardly surprising that the process produced that monument to central bank oligarchy, the European Central Bank.[64] Research on the comitology of environmental policy suggests that this is not an aberration.[65] Oligarchy is, thus, engrained in much European regulatory decision making.

I have argued in this account that the impact of what is for shorthand called 'Europeanization' on the new British regulatory state parallels the ambiguous impact of globalization. On the one hand, powerful forces have contributed to the modernizing process that lies at the centre of the changes we have experienced during the 1970s to the 1990s: that is, have contributed both to the destruction of the world of club government and to its replacement by more formally organized, codified policy worlds. But Europeanization, like globalization, has also contributed to another part of the process of destruction: the fragmentation of the governing system so that it loses the settled, homogenous character that was once a distinguishing mark. In this way, both globalization and Europeanization have strengthened the system's chronic tendency to hyper-innovation.

THE AGE OF FIASCO

Hyper-innovation; justifying innovation as the search for policy effectiveness; policy fiascos: these three have all marked the history of the new regulatory state. The obvious question is: what, if anything, is the connection between them?

Since the first two—hyper-innovation and its legitimation by a 'modernizing' language of effectiveness—have been central features of this book, we concentrate here on the third, so far neglected, feature: policy fiasco. Policy fiascos are hardly unique to the modern British state, nor are they unique to Britain. The notion of a policy fiasco is indeed itself an elusive one. In the standard modern study of the phenomenon, Bovens and 'tHart show that the perception of fiasco is dependent on a large number of contingent factors: among the more obvious are the time frame employed to assess the outcome of a policy and the criteria of success or failure applied.[66] Nevertheless, policy fiasco is hardly a mere subjective construction. There undoubtedly are contestable cases—contestable because we are uncertain of the appropriate criteria of success or failure, or are unsure whether we have given the policy enough time to succeed or fail. But there are also indubitable fiascos that fail to measure up either to the criteria of success or failure that guided the original project or have had patently lamentable outcomes.

Club government had a rich history of policy disaster in Britain in the first two-thirds of the twentieth century. The failures included some huge strategic miscalculations in the management of foreign and economic policy, stretching from the mismanagement of sterling in the 1920s to the mismanagement of policy over European unification in the 1950s.[67] They included some classic organizational disasters, in which military history stretching from the Boer War to the Second World War is particularly rich.[68] They included recurrent disasters of project mismanagement in the field of high technology, ranging from the commissioning of the Concorde supersonic airliner to a series of missile procurement projects that produced stunning cost overruns, grossly delayed delivery, and sub-standard performance.[69] They included disastrous attempts simultaneously to engineer massive social and natural change like the Labour Government's groundnuts scheme in east Africa in the late 1940s.[70] They included massive regulatory failures in the very heart of the club system of self-regulation in the 1970s, notably the great secondary banking crisis of the mid-1970s and the disastrous catalogue of prudential failures and fraud in the Lloyd's insurance market.[71] They included long drawn out histories of poor public sector performance, which, though never revealing themselves in a single catastrophic moment, inflicted damage as great as any high-profile disaster: obvious examples included the mediocrity of so much of the school system, which allowed up to 40 per cent of pupils (already disproportionately from the poorest families) to leave education with few basic skills and without any formally measured achievement;[72] and the manipulation of patients' lives resulting from the unacknowledged power of doctors in health care rationing for much of the early history of the National Health Service.[73] And they culminated in what might be called grand systemic fiasco—the near meltdown of the whole system in the wake of the great economic crisis of the mid-1970s.

It is precisely this history that makes the recurrence of fiasco so damaging to the regulatory state, for its modernist ideology rests heavily on an achievement claim—that the design of new institutions and practices frees us from this disastrous past. Fiascos, thus, resemble scandals of the kind analysed by Thompson—indeed, they are often constructed as scandals—in that they deplete the symbolic capital of governing elites.[74] In Scott's study of authoritarian high modernism, fiascos that inflict untold human suffering are inscribed in the very nature of the modernist enterprise. But, as Scott notes, these fiascos derive not from modernist ideology itself but from its implementation by authoritarian regimes in circumstances where civil society is 'prostrate'.[75] Plainly neither of these conditions exist in Britain. The obvious question, therefore, is: to what extent can the greatest recent fiascos in British government be traced to what I have argued is the key feature of the regulatory state—that it is a characteristically modernist enterprise in its search for synoptic surveillance and control? Do these fiascos, in other words, reveal the limits of high modernism as a governing strategy?

I have selected six high-profile fiascos from the age of the new regulatory state to explore this question. I first present them in thumbnail sketches below.

The Millennium Dome cost over £700 million in public money, never remotely achieved the visitor numbers projected in its business plan, was a public relations disaster on its grand opening, and continues to prove a poisonous (and expensive) political legacy for government.

Rail Privatization left Britain without a reliably timetabled railway network, the highest fares in Western Europe, railways more deeply in debt even than the old nationalized British Rail, and a bankrupt manager of the rail network (Railtrack).

The Community Charge (Poll Tax) was the centrepiece of the Thatcher Government's reform of local government finance in the late 1980s. It was completely abandoned within a year of attempted implementation in England and Wales. The attempt to implement it wasted, directly, £1.5 billion of public money, produced widespread defiance of the law, permanently damaged the finances of local government, and contributed to the fall from office of one its main supporters, Mrs Thatcher.

The Barings bank collapse in 1995 was a major disaster in banking regulation: it destroyed an elite City institution; greatly damaged confidence in the security of the whole banking system; and contributed to a major humiliation for the Bank of England—its loss of responsibility for banking supervision in the new regime introduced on Labour's election in 1997.

BSE (mad cow disease) inflicted catastrophic economic damage in agriculture and caused a public health disaster.

IT fiascos bring us to a particularly rich source, for the case encompasses not a single disaster but several. The last decade is particularly rich in IT fiascos in British government, typically involving a range of catastrophic outcomes: massive cost over-runs; crippling implementation delays; and the total breakdown of policy delivery.

The modern history of fiasco in Britain has produced, obviously, a number of attempted explanations. Two particularly important accounts see the system as having a comprehensive, chronic vulnerability to fiasco. Dunleavy, reviewing disasters in the mid-1990s, concluded that British government was uniquely highly prone to fiascos by west European standards, and traced it to three engrained features of the governing system: extreme majoritarianism in a unitary state; the persistence of many of the features that I have identified as traits of club government, especially a devaluation of formally acquired skills and explicit knowledge at the top of government, notably in the civil service elite; and some of the very features associated with the revolutionary changes in government documented in earlier chapters of this book, notably the craze for downsizing that denuded organizations of the analytical resources needed for systematic policy evaluation, and a cult of 'macho management' that encouraged imprudent and ill thought out decision making.[76] Rhodes foretells fiasco from the very character of the new modernity. Government lives in an age of high social complexity in which dispersed networks cannot be managed by hierarchical command and control.[77] The brutal character of the Thatcher revolution in the 1980s produced precisely this kind of command mode and led to numerous policy failures.[78] According to this account, therefore, there is an engrained potential for fiasco because of the incongruence between the social circumstances of government and its governing tools: 'government will have to learn to live with policy networks, but its tool kit of controls was designed for an era of line bureaucracies, not for steering differentiated, disaggregated policy systems.'[79] The high modernism of the new regulatory state is flying in the face of complex social reality.

We are, therefore, not short of general explanations of fiasco, and these general explanations connect closely to the modernist impulse as it has revealed itself in British government during the 1970s to the 1990s. The evidence of the fiascos examined here suggests, however, that it is hard to offer a single comprehensive explanation linking policy fiascos to engrained features of the governing system. And there is a good reason for this, connected to the very character of the age we are living through. In an age of turmoil and hyper-innovation, British government has lost the kind of homogenous character that marked it in the era of club government. And, as we saw above, this diversity is magnified by the way the consequences of Europeanization and globalization are being absorbed into the system, creating further fragmentation. In short, it is hard any longer to have a single over-arching theory of the origins of policy fiasco in Britain. And, as a consequence of this, it is hard either fully to exonerate or fully to implicate the new regulatory state in these affairs. Thus, we shall now find that the six fiascos examined here fall into three distinct categories. Two (BSE and the Barings bank collapse) are explicable as residues: in other words, as either the policy legacy of the incompetent club world, or the result of persistence of the old club attitudes despite institutional reform. Two (the Poll Tax and the Millennium Dome) are the result of contingent features of the new regulatory state: in other words, they arise, not from attempting to realize its central ambitions, but from features of the policy-making system that have accompanied the sustained crisis of the old world. They arose, in particular, from the hyper-politicization that occurred in the wake of the collapse of club government. Two (rail privatization and IT) do arise from features intrinsic to the teleology of the regulatory state, notably its massive reform ambitions and its drive to create the means of synoptic, comprehensive observation.

The two episodes that unambiguously reflect either a club legacy, or the direct persistence of the club world, are the BSE catastrophe and the Barings collapse. Some of the contingent features of the actual handling of the BSE crisis, as revealed in the reports of the BSE Inquiry, show the persistence in MAFF and some other parts of the civil service of many cultural traits of the club world: obsession with secrecy; unwillingness to divulge much systematically collected information; and, where divulged, its selective release so as to manipulate public expectations.[80] Faced with growing evidence of risks to human health, the official strategy in responding to public worries was one of 'sedation'.[81] But these merely helped prolong the public revelation of the fiasco, further undermined public confidence in the food safety regime, and helped destroy MAFF itself as an independent Ministry.[82] The roots of the catastrophe lie much further back: in the closed world of agricultural politics created during and immediately after the Second World War; in the symbiosis that existed in this closed world between bureaucratic and farming interests; and in the ideologies of agricultural production that elevated food production to a supreme position over values like human health.[83] This fiasco and its aftermath—the most important institutional feature of which has been the creation of the Food Standards Agency described in Chapter 6—is, therefore, best considered as a late episode in the crisis of club government and a contribution to the further expansion of the new regulatory state.

A similar story can be told about the Barings fiasco. The initial official reaction to the collapse—for instance, by the Bank of England—stressed the complexity of modern global financial markets and the difficulty of regulating their sophisticated processes.[84] The official inquiry revealed a different state of affairs. Both within Barings and the Bank of England the catastrophe was allowed to develop because of entirely elementary failings. The failings were, in the words of the chairman of Barings at the time, 'absolute':[85] failure to reply to letters of enquiry; failure to chase up those failures; failure on the part of the Bank to enforce on Barings standards which were routinely imposed on other financial institutions.[86] In the words of the report of the Board of Banking Supervision: 'The Bank regarded the controls in Barings as *informal but effective*. It had confidence in Barings' senior management, many of whom were longstanding Barings' employees. Accordingly, it placed greater reliance on statements made to it by management than it would have done had this degree of confidence not existed.'[87] In short: it believed what Barings told it, without checking, and this at the high tide of the regulatory state. In other words, even after two decades of financial failure and institutional reform, a central value of the club world in banking regulation—that there existed a small category of elite institutions who could be trusted with light touch, informal regulation—still persisted. The consequences have included, in a manner analogous to the outcome of the BSE affair, an extension of the domain of the regulatory state: as we saw in Chapter 4, the Bank of England was stripped of responsibility for prudential supervision and a new Financial Services Authority was created.

Two features link the catastrophes of the Millennium Dome and the Poll Tax: their incorporation into the world of high politics and the way even quite elementary features of systematic policy analysis were swept aside as a result. In short, they show how what I have called hyper-politicization, though an engrained feature of new world of British government, frustrates the ambition central to the regulatory state: to subject policy choice to systematic rational analysis. The case of the Poll Tax exemplifies one of the central features of the changed world of British government that has recurred in the pages of this book: local government finance is one of the best-documented cases where a world of low politics dominated by a well-integrated policy community was destroyed, and was exposed to intervention from actors in the highest reaches of high politics, senior Ministers.[88] The study by Butler and colleagues of how the poll tax was developed shows how the issue of local government was absorbed into the highest sphere of high politics, the sphere of Prime Ministerial concern.[89] They show how any contributions from those with expert knowledge of either local government finance or the world of local government itself—the very sources of the kind of analysis associated with the formal values of the regulatory state—were deliberately excluded. And they show how this exposure to politicians produced a casual mode of decision making based on no serious consideration of evidence or issues. The critical commitments, for example, were made at a meeting at Chequers, which received a glitzy presentation from the two senior Ministers responsible with only about half the Cabinet present. The process was marked by exactly the absence of the kind of systematic analysis of data and options that are one of the hallmarks of the new world of regulation: Ministers 'acted after cursory investigation and virtually no consultation with interested parties.'[90]

The Millennium Dome is an even clearer example of the consequences of hyper-politicization. It was driven from the start by high politics, initiated and conceived as an iconic project by the then Deputy Prime Minister, Michael Heseltine. When it seemed endangered by the impending Conservative election defeat of 1997, Mr Heseltine, in turn, substantially committed the likely incoming Prime Minister (Mr Blair) to the project.[91] This history of commitment from high politics explains one critical feature of the whole affair. The business plans supporting the Dome at different stages were all subjected to the analytical apparatus of the new regulatory state, and were found wanting. As the National Audit Office inquiry into the episode shows, the critical decision to further fund the project was made by the Millennium Commissioners in defiance of their own independently commissioned consultant's report that expressed scepticism about the visitor number targets. (These unrealized targets were the root cause of failure.[92]) What is more, in continuing to fund the business plan as more financial holes appeared, they overrode the views of their own Accounting Officer, who advised that the project was inherently high risk and 'that a further grant could not be made on value for money grounds when set against the normal judgments which the Commission had sought to make over its lifetime.' The Accounting Officer asked that he be directed, and was done so on wider symbolic grounds, notably the impact of cancellation on the reputation of the UK.[93] Nor were these accounting reservations especially stringent or novel; they arose from 'value for money' caution of a sort traditionally second nature to Accounting Officers. But by then all rational caution was swept aside by the absorption of the issue into the high politics of Prime Ministerial commitment and the political ambitions of the Dome 'Minister' Peter Mandelson.[94]

Of course, these cases of hyper-politicization are not 'accidental' frustrations of the analytical capabilities of the new regulatory state. They arise from the conditions that accompanied its birth, notably the collapse of old worlds and old understandings: from the penetration of formerly enclosed domains, and from the passing away of the kind of constitutional understandings dividing ministers and civil servants discussed in Chapter 6. While hyper-politicization is the very reverse of what is intended in the new regulatory state, it is inextricably part of its rise, for it is a legacy of the crisis that led to its creation. (In the case of the Dome, one might add also that its location in London echoes one of the obsessions noted by Scott as characteristic of authoritarian high modernist regimes: endowing national capitals with grandiose, fatuous design projects.[95])

The final two examples of fiasco do, I suggest, arise from the ambitions central to the teleology of the new regulatory state. Scott's study of high modernism is filled with examples of two kinds of modernist project: 'great leaps forward', which rely on clearing away the clutter of existing institutions in the hope of making a radical break with the past, and projects that apply both the imagery and the hardware of high technology to expand the surveillance and control capacities of the state.[96]

The catastrophic condition of the present British rail system has its roots precisely in such a 'great leap forward' mentality, a mentality that shaped the mode of rail privatization that was carried out in the mid-1990s. The great leap forward that produced this catastrophe was remarkable for the haste with which it was enacted and the sketchiness of the preparation with which complex institutional changes were introduced. Hasty implementation, designed, in part, to cut off the option of public ownership to an incoming Labour Administration, lay behind the decision to rush the privatization of network management in 1996.[97] Privatization was achieved by stock market flotation of Railtrack as a single issue, rather than in the staged flotations that had been used in the other big measures like gas and electricity privatization. The National Audit Office report on this process estimates that the cost of this rushed decision to the public purse was £1.5 billion—the difference between the return from a single giant flotation and the higher return that the Office estimated would have accrued from a staged flotation.[98] Thus, even this sidelight on the catastrophe shows costs to the public purse that already match those of the Poll Tax and are double those of the Dome. Above all, the great leap forward meant that detailed technical preparations to support the complex new institutional arrangements were all neglected. Terry's analysis of the planning documents produced in advance of privatization shows that they contained only the sketchiest analysis of the modalities of transition. For example, the planning paper for one of the most complicated and contentious parts of the process—the sale of passenger rolling stock to the new operating companies—was a mere five pages long.[99]

There were particular features of the history of rail privatization that contributed to this fatally pathological process, notably the perceived need to extract the maximum short-term revenue for the Treasury from the sale, and the calculation that the best way to do this was to break up the system for sale in job lots. But, fundamentally, the mode of rail privatization was not an aberration. It sprang from a distinctive style of politics that marked decision making after 1979, a mode that put a premium on pushing through radical measures rapidly and with the minimum of preparation. After 1979, there occurred a counter-revolution produced by the conviction that there was needed a series of radical transitions—sudden leaps that would produce irreversible cultural and institutional change.

The rich recent history of IT project disasters includes the fiasco at the Passport Agency in 1999, when the failure of a newly introduced system caused an almost complete breakdown in the service of passport issue,[100] and the cancellation in 1999 of a 3-year project costing more than £1 billion to encode benefit data in a smart card and thus automate benefit payments via the Post Office network.[101] But these are merely emblematic of a wide range of IT-related problems. Many of these fiascos actually resemble another policy area rich in project disasters: defence procurement. Not only are many of the particular sources of problems in defence replicated (huge cost overruns, huge delays in delivery, serious malfunctions in both the delivered hardware and software), but the economic relationships that lie at the heart of the projects (notably the dependence of the state on a small number of oligopolistic multinational suppliers) are also strikingly similar.[102] But what makes recent IT fiascos of analytical importance is the way they link to central ambitions of the regulatory state, notably to the ideology of high modernism that drives it. The ideology of the steering state that so influenced policy makers 'reinventing government' on both sides of the Atlantic in the 1990s was essentially cybernetic in inspiration: it relied on faith in advanced IT as a technology that would allow accurate synoptic observation and control.[103] Margetts has explored how an ideology of what she calls 'hyper-modernism' is used to picture the transformative capacities of IT, offering government the vision of an escape from old organizational limits.[104] And sure enough, in looking at the recent detail of steering in the core executive, Holliday has found that organizing the state so as to exploit digitalized technology for purposes of steering and surveillance has become an increasing preoccupation of the core executive over the last two decades.[105] That preoccupation has loomed even larger in the years since the publication of *Modernising Government*, with its self-conscious presentation of modern government as an institution in which digitalization is a key feature.[106] More immediately still, IT is now what Bastow and colleagues summarize as 'mission-critical' to government agencies.[107] It is mission-critical for a very obvious reason: because it offers the huge gains of modernity, massive increases in the capacity of the state to perform some of the great tasks of statecraft. It potentially greatly increases state capacity to subject civil society to rationalizing and standardizing processes. It can, thus, allow much more finely tuned performance of functions like extraction of resources (e.g. through taxation); direct surveillance (for instance, electronic tagging of offenders or 'smart card' based surveillance of motorists' movements); and delivery of services (for instance, more comprehensively integrated and finely calibrated benefit delivery systems).

There are general social limits to these potential gains, and they are set by the need to reduce everyday complexity to the standardized and the legible, but these limits do not seem to lie at the heart of British IT fiascos. British disasters like the passports and benefit card fiascos have to do with an inability to exploit the potential benefits of modernization: poor project management skills within government and failure to commit the resources needed to build effective IT systems. A striking example of the latter is provided by the case of the Child Benefits Agency, a fiasco-prone institution, where, for all the rhetoric of digital-ization, staff were left operating an antiquated technology: for instance, when the Agency was established in 1993, the computing systems provided to staff were only dumb terminals instead of networked PCs. Dunleavy and Margetts's first study of *Government on the Web*, from which this example is drawn, showed some extraordinary examples of how backward were public agencies in their ability to adopt web-based innovations despite all the rhetoric of *Modernizing Government* and the commitments to targets for web-based dealings with cit-izens.[108] Their follow-up study, based on case studies of HM Customs and Excise and the Department of Transport, Local Government, and the Regions, though it showed some progress, still paints a picture of patchy coverage of even basic IT capacities.[109] When IT is 'mission-critical', as it is bound to be in the British version of high modernism, and the IT is incompetently managed, then the mission fails. Thus, what is special about recent IT fiascos, setting them aside from old-fashioned British fiascos of the sort that involve expensive missile systems that refuse to work, is that IT projects lie at the heart of the search for a synoptic vision and the control that flows from that vision.

THE FATE OF THE BRITISH REGULATORY STATE

The heart of the argument of this book is that the emergent British regulatory state amounts to an incomplete reconciliation with the conditions of modernity: in other words, with governing arrangements where codified knowledge matters more than tacit knowledge; where codified rules matter more than understand-ings; where instrumental achievement matters more than traditionally occupied position; and where measurable accountability matters more than elite solidarity.

Why is this reconciliation incomplete? There are broadly three reasons: the historical circumstances of the reconciliation itself; the inherent problems in real-izing the ambitions of high modernity, especially in Britain; and the evolving character of the animal that is being reshaped—the British state itself.

The first and most important mark of the historical changes described in these pages is that they amount to a forced reconciliation: a shotgun marriage between the new state and the old oligarchies who ruled Britain even in the half-century of formal democracy after 1918. That shotgun marriage was forced, to emphasize another dominant theme of this book, by the revolutionary consequences of twin crises: the crisis of economic (under) performance and the crisis of the system of government itself. It was also a revolution with a distinctive political cast, because it was largely a revolution from above: the great changes in market practices, state structures, and self-regulatory arrangements were largely initiated by one set of elites—notably in the great Thatcher reforms—against some of the interests at the heart of the old club system. Some of the most important sources of resistance included: parts of the civil service elite that the Thatcherites encountered when they first entered office; traditional domestic economic elites, such as those who ruled in the City before the great competitive reforms of the 1980s; professional elites such as the consultants who ruled so much of the old NHS; and parts of the academic elite that we encountered in our examination of the new world of university assessment. The consequences of the ensuing struggles between these elites and the forces of high modernism are scattered through the pages of this book.

These consequences include the creation of tortuous, bizarre institutional formulas and constitutional ideologies that serve the function of preserving elite autonomy even after crises have forced the abandonment of the heart of club government. That, in summary, is the history of the strange evolution of 'self-regulatory' institutions in the financial markets from the 1980s to the present day, and of the reconstruction of accountancy regulation also documented in Chapter 4. In financial markets, the language of self-regulation was used to describe the old club world; it was then used to describe the very different structure created in 1986 in the Financial Services Act; and it is even used to describe the system now presided over by the Financial Services Authority, the most comprehensively empowered financial regulator in any of the leading world financial centres. In the new world of accounting regulation—in the institutions organized under the umbrella of the Accountancy Foundation—we have seen such a blurring of the line between the public and private that nobody could possibly tell where the public sphere begins and private interests end. That arrangement is ideal for protecting powerful interests from public accountability. But the language is not mere fiction, though mystification is part of its purpose. Even the Financial Services Authority, as we have seen, has maintained important institutional features—such as its status as a company limited by guarantee—to try to preserve it as the property of interests in the markets; and even in 1995, as we saw in the last section, banking regulators were still working with many of the key assumptions of the old club world.

The incomplete reconciliation has also included reforms—like the regulatory framework for the privatized industries—that involved attempts to preserve the discretion and 'flexibility' that had been the hallmark of club rule. In some other cases, old elites have reconstituted, regrouped, and captured the new world of regulation: that, as I argued in Chapter 6, has been the story of the regulation of higher education.

The incomplete reconciliation is also due to the persistence of powerful cultural traits from the old governing order. The single most important of these is what Dyson has nicely characterized as constitutional anthropomorphism, a trait that lies at the base of much of the hyper-politicization in the newly emergent system.[110] Constitutional anthropomorphism refers to the extreme personalization of authority at the heart of British government, and it is a spoor of one of the most traditional traits of all—the original historical expression of public authority in the person of the monarch. Its traditional constitutional expression is in doctrines of individual ministerial responsibility; its institutional expression is in the way ministerial heads of departments are little monarchs in their own kingdom; its everyday political expression is in the way individual ministerial reputation—both its advancement and its destruction—lies at the heart of partisan politics. One consequence is that in a crisis new modes of arms length regulation are swept aside by the reassertion of ministerial authority. That is the lesson of the great crisis of rail privatization in 2001/2 discussed in Chapter 5, and the crisis in the government of prisons discussed in Chapter 6. Nor could it have been otherwise: given the persistence of constitutional anthropomorphism, it would have been political suicide for any Secretary of State to have maintained a hands off relationship with the railways. (The fact that it was also suicidally dangerous to intervene only shows the way agents are trapped by historical circumstance. The rail crisis did, indeed, contribute to the resignation from office of the Secretary of State, Stephen Byers, in 2002.[111]) But the influence of constitutional anthropomorphism is not confined to moments of high crisis. It has reshaped the everyday conduct of policy from the centre. The destruction of the autonomy of so many of the old club domains—in the professions, in service markets, in key public institutions like health and school education—has exposed those domains to the attentions of the central state. The result—as we saw in Chapter 6 in domains like education and health—is a series of linked developments: micro-management of policy, involving Ministerial attention to the minutiae of policy delivery, especially across the span of the welfare state; the multiplication of policy initiatives needed to serve the symbolic demands of the partisan battle; and the manipulation of some of the key features of the new modernity—such as performance indicators—to serve that partisan battle. Hyper-politicization and hyper-innovation, thus, go together.

The dilemma for the new regulatory state, however, is that neither a partial nor a full reconciliation with modernity provides a stable resting point. This brings us to the second main source of the incomplete reconciliation with modernity. I have sought throughout to argue that the regulatory state in Britain amounts to a quintessential project of high modernism. As such, its ambitions are ensnared in the problems of high modernity: in the problems of achieving a central synoptic vision, and of converting that vision into control. The signs of the ambition are everywhere, and form much of the substance of earlier chapters: the investment in intelligence gathering and in surveillance of both individuals and institutions; the colonization of new domains, like the formerly relatively autonomous domains of sport and the arts; the symbiosis between different regulated domains in the attempt to realize new modes of social engineering, such as the crossover between the regulation of sport and the regulation of diet in pursuit of creating a healthier population; the drive to shape the capacities and substantive knowledge of the population through close control of the school system; the rise of a new era of grand projects, ranging from symbolic edifices like the Millennium Dome to prestigious high-technology enterprises like the great IT programmes discussed in the last section. Scott's study of authoritarian high modernism in the twentieth century showed how and why modernism and policy fiasco go together. In a society marked by liberal freedoms and democratic institutions, nothing on the scale of the 'great leap forward' fiascos of authoritarian high modernism is possible. But, as the preceding section showed, at least some of the fiascos in the new regulatory state are a reflection of the limits of the modernist enterprise.

But there are also more contingent problems that are special to Britain, and these bring us to the third and final source of the incomplete reconciliation: the changing character of the British state itself. The greatest burst of modernism that administered the death blows to club government came with Thatcherism. The great Thatcherite reforming programmes were, however, only realizable through the exploitation of entirely traditional features of the British state: notably, empowerment of a new metropolitan elite through the old conventions of Parliamentary majoritarianism. Throughout the 1980s and 1990s that very constitutional settlement dissolved. One process of dissolution, against which Thatcherites railed, but with which in government they had been forced into complicity, came from outside: from the increasing transfer of policy competence to new centres like Brussels and (after the creation of the Euro-Zone) to Frankfurt. The contradictions of the Thatcherite position are epitomized by the case of the Single Market Programme: a massive step in the transfer of policy competence from the domestic arena, the legislation enabling its domestic implementation was passed through the Commons by Mrs Thatcher's government in 1986 using the huge majority that had been a product of the Falklands-inspired victory in the General Election of 1983. A second process of dissolution was quickened by the very successes of Thatcherite radicalism, and by reaction against the way Thatcherism exploited the conventions of Parliamentary majoritarianism. The reforms that were nominally carried out in the name of a United Kingdom government were in reality the work of a government whose political base, and whose interest group base, gradually shrank to the metropolitan world of south-east England. The extraordinary electoral geography revealed after the 1997 general election—with the Conservatives annihilated as a parliamentary force in Scotland and Wales—thus completed the conditions for the devolution reforms introduced by the new Labour Government. Midwinter and McGarvey, for example, present convincing evidence that the onward march of the regulatory state has indeed been halted in Scotland.[112] And, as a bonus, the removal from office of a Conservative Party with residual attachments to Northern Irish Unionism also completed the conditions for the beginnings of devolved government in Northern Ireland after the 1998 Good Friday Agreement. In short, the very state that the Conservatives had modernized after 1979 itself began to dissolve.

The twin processes of devolution of policy competence 'upwards' to Europe, and 'downwards' to the formerly subject national components of the United Kingdom, are of course part of Rhodes's famous image of a 'hollowed out' state.[113] That hollowing out has left the new British regulatory state in a strange condition. After the revolution that swept away the old world of club government, the state has endowed itself with modernist ambitions, and with many modernist institutions and practices. But it is doubtful that it any longer has the capacities—either the policy competence or the symbolic capital—to effectively realize those ambitions.

NOTES

1. INTRODUCTION: FROM STAGNATION TO HYPER-INNOVATION

1. In the case of France, the reference to dictatorship concerns Vichy.
2. Esping-Andersen (1990: 26–78).
3. The diversity is sketched in, for instance, Hood (1991: 55).
4. Pollitt et al. (1999: 42).
5. R. Rhodes (1997: 87); see also R. Rhodes (2000a: 256).
6. Marquand (1988: 175–206).
7. Scott (1998: 87–146).
8. Osborne and Gaebler (1992: 25–48).
9. Hood et al. (1999, 2000).
10. Majone (1996).
11. Scott (1998: 219). These words come in Scott's discussion of authoritarian high modernism, specifically in his account of Soviet collectivization. I should, therefore, state the obvious: I am not suggesting that we have been living through an authoritarian terror. Authoritarian high modernism has been catastrophic, but the ideologies of high modernism have been liberating: they democratize and they create the conditions for purposive social reform.
12. Porter (1995: 76).
13. Oakeshott (1962: 8–13).
14. Porter (1995: 84–5) discusses both the traditional anti-democratic opposition to standardization and quantification, and a more modern source in the post-Marxist theories of the Frankfurt School. The hostility to quantification bequeathed to much British social science from the influence of the Frankfurt School also holds a clue to the opposition to modernization coming from so much nominally 'progressive' British social science.
15. I owe the image and the thinking behind it to Foley (1989).
16. Hood et al. (1999: 3–19).
17. Beer (1982: 119) summarizes the evidence from the 1960s and 1970s of a contemporary decline of the civic culture, concluding that there had been a 'collapse'.
18. See Larkin (1988: 167) for the original.

2. IMAGES OF THE REGULATORY STATE

1. See Feigenbaum et al. (1999) for a comparative survey.
2. See Coates (2000: 23–74) for the revival of liberal models.
3. See Nolan (2001) for an international survey.
4. For the global reshaping that stresses the centrality of central banks, see Jayasuriya (2001); for the more general rise of new agencies in Western Europe, see Thatcher and Stone Sweet (2002).
5. Kooiman (1993). The many (ambiguous) meanings of governance are debated by the contributors to Pierre (2000).

6. R. Rhodes (1997: 198–9); see also R. Rhodes (2000*a*: 254–66).
7. Courpasson (2000).
8. Osborne and Gaebler (1992: 35).
9. Teubner (1987: 20, 1993: 9–10) and Luhmann (1990: 1–20, 1995: 12–50, 437–77). I examine the consequential theories of autopoiesis more closely in Chapter 4.
10. Hofstadter (1962) is still a standard, if polemical, interpretation; for a more celebratory account, see Schlesinger (1960, 1961); see Duxbury (1995: 149–58) on the legal face of the regulatory state, especially on its 'statutorification'.
11. D. Vogel (1986: 231).
12. Morone (1990: 107–8).
13. The figure is from Morone (1990: 117); the classic insider's account of the New Deal agency creation is Landis (1938).
14. This draws on the historical table of measures in Machlup (1952: 187–93).
15. Hofstadter (1962: 232).
16. Hofstadter (1962: 232).
17. The phrase is from Landis's classic insider's account of the process: Landis (1938: 14); the figure is from Morone (1990: 131).
18. See McCraw (1984: 300–9) for this distinctive tradition.
19. Seligman (1982: 39–72).
20. I rely on Cushman (1941: 327–46).
21. On the former, Kelman (1980) and Noble (1986); on the latter, Marcus (1980).
22. Sunstein (1990: 12–13).
23. For the nature of the historical turn represented by the new social regulation, see D. Vogel (1981) and G. Wilson (1984: 211–15).
24. R. Stewart (1988: 107).
25. R. Stewart (1988: 108).
26. I rely on the classic comparative study of American regulatory 'exceptionalism', Kelman (1981: 5–6, 221–37), and D. Vogel (1983, 1986: 10–14).
27. The key source of the argument about American structural power is Strange (1994).
28. The evidence of US state power in global regulatory processes is impressively compressed in Braithwaite and Drahos (2000: 475–9).
29. Majone (1996) is canonical; for subtly different, compressed versions, see Majone (1991, 1999).
30. Majone (1996: 54–5).
31. Majone (1996: 287).
32. Majone (1996: 286).
33. Majone (1996: 286); for the Dahl original, Dahl (1956/1963: 4–33).
34. Thatcher and Stone Sweet (2002: 1).
35. Heclo (1977: 84–112).
36. I have assembled this summary view from: Cram (1994), Peters (1994), Sun and Pelkmans (1995), Caporaso (1996), Christiansen (1997), and Richardson (2000: 1013–17).
37. The most intellectually influential account is Nonet and Selznick (2001), originally published in 1978.
38. Teubner (1987: 19).
39. Teubner (1987: 21), italics in original.
40. Durkheim (1933/1964: 211).
41. McBarnet and Whelan (1991, 1999) and Picciotto (1992: 77–96, 171–229).
42. This literature of disenchantment spans more than two decades. For some landmarks, see Pressman and Wildavsky (1973), Hood (1976, 1994), and Bovens and 'tHart (1996).
43. Ayres and Braithwaite (1992).
44. Ayres and Braithwaite (1992: 157–62).
45. Ayres and Braithwaite (1992: 101–32).
46. Ayres and Braithwaite (1992: 35–41).
47. Braithwaite (2000) and Braithwaite and Drahos (2000).

48. Braithwaite and Drahos (2000: 479–88).
49. See Gunningham and Rees (1997: 363–414) for an introduction to a special issue of *Law and Policy* on this; and Furger (1997), Rees (1997), and Sinclair (1997) for cases.
50. Gunningham et al. (1998: 37–91).
51. Gunningham et al. (1998: 4, n. 5).
52. Gunningham et al. (1998: 51).
53. Gunningham et al. (1998: 56–69). The words in quotation are on p. 56.
54. Gunningham and Johnstone (1999).
55. Department of Energy (1990: ii. 355–86). I discuss this report and the wider issues of safety inspection in Chapter 6.
56. Gunningham and Johnstone (1999: 38).
57. Gunninngham and Johnstone (1999: 93).
58. Clarke (2000: 23).
59. Clarke (2000: 25).
60. Ericson and Haggerty (1997: 48).
61. Giddens (1990); and for a more recent restatement, Giddens (1999).
62. Giddens (1990: 124–34).
63. U. Beck (1992: 19). Beck has prompted a large critical literature in both English and German. For a sample, see Adam et al. (2000).
64. For his reflections on some British risks, notably BSE, see Beck (2000).
65. Notably Wildavsky (1989) and Wildavsky and Dake (1990); Douglas (1990, 1994).
66. See Sapolsky (1990) on the general politics of risk; Kleidman (1990) for a media case study.
67. Douglas (1994: 4). The work referred to is Douglas (1966); see also Douglas (1990).
68. Douglas (1994). The first quotation is from p. 33, the second from p. 15. Douglas's biggest influence on risk research in Britain has been via the work of Christopher Hood and his collaborators: see especially Hood et al. (2001: 4) and Hall et al. (2000).
69. Royal Society (1992).
70. Power (1997).
71. Power (1997: 138).
72. Power (1997: 138–9).
73. I discuss the BSE case in more detail in Chapter 7; for food processing, see Flynn et al. (1999); for the traditional regulatory community in biotechnology, see van Zwanenberg (1998).
74. van Zwaenberg and Millstone (2000: 273) and van Zwanenberg (1998).
75. Stirling (1998); see also Stirling (1997, 1999).
76. Stirling (1998: 98–100).
77. Weale (2001: 358); cf. Weale et al. (2000: 181–2).
78. Knight (1933: 19–20).
79. The list is from Giddens (1999: 1).
80. Hood et al. (2001).
81. Hood et al. (2001: 136).
82. Hood et al. (2001: 171), italics in original.
83. Hood et al. (2001: 171–2).
84. Marquand (1988: 178).
85. For an account of the hegemonic constitutional ideology at the moment of flux, see Norton (1984: 10–19).
86. Sharpe (1982: 136). Compare Howell (1986: 7): 'From some point in the 1920s, most Socialists within Britain were also British socialists.'
87. Heclo and Wildavsky (1981: 7).
88. H. Dale (1941: 29–30, 50–1).
89. Bulpitt (1983: 29–30). Bulpitt is here criticising the adequacy of the distinction in explaining centre–periphery relations. My point is that, as a construct, it served to consign important policy domains to the sphere of low routine.

90. See Gamble (1994: 47–63) for a survey.
91. Ingham (1984: 96–127).
92. For illustrations, see Jessop (1971).
93. Almond and Verba (1965: 315).
94. On decline, Kavanagh (1980); and Beer (1982: 110–20) for particularly compelling evidence of change.
95. A major theme of both Shonfield (1965: 88–120) and Dyson (1980: 36–44).
96. D. Vogel (1986: 193–225).
97. See Martin (1997) for a study of a key figure in the Nuffield School, W. E. J. McCarthy—particularly revealing for the way it charts the gradual modification of the original 'voluntarism' in the light of the problems of the 1970s and 1980s.
98. Professor Hugh Clegg, the most important figure in the foundation of the 'Nuffield' school, was a member of the Royal Commission; W. E. J. McCarthy was its director of research.
99. See the 'Addendum by Lord Donovan', the 'Supplemetary Note by Lord Tangley', the 'Supplementary Note by Lord Robens, Sir George Pollock and Mr John Thompson', and the 'Note of Reservation by Mr Andrew Shonfield', all in Royal Commission on Trade Unions and Employers' Association (1968: 279–302).
100. Hawkins (1984).
101. The most obvious connection is via the distinguished series Oxford Socio-Legal Studies in which have been published some of the key 'soft' and 'smart' regulation studies discussed earlier: Gunningham et al. (1998) and Gunningham and Johnstone (1999). Hawkins is the general editor of the series, but this institutional role reveals only a glimpse of his importance, which derives from the power and originality of the systematization of regulatory ideology in *Environment and Enforcement*, and the way it shaped the thinking of a generation of legal scholars of regulation.
102. Hawkins (1984: 27).
103. Hawkins (1984: 190).
104. Hawkins (1984: 207).
105. Hawkins (1984: 193).
106. Hawkins (1984: 204).

3. CREATING CLUB REGULATION

1. Machlup (1952: 181).
2. Ogus (1992: 2–3).
3. Elton (1969: 415–30).
4. Keir (1966: 3), from which the words in the quotation are taken.
5. Ogus (1992: 2).
6. Haas (1970: 191).
7. Ogus (1992: 9).
8. Dyson (1980: 37).
9. Roberts (1969: 12).
10. Arthurs (1985: 15–25).
11. Ogus (1992: 11–13).
12. Ogus (1992: 7, 12).
13. Haas (1970).
14. Hobsbawm (1962/1997: 42–100).
15. Much of this turns on debates about the character of the 'nineteenth-century revolution in government': see MacDonagh (1958) and Parris (1960), and for an attempt to unravel the skeins in the arguments, see Cromwell (1966).

16. See Brebner (1948).
17. Perkin (1969: 107–8).
18. MacDonagh (1961, 1977: 1).
19. Arthurs (1985: 15).
20. Parris (1969: 281).
21. Redlich and Hirst (1970: 116–38) on the former; Parris (1969: 134–59) on the latter.
22. MacDonagh (1977: 6), and recurring theme of MacDonagh (1961).
23. Arthurs (1985: 42).
24. On this central theme viewed through the problems of the fulcrum institution of the old order, the House of Lords, see Le May (1979: 127–51).
25. A fuller list of institutional innovation is in Roberts (1969: 93–5).
26. Larson (1977: 87–8) confirms this.
27. Perkin (1969: 255).
28. M. Thomas (1948: 9–13, 65–70).
29. Quoted, M. Thomas (1948: 76).
30. Bartrip and Fenn (1980, 1983) document.
31. Ashby and Anderson (1981: 28).
32. Quoted, Ashby and Anderson (1981: 28).
33. Parrris (1965: 34–7, 92, 190–1) and Alderman (1973: 48).
34. Parris (1965: 92).
35. Gourvish (1980: 49).
36. Dobbin (1994: 158–65).
37. Paulus (1974: 38).
38. Paulus (1974: 38).
39. On the struggles with the older tradition of business autonomy, see Arthurs (1985: 50–88).
40. Alderman (1973: 161, and 232–50).
41. Bartrip (1980) tells this story.
42. The significance of the social composition of the magistracy is examined in Bartrip and Fenn (1980) and Bartrip and Burman (1983: 59).
43. Ashby and Anderson (1981: 40–3), see p. 130 for the quotation.
44. Porter (1995: 99).
45. For instances Bartrip and Fenn (1980, 1983).
46. M. Thomas (1948: 130).
47. Quoted, M. Thomas (1948: 119–20), italics in original.
48. The whole problem of business eluding the law is a central theme of Arthurs (1985: 50–88).
49. Carson (1970a,b, 1974, 1980).
50. Carson (1979).
51. Carson (1980: 162).
52. Perkin (1969: 428).
53. Larson (1977: 88).
54. Millerson (1964: 120–47).
55. Reader (1966: 50–2).
56. Murphy (1988: 161–91).
57. This brusque summary, nevertheless, glosses over considerable variation in success in realizing professionalization strategies: for some sense of this variation at mid-century, see Reader (1966: 59–72).
58. Millerson (1964: 148).
59. Berlant (1975: 130–8).
60. Waddington (1984: 135–52, 1990).
61. Merrison (1975: 2).
62. M. Stacey (1992: 23).
63. Merrison (1975: 13–14).

64. This relies on M. Stacey (1989*a,b*, 1992: 203–55).
65. On archaeology, see Hopwood (1987).
66. Hein (1978: 139–83) and Sugarman (1995: 227–8).
67. Miller and Power (1995: 6).
68. Armstrong (1987: 420) and Edwards (1989: 109–25).
69. N. Stacey (1954: 24–36).
70. Willmott (1985: 48).
71. Also confirmed in Zeff (1972: 7).
72. Kynaston (1995: 21).
73. Reader (1966: 47).
74. Carr-Saunders and Wilson (1933: 329) confirm.
75. The list is from Millerson (1964: 92).
76. Sugarman (1995: 227–30).
77. Porter (1995: 109).
78. Porter (1995: 109–10).
79. Ingham (1984) is a classic study.
80. The most economical way to get a picture of this uniqueness is via the landmark official reports on the financial system in the twentieth century: Committee on Finance and Industry (1931*a*: 25–45), Committee on the Working of the Monetary System (1959: 42–109), and Committee to Review the Functioning of Financial Institutions (1980: 288–318).
81. On this ideology and the way it allowed crooks to prosper, see Kynaston (1995: 148–9).
82. Morgan and Thomas (1962: 140–55) and Kynaston (1994: 151–64, 250–63).
83. Kynaston (1995: 319).
84. Quoted, Stock Exchange (1979: 17); see also Kynaston (1994: 277–86) for the history of this inquiry.
85. Clapham (1970) is virtually organized around the sets of crises. See Presnell (1956: 501–10) for earlier crises and the decline of provincial banking.
86. Clapham (1970: 95–102, 199–211, 226–34, 326–9).
87. Sayers (1976: i. 13–27, ii. 593–602).
88. Fletcher (1976: 17–34, 43–51).
89. See Blunden (1975) on this.
90. Authoritative on this is Sayers (1976: i. 13–17).
91. Hirsch (1977).
92. Bagehot (1873/1910: 162–307).
93. Committee on Finance and Industry (1931*a*: 15).
94. On the 'closure' of markets, especially of the Stock Exchange, see Kynaston (1995: 400–1, 526–9).
95. Lisle-Williams (1984: 337–8); see also Kynaston (1995: 324) on dynastic marriage as a key to social fusion.
96. For a bruising early encounter between the City and the nascent democracy, see Kynaston (1995: 494–7) on the City and Lloyd George's People's Budget.
97. This relies on Kynaston (1999: 185–211, 323–53) and Sayers (1976: ii. 501–60), which is particularly important on the connection in the 1930s between domestic financial system management and the wider problems of international financial diplomacy.
98. For the sudden and alarming culmination of this wave of socialist rhetoric by the end of the First World War, see McKibbin (1974: 91–106).
99. Clay (1957: 272–317).
100. Clay (1957: 160–3) and Kynaston (1999: 193–202).
101. Committee on Finance and Industry (1931*a*: 5).
102. Committee on the Working of the Monetary System (1959: 120).
103. See Sykes (1926: 73–93) for the critical phase.

104. The history of the consolidation of the clearing banks into a London-focused 'big five' is condensed in Truptil's classic (1936: 59–109).
105. Sayers (1976: i. 13–17, ii. 639–54).
106. For a characteristic official account of practice and its underlying cultural understandings, see Committee on the Working of the Monetary System (1959: 269–79), especially p. 274.
107. On Norman's style, see Clay (1957: 474–89) and Sayers (1976: i. 160).
108. Committee on Finance and Industry (1931c: 296).
109. Committee on the Working of the Monetary System (1960: 52).
110. For a vivid account of how far the Bank (and especially the Governor) was informally managing competition across markets in the wake of the Great Crash, see Kynaston (1999: 380–429); for a more formal study of the growth of restrictive practices in one key part of the financial system, see Griffiths (1973).
111. Committee on the Working of the Monetary System (1960: 52).
112. Committee on Finance and Industry (1931b: 2).
113. Tropp (1957: 3).
114. Carr-Saunders and Wilson (1933: 334, 342, 387).
115. Johnson (1972) is the classic on the resulting variety of modes of occupational control.
116. Merrison (1975: 5, 13–14).
117. Abel (1988: 35).
118. Abel-Smith and Stevens (1967): Part II on the era of consolidation and stagnation.
119. See Webster (1988: 107–20) for the authoritative official history of these struggles.
120. Perkin (1990: 155–70).
121. See Tropp (1957: 269) for a passage on the growth of teacher autonomy in the classroom by the 1950s—a passage that will read bizarrely to any teacher subjected to the regulatory regime of the last decade discussed in Chapter 6.
122. Berdahl (1959: 56).
123. G. Rhodes (1981: 174–6) and Robens (1972: 64).
124. Robens (1972: 63). Robens used this passage to dismiss the (unnamed) advocates of stricter legal enforcement.
125. D. Vogel (1986: 162).
126. D. Vogel (1986: 171).
127. G. Rhodes (1981: 76–8).
128. Carson (1982), especially pp. 231–84.
129. Ashby and Anderson (1981: 102).
130. Hawkins (1984: 191).
131. Hutter (1997: 187–94, 2001: 103–4, 123). Hutter's work on the inspectorate shows, however, a more recent growth of adversarialism (Hutter 1997: 271–2). I discuss this more fully in Chapter 6.
132. See Wilcox and Gray (1996: 25) for the words in quotation marks.
133. See Wilcox and Gray (1996: 25–7) for the Arnoldian ideology and its aftermath.
134. G. Rhodes (1981: 176).
135. Robens (1972: app. 6, p. 184).
136. Weale (2001: 357).
137. The authoritative exposition, and critique, of this historically embedded ideology is in Committee on the Civil Service (1968), especially pp. 9–15; the historical development of the ideology is well described in R. Thomas (1989: 33–71); and an entertaining exposition of the ideology is Sisson (1959: 13–37, 132–49).
138. Examined in Arthurs (1985: 115–31).
139. See Prosser (1997: 36–7) and Cushman (1941: 510–29) for a detailed history.
140. Arthurs (1985: 134).
141. Parris (1969: 98–100).
142. Royal Commission on Trade Unions and Employers' Associations (1968: 10).
143. On the Commission and its fate, see R. Taylor (1993: 151–7).

4. TRANSFORMING SELF-REGULATION

1. Dyson (1992: 16–18).
2. See Coleman (1996: 167–9) for this.
3. For shifting UK meanings, Gower (1984) is illuminating at a moment of change.
4. Baggott (1989: 436–8).
5. Ogus (1995: 99–100).
6. Notably, Ayres and Braithwaite (1992).
7. Baggott (1989: 438).
8. D. Vogel (1986: 24), Baggott (1989), and Graham (1994). For a contrasting culture, see D. Vogel (1996).
9. For the 'purest' cases of club markets, see Collins (1999: 212–18).
10. Millerson (1964: 148).
11. Graham (1994); but Black (1996) examines the critical point of change in this understanding.
12. In legal theory, 'juridification' is associated with critical accounts of the explosion of law; I use it here neutrally to signify the rise of legal rules, legal reasoning, and resort to legal institutions to administer regulation. For the critical history, see Teubner (1987: 6–7, 1993: 74).
13. For example, Collins (1999: 111).
14. An economical sketch of regulatory patterns in the range of financial markets before the era of hyper-innovation is Committee to Review the Functioning of Financial Institutions (1980*a*: 228–300); Wilding (1982) does a similar job for the professions.
15. For characteristic examples, see Cabinet Office (2000) and Office of Fair Trading (2001*a*).
16. The two key collections are Schmitter and Lehmbruch (1979) and Lehmbruch and Schmitter (1982). The words quoted are Schmitter's in Schmitter and Lehmbruch (1979: 13).
17. See Black (1996: 43–51) for a normative case for governing self-regulation by the principles of reflexive law; and Prosser (1999) for an argument about the relevance of theories of autopoiesis to utility regulation.
18. Ayres and Braithwaite (1992) and Grabosky and Braithwaite (1993). See also Gunningham et al. (1998).
19. The modern theory of autopoiesis is theoretically heavily indebted to Luhmann (1990, 1995) (esp. 1995); its most influential exponent in legal theory is Teubner (1987, 1993).
20. Teubner (1993: 69).
21. Robens (1972: 43–6).
22. Gunningham and Johnstone (1999), esp. pp. 308–40.
23. For accounts that invoke theories of autopoiesis and reflexivity in industrial safety and environmental regulation outside Britain, or in comparisons of Britain with other systems, see Born and Goldschmidt (1997) and Alders and Wilthagen (1997).
24. The quotation is from Office of Fair Trading (2002*a*: 1). The full list is: used cars, car repair, credit, funerals, travel, estate agents, direct marketing.
25. This is a count based on a search of the trade associations directory maintained by the Trade Association Forum, a body part sponsored by the DTI: Trade Association Forum (2002).
26. Public Relations Consultants Association (2001).
27. Catholic Bishops' Conference (2001).
28. Holt and Mason (2000: 166).
29. Collins (1999: 212–18).
30. See Committee to Review the Functioning of Financial Institutions (1980*a*: 288–344, 1980*b*: 486–520) for an overview at a moment just before great change in the whole system; see Baltic Exchange (2002) for a description of a typical specialist club market.
31. Kynaston (1994: 12–13).
32. For instance, Panel on Take-Overs and Mergers (1979: 3–11, 22–4), Stock Exchange (1979: 16–28), and Committee to Review the Functioning of Financial Institutions (1980*a*: 288–300).

33. For some of the accumulation, see Blunden (1975: 788).
34. For a summary official sketch by the responsible officer at a moment of crisis, see Blunden (1975).
35. For a typical authoritative statement dating from the 1950s, see Committee on the Working of the Monetary System (1959: 118–21).
36. Reid (1982) is a gripping account.
37. Blunden (1975) is an official, authoritative account.
38. See Board of Banking Supervision (1995) for the report; discussed in more detail in Chapter 7.
39. The details are in HM Treasury (1997).
40. For characteristic examples, see Collins (1999: 212–18) and Committee to Review the Functioning of Financial Institutions (1980a: 301–18).
41. See Reid (1988: 243–60) for the institutional details.
42. See Wilks (1999: 209) on the relationship between the MMC and the Panel.
43. Panel on Take-Overs and Mergers (1979: 3–11) summarizes the history.
44. The most recent version at the time of writing is Panel on Take-Overs and Mergers (2002).
45. See P. Davies (1997: 774–805) for the full, complex apparatus of regulation; see p. 775, n. 23 for the key legal decision.
46. Analysed in particular in Clarke (1981, 1986).
47. Lloyd's (2000).
48. See Lloyd's (2002) for latest.
49. S. Vogel (1996: 93–117) is authoritative.
50. Reid (1988) tells the whole story.
51. Financial Services Authority (2001a).
52. Financial Services Authority (2001a: 9–19).
53. Financial Services Authority (2002).
54. Millerson (1964: 246–58) and Reader (1966: 164–6).
55. Wilding (1982: 12).
56. Tropp (1957: 3).
57. Tropp (1957: 268–9).
58. Power (1997: 15–40) is a summary account.
59. This relies on Matthews et al. (1998: 38–88), Armstrong (1987), and Miller and Power (1995).
60. Loft (1986) and Matthews et al. (1998: 142–54).
61. Willmott (1985) and Zeff (1972: 7, 68–9).
62. Cheffins (1997: 372–3).
63. Financial Reporting Council (2001, 2002).
64. Accounting Standards Board (2001) and Financial Reporting Council (2001, 2002).
65. Accountancy Foundation (2002: 2).
66. Accountancy Foundation (2002: 3).
67. Accountancy Foundation (2002: 4).
68. Department of Trade and Industry (1998a, 2000: 241–93); and for the negotiations following the publication of the consultative document in 1998, see Accountancy Foundation (2002: 1).
69. Accountancy Foundation (2002: 2). Compare the new Financial Services Authority described earlier in this chapter.
70. Accountancy Foundation (2002: 5). The document also gives details of all other Board memberships, from which these generalizations are drawn.
71. See Hewitt (2002).
72. Berlant (1975: 130–53).
73. Waddington (1984: 96–132, 1990).
74. See M. Stacey (1992: 203–16) for this.
75. See Merrison (1975) for the ensuing report; see Stacey (1992: 29–44) for the revolt.
76. See R. Smith (1989) on these cases.
77. M. Stacey (1992: 51–85).
78. Klein (1990).

79. See Harrison et al. (1990: 86) on the growth of 'top down' control.
80. Salter (2001: 871).
81. Abel (1988: 35).
82. Abel-Smith and Stevens (1967: 187–243).
83. Abel (1989: 133).
84. Stacey M., (1992: 181–99).
85. Abel (1989: 134–5).
86. Abel (1988: 117–9, 227–8).
87. See O'Brien and Epp (2000: 304) for the words in quote marks.
88. Hanlon (1997) summarizes the economic setting and the consequences.
89. See Brazier et al. (1993) for the key reforms; see Hanlon (1997) for the economic interests at work.
90. Bar Council (2001) and Law Society (2000).
91. Office of Fair Trading (2000).
92. Law Society (2000).
93. Office of Fair Trading (2001b).
94. Office of Fair Trading (2002a: 13–17).
95. Holt and Mason (2000: 93–120) summarize this.
96. Teubner (1987, 1993).
97. Teubner (1993: 69).
98. Holt and Mason (2000: 146).
99. For examples, see Allison and Monnington (2002: 113).
100. Holt (1989: 202–79) and Jones (1988: 15–41).
101. Birley (1995a,b) surveys widely.
102. See Coghlan and Webb (1990: 21) for the early history; and Holt and Mason (2000: 150) on the gradual acquisition of more executive functions after 1970.
103. Sport England (2002) is the source for the details.
104. UK Sport (2002a) is the source for the quotation and for this institutional description.
105. See Rugby Football League (1999) for the details.
106. See Morrow (1999: 4–29) for the 'new business of football.'
107. For *Raising the Game* and its institutional consequences see Department of National Heritage (1995, 1996).
108. Department of National Heritage (1996: 2).
109. Department for Culture, Media and Sport (2000).
110. Department for Culture, Media and Sport (2000: 11).
111. Department for Culture, Media and Sport (2000: 19).
112. Department for Culture, Media and Sport (2000: 44).
113. Department for Culture, Media and Sport (2002).
114. The full list of allocations for all sports in UK Sport (2002a).
115. National Ice Skating Association (2002).
116. Parrish (2001: 172–84).
117. Parrish (2001: 162–5).
118. Home Office (2000a); on hare coursing, HC Debates, vol. 373, cols 727–34, 29 October 2001.
119. On fox hunting, see the submission to the Burns Inquiry by the Association of Masters of Harriers and Beagles (2000); for boxing, see Hoey (2001).
120. Department for Culture, Media and Sport (2001b).
121. Arts Council (2001, 2002).
122. The debt of my argument here to Gamble's (1994b) well-known thesis about the free economy and the strong state will be obvious.
123. Office of Fair Trading (2002b: 22; and 2001c.).
124. For this case, see Clarke (1990: 162–3, 178–9).
125. Scott (1998: 4–6).

5. REGULATING PRIVATIZATION

1. Feigenbaum et al. (1999: 1, 62).
2. Thatcher, Mark (2002: 128–30, 137).
3. Graham (2000: 7–21).
4. See Holmes (1985: 170–1) for details.
5. Berle and Means (1932/1992: 112–16).
6. Hutton (1996: 298–31).
7. A major theme of Parkinson (1993: 3–50); see also Atiyah (1979).
8. Hadden (1977: 19–22).
9. Stokes (1986: 160–1).
10. Cheffins (1997: 39).
11. Parkinson (1993: 25–32).
12. Parkinson (1993: 27–30).
13. Reich (1964).
14. See Parkinson (1993: 27) on the way more or less automatic access to the privileges of limited liability led to the wasting away of the concessions model.
15. Self and Storing (1962: 111). I owe this reference to R.E.Goodin: see Goodin (1990). And for a similar US observation, see Reich (1964: 778).
16. For a brief history, see Gibbons (1998: 150–78).
17. Cheffins (1997: 96–7).
18. Wilks (1999: 208–13).
19. Wilks (1999: 10).
20. Two particularly devastating accounts, based on official inquiry, are Select Committee on Nationalised Industries (1968: 183–90) and National Economic Development Office (1976: 22–41).
21. See Craig (1991) for this 'forgotten' tradition: his word, 538; and on its modern invention following privatization, see Prosser (2000).
22. Prosser (2000: 65).
23. Letwin (1988: 50). Oliver Letwin was a member of Mrs Thatcher's Policy Unit; subsequently a Conservative MP, presently a member of the Conservative Shadow Cabinet. The introduction to Letwin in this volume (p. 49) provides a striking example of how involved the British pioneers of privatization had become by the close of the 1980s in the world privatization movement, especially via the City of London. When he delivered the words quoted here, Letwin was an Assistant Director of N.M. Rothschild with special responsibility for privatization.
24. Conservative Party (1989).
25. Ridley (1991: 14–16, 62). Ridley gives no exact date for his report, but notes (16) that it was almost a replica of a report he had produced for Mr Heath's Shadow Cabinet in 1970. Denham and Garnett (2001: 304, n. 61) date the report to 1978 from Keith Joseph's papers.
26. An authoritative study of the government of the old nationalized sector is Prosser (1986).
27. National Economic Development Office (1976: 22–41).
28. See Swann (1988: 236–8) and Lawson (1992: 203–6) on these passages to disenchantment.
29. Wilks (1999: 245).
30. Hoskyns (2000: 202), quoting his own memo to the Prime Minister on 8 July 1980. Hoskyns was the first head of Mrs Thatcher's Policy Unit after the election of 1979.
31. Foster (1992: 112–14, 355).
32. See Abromeit (1988) for how action preceded theory.
33. Foster (1992: 124–5).
34. Ridley (1991: 62–3).
35. Ernst (1994: 37–53) documents these assertions.
36. Self and Storing (1962: 111).

37. Baldwin and Cave (1999: 234).
38. Foster (1992: 125).
39. For a similar argument about the connection between national cultures of economic regulation and the mode of privatization, this time in a comparative study with France, see Prosser (1990).
40. Littlechild (1983, 1986).
41. Ridley (1991: 62) and Lawson (1992: 223).
42. Littlechild (1983: 7). For sceptical accounts of his argument, see Prosser (1997: 7–9) and Graham (2000: 151–3).
43. Littlechild (1986: 5).
44. Littlechild (1983: 16–20).
45. Littlechild (1983: 36).
46. See Foster (1992: 124) on pressure of time.
47. Thatcher, Margaret (1993: 681–2) and Walker (1991: 188–91).
48. Department of Energy memorandum in Select Committee on Energy (1986: 87).
49. Secretary of State in oral evidence, Select Committee on Energy (1986: 71).
50. For criticims of the personal nature of the system as an obstacle to accountability, see Velijanovski (1990: 302) and Hansard Society (1996: 12, 51); and for a studied rejection of American style commissions as prone to bureaucracy, see Department of Energy in evidence to Select Committee on Energy (1986: 87).
51. A canonical statement of this anti-legal stance, and a defence of a light touch regulatory regime, occurs in the Second Reading speech of the Secretary of State for Industry (Patrick Jenkin) of the Telecommunications Bill that established the new regime: 'For the ordinary citizen, statute and common law may represent an impenetrable mesh of legal duties and prohibitions, but, happily, most of us can get through our lives without any overt enforcement of these provisions against us. So it will be with this regulatory system. It provides a framework, states the duties and constraints and provides the powers to see that they are observed. However, in practice the BT board will be free to conduct its affairs with a minimum of interference and control.' HC Debates, vol. 33, cols 38–9, 29 November 1982.
52. Young (2001: 107–29) is an examination of the issue of Parliamentary accountability.
53. For a hostile account of American 'legalism' by an insider, see Foster (1992: 6–7, 259–67).
54. Littlechild (1986: 36).
55. Littlechild (1986: 28).
56. McKinnon (1993: 120).
57. Graham (2000: 153).
58. Documented in Prosser (1997: 88–116); and for reflections on where this left the wider energy regime, see Dow (2000).
59. For a narrative of Labour's convoluted policy history, see Young (2001: 67–9, 150–2). See Gamble and Kelly (2001: 175, 167–83) on the more general setting of economic policy after 1997.
60. Thatcher, Mark (1997: 123).
61. Thatcher, Mark (1997: 139).
62. For examples from the Rail Regulator, see Swift (1999: 175–6).
63. The details are described in Utilities Law Review (2000); an official text is in Office of Gas and Electricity Markets (2002a).
64. On American regulatory professionalization, the careerism of regulators and the way this shapes regulatory politics, see J. Wilson (1980).
65. On this, see Graham (1998a) and Corzine (1998).
66. See Department of Trade and Industry (1998b) for the 'Green Paper' text; see also Graham (1998b).
67. My account relies on journalistic reporting, notably Corzine (1998) and Cooper (2000).
68. For details, see Utilities Law Review (2000) and Riley (2000).
69. Office of Gas and Electricity Markets (2002b: 23–5).

70. See Prosser (2000) for the details.
71. Department of Energy (1986: 5).
72. See McHarg (1998) on its decay.
73. See the Prime Minister's condemnation of the scale of executive remuneration as 'distasteful': HC Debates, 28 February 1995, col. 837.
74. See Select Committee on Employment (1995: v, xviii).
75. See Corporate Governance (1996) and Young (2001: 123) for a summary of the affair.
76. Concurrency as an issue is built into the structure of the regulatory system because of the simultaneous and often overlapping regulatory responsibilities of sectoral regulators, responsible for particular industries, and the increasingly powerful regulators of competition across the whole economy, such as the Office of Fair Trading.
77. Documented in Wilks (1999: 243–81).
78. Riley (2000) has details.
79. Utilities Law Review (2000) has details.
80. Riley (2000).
81. Cram (1994), Peters (1994), Christiansen (1997), and Richardson (2000) are sources of the general observations; Coen and Thatcher (2000) apply the insight to utility regulation.
82. Nugent (2001: 72–8).
83. See Armstrong and Bulmer (1998: 15–27) for an overview of the issues.
84. See Wilks (1999: 300) for the quotation; see also Wilks and Bartle (2002).
85. See Slot and Skudder (2001) on this.
86. For telecommunications, see Sauter (1996); for more general universal service pressures, see Prosser (2000: 77–81).
87. Prosser (2001: 506).
88. Thatcher, Mark (2000: 391).
89. Botchway (2001: 19).
90. Knill and Lehmkuhl (2000: 71–4).
91. Postal Services Commission (Postcom) (2001: 6–9).
92. Hunt (1997: 114).
93. I rely heavily on the most authoritative summary, based on questioning of key witnesses: Select Committee on Transport, Local Government and the Regions (2002a).
94. Select Committee on Transport, Local Government, and the Regions (2002a): 'The decision to place Railtrack in Administration', paras 4–9.
95. See Select Committee on Environment, Transport and Regional Affairs (2000) for these.
96. For a close examination of the problems of arriving at a considered conclusion on this difficult subject, see Hutter (2001: 49–69).
97. Select Committee on Transport, Local Government, and the Regions (2002a): 'Major structure enhancements', paras 27–34.
98. Select Committee on Transport, Local Government, and the Regions (2002a), 'The decision to place Railtrack in Administration', paras 5–7.
99. There are serious puzzles over Railtrack's strategies and whether they necessarily led to bankruptcy, summarized in Select Committee on Transport, Local Government, and the Regions, 'The decision to place Railtrack in Administration', para 7. Texts of key documents, including minutes of key meetings, can be read at Department for Transport (2002a).
100. The statement is at HC Debates, cols 954–6, 15 October 2001.
101. Select Committee on Transport, Local Government and Regions (2002a), 'The Strategic Rail Authority and Franchise Replacement', paras 6–13 document.
102. Select Committee on Transport, Local Government, and the Regions (2002a), 'The decision to place Railtrack into Administration', para 7.
103. Sir Alistair Morton, at Select Committee on Transport, Local Government, and the Regions (2002b)—at question 144.
104. See Department for Transport (2002b) for these details.

105. A striking example is provided by the furious partisan exchanges which accompanied the Secretary of State's announcement of Railtrack's plunge into Administration: HC Debates 954–73, 15 October 2001.
106. Examined in Shaoul (2000) and Graham and Vass (2000).
107. Bannister (2000).
108. Department for Transport (2002*b*).
109. On the National Lottery, see Miers (1996) and National Lottery Commission (2002: 6–9).
110. See Hay (1999: 127–30) and throughout for an excellent account of Labour's odyssey to post-Thatcherism.
111. See Maloney (2001) on the history of the growth of an increasingly elaborate regulatory regime in water; see Melville (1994) on the manipulative strategies of a particularly troubled water company (Yorkshire Water) in the early years of privatization.
112. Marsh (1992: 238–49).
113. See Chapman and Temple (1998: 309–15) for a summary.
114. Hay (1999).
115. Philpot (1998) documents.
116. For a discussion and summary of the evidence supporting these assertions, see Warren (1999) and Moran (2001).
117. The historical context of this problem of legitimation in Britain is examined in Boswell and Peters (1997).
118. Cadbury (1992*a,b*) was set up by the Financial Reporting Council, the Stock Exchange, and the accounting profession; Greenbury (1995) by the CBI; Hampel (1998) by the Financial Reporting Council.
119. See Heseltine (2000: 468–9) for an account of Greenbury's unhappiness as he encountered an unfamiliar world of politics.
120. Hampel (1998).
121. Select Committee on Employment (1995: Xliiii).
122. See Department of Trade and Industry (2001: 38–59, 2002).

6. REGULATING AND COLONIZING PUBLIC WORLDS

1. The authoritative accounts of the revolutionary transformation are in the reports of the 'Whitehall' programme: for an overview see the summary account offered by R. Rhodes (2000*a*: 245–66).
2. The debt of this argument to Bulpitt's (1983) 'dual polity' model will be obvious here.
3. For Warren Fisher, see Fry (1969: 55–8).
4. Ministry of Reconstruction (1918: 7–10).
5. Ministry of Reconstruction (1918: 11).
6. On this, see Parris (1969: 131–3).
7. For long-term influence of the 'Haldane' model, see Foster and Plowden (1996: 74) and Richards (1997: 235–42).
8. See Parris (1969: 98–100, 131–2).
9. Heclo and Wildavsky (1981: 76–128).
10. Hood et al. (1999: 50).
11. Scott (1998: 219).
12. Jenkins et al. (1988); I put 'Ibbs' in quotation marks because the report is popularly identified with Ibbs, or alternatively known in shorthand as the Next Steps Report.
13. Jenkins et al. (1988: 9). Italics added by me.
14. Hogwood et al. (2000).

15. For evidence I rely on: Oliver and Drewry (1996: 87–114), Daintith and Page (1999: 37–46), and Hogwood et al. (2000: 215–18).
16. Hood et al. (1999: 79).
17. Hood et al. (1999, 2000).
18. A key moment in the rise of the indicators was the appearance of the Citizens Charter in 1991: Her Majesty's Government (1991).
19. R. Wilson (1999).
20. Her Majesty's Government (1991).
21. Drewry (2000: 185) is the source for these figures.
22. Farnham and Horton (1996: 63–5, 112) and McHugh et al. (2001); and for an overview of industrial relations, more generally, Duncan (2001).
23. Farnham and Horton's phrase (1996: 175–6).
24. See F. W. Taylor (1985/1911: 115–19) for the core of Taylor's 'science' of management: the minute management of the tasks of subordinates.
25. R. Wilson (1999).
26. The plastic nature of the rules, especially as they affected the critical issue of the doctrine of Ministerial responsibility, is well discussed in Le May (1979: 108ff).
27. For an economical summary of this model, for its growing crisis, and for the way it views the model from a comparative perspective, see Campbell and Wilson (1995: 1–71).
28. Foster and Plowden (1996: 74). This book is indeed an extended defence of the Haldane doctrine of informal partnership in the face of the changes introduced by the Next Steps Programme.
29. See Foster and Plowden (1996: 224–5) on overload.
30. Home Office (1995).
31. Lewis (1997: 97–119).
32. Home Office (1995: 93). My italics.
33. On this Talbot (2000: 68); see also Talbot (1996).
34. The dismissed head of the Agency, Derek Lewis, went highly public with a critical, partisan account of his relations with the Home Secretary: Lewis (1997: 97–119).
35. Gains (2001) surveys these.
36. Jenkins et al. (1988: 9).
37. On these origins in incarceration and education, see Roberts (1969: 47–8, 122–4, 155–7, 155–61, 186–202).
38. For three cases, see Hughes, Mears and Winch (1997).
39. A. Smith (1997, 2000), O'Riordan and Weale (1989), Skea and Smith (1998), and Jordan (1993) are the sources for this account.
40. See A. Smith (1997: 53) for the phrase.
41. Royal Commission on Environmental Pollution (1976: 76–90).
42. A. Smith (1997: 76–89).
43. A. Smith (1997: 76–7).
44. Weale et al. (2000: 225–6).
45. Weale et al. (2000: 226).
46. Weale (2001: 358).
47. Hood et al. (1999: 140).
48. The phrase is from Hood et al. (1999: 139).
49. Cited in Hood et al. (1999: 147).
50. Gray and Wilcox (1995: 133–48) summarize the history of this transformation.
51. Hood et al. (1999: 143–4).
52. Pring (2001) documents this intensification.
53. See, for instance, the targets-dominated strategy document: Department for Education and Skills (2002).
54. For example, the (then) Secretary of State's views on the need for a daily 'literacy hour' in primary schools: Blunkett (2001).

55. Wilcox and Gray (1996: 2).
56. Laughlin and Broadbent (1997: 278–80) summarize this context.
57. I borrow this phrase from Pollitt et al. (1999: 1).
58. I rely on Normanton (1966: 20–21).
59. National Audit Office (2002).
60. For evolution and activities, see Audit Commission (2002: 2).
61. Normanton (1966: xviii).
62. Pollitt et al. (1999: 234–5).
63. This case is argued in Barzelay (1997: 236–42).
64. Pollitt et al. (1999: 72, Table 5.2).
65. Power (1997).
66. Power (1997: 15–40).
67. See Power (1997: 91–121) on the general transformation, and pp. 104–9 on the particular case of medical audit.
68. Hutter (2001: 266–72).
69. The quotations are from Department of Energy (1990: 253).
70. On the institutional aftermath of Piper Alpha, see M. Beck et al. (1998: 19).
71. Gunningham and Johnstone (1999: 369).
72. Robens (1972: 31–9).
73. Gunningham and Johnstone (1999: 344).
74. Carson (1983: 84–138); see Department of Energy (1990: 221–38) on Occidental's management of safety; M. Beck et al. (1998).
75. D. Smith (1995).
76. James (1992: 91) and James and Walters (1997: 46–7).
77. A. Smith (1997: 163–206, 2000: 108–1).
78. Hague et al. (1975) and Hood (1982: 44).
79. Klein (1990) summarized this as the 'politics of the double bed', a system I have described in passing in discussing the medical profession in Chapters 3 and 4.
80. The impact of regionalism is a key theme of Webster's monumental history of the Service: see Webster (1988: 262–70, 1996: 765–77).
81. The classic study of how rationing was 'hidden' is Aaron and Schwartz (1984: 101).
82. See Royal College of General Practitioners (1992: 1–2) on the uniqueness of this British gatekeeping arrangement.
83. See Aaron and Schwartz (1984: 101).
84. Harrison et al. (1990: 75–87) document.
85. Two key histories are Klein (1995) and Mohan (1995: 44–72, 129–53).
86. Department of Health (1989).
87. See Klein (1995: 138–40) and Cairney (2002).
88. Wood (2000).
89. Department for Health (1999) and Health Development Agency (2002: 7–8).
90. A very good flavour of the impact of hyper-politicization can be had from Butler and Kavanagh's (2002) account of the role of health policy in the General Election of 2001: 4, 23, 26, 51, 84, 92, 94, 112, 113, 119, 172, 181.
91. Berdahl (1959: 57–62).
92. Halsey and Trow (1971: 63).
93. The polytechnics had originated from colleges under local authority control, see Robinson (1968).
94. See Higher Education Funding Council for England (1995) for the early development of this.
95. Neave (1988).
96. Quality Assurance Agency (2002) has the details of the latest scheme.
97. Higher Education Funding Council For England (2002) has details.
98. There is a brief history of the evolution of the RAE rules of the game at Select Committee on Science and Technology (2002a).

99. Calculated from www.hero.ac.uk/rae/members
100. This is based on the Guardian ratings of institutional outcomes: at www.guardian.co.uk/researchratings/table (accessed 22 Aug. 2002).
101. See Berdahl (1959: 51–7) for history. The Medical Research Council was established in 1913.
102. The background and history of these developments are summarily described in Office of Science and Technology (1998).
103. Calculated from Engineering and Physical Sciences Research Council (2002: 47–9).
104. Biotechnology and Biological Sciences Research Council (2002: 5).
105. Economic and Social Research Council (2002).
106. This version of a 'captured' process is powerfully contested by Baker and May (2002) who view the processes I describe here as a Foucauldian growth of 'regulated liberty'.
107. The two reports were those of the Sykes Committee (1923), which prepared the ground for broadcasting, and the Crawford Committee (1926), which prepared the way for corporate status and the Royal Charter for the BBC: on these and the early politics, see Briggs (1961: 164–83, 327–48).
108. Briggs (1961: 348–60).
109. On the significance of this, I rely on Born and Prosser (2001: 661–2).
110. See Scannell and Cardiff (1991: 277–303) on this creation and on the unease and uncertainty about non-metropolitan identities, such as that represented by St Patrick's Day.
111. Scannell and Cardiff (1991: 181–223) are exceptionally illuminating on the strangely donnish stratification of musical tastes in the Corporation. See Briggs (1965: 123) for an obsession with voice style.
112. Most comprehensively in Humphreys (1996).
113. The complex institutional architecture before the upheaval represented by the proposals of 2002 are summarized in Gibbons (1998: 243–74).
114. See Department of Trade and Industry/Department for Culture, Media and Sport (2002) for details.
115. See Wright (1991) on the shape of community in pharmaceutical regulation; Hancher (1990: 118–9, 122–4) on narrower issues of pharmaceutical regulation; Abraham (1995: 61–4) on the particular significance of Thalidomide; and van Zwanenberg (1998) and van Zwanenberg and Millstone (2000) more generally on the regulatory styles in this area.
116. Human Fertilisation and Embryology Authority (2000).
117. Human Fertilisation and Embryology Authority (2001a: 16).
118. Human Fertilisation and Embryology Authority (2000).
119. Human Fertilisation and Embryology Authority (2001b).
120. For a particularly bruising encounter with the Parliamentarians, see Select Committee on Science and Technnology (2002b).
121. Notably Paulus (1974: 38).
122. BSE Inquiry (2000). In Chapter 7, I examine the BSE episode more closely as a policy fiasco; here I am primarily interested in its regulatory aftermath.
123. M. Smith (1990: 87–146, 1991); see also Flynn et al. (1999).
124. This summary history is taken from Food Standards Agency (2000a).
125. The figure is from Food Standards Agency (2000a).
126. Food Standards Agency (2000b), quoting the Act.
127. Food Standards Agency (2002a).
128. Food Standards Agency (2002b: 34–7).
129. Thus, the two classic studies of the regulation of political competition after 1918 concentrate, respectively, on the rules of the electoral system—Butler (1953)—and the regulation of sources of party finance, Pinto-Duschinsky (1981).
130. This account is from Home Office (2000a).
131. O'Leary (1962: 229).
132. The three chairmen to date have been: Lord Nolan, Lord Neill, and, presently, Sir Nigel Wicks.

133. Committee on Standards in Public Life (1995) is the First Report; Committee on Standards in Public Life (2000*a*) reviews its fate.
134. Committee on Standards in Public Life (2000*b*, 2001).
135. Committee on Standards in Public Life (1996, 1997*a,b*).
136. Committee on Standards in Public Life (1998).
137. The relies on Electoral Commission (2001: app.).
138. Electoral Commission (2001: 3–4).
139. Tempest (2002).
140. Hinsliff (2002).
141. Committee on Standards in Public Life (2002).
142. The accusation is sceptically analysed against appointments data in Richards (1997: 72–84); but he assembles convincing evidence of mandarins' perceptions that she had a unique appointment style: pp. 110–32. This book is the most subtle examination of the 'Thatcher effect' in this sphere.
143. The details and issues are examined in Select Committee on Public Administration (2002); and, for the modernizing rhetoric, see Cabinet Office (1999: throughout).
144. The authoritative account, based on questioning of witnesses, is Select Committee on Public Administration (2002).
145. Committee on Standards in Public Life (2002).
146. A case for this kind of codification is made in Select Committee on Public Adminstration (2002).

7. FROM STAGNATION TO FIASCO: THE AGE OF THE REGULATORY STATE

1. Searle (1971: 54–106).
2. S. George (1998: 42–70).
3. Surveyed in Radice (2000).
4. Cannadine (2002: 121–35).
5. Colley (1996: 388).
6. The definitive study of the high politics of this transformation is Cowling (1971).
7. Cannadine (2002: 181).
8. As will be all too obvious, this part of my argument is heavily influenced by Cannadine (2002), and the reading prompted by his book, notably. B. Tomlinson (1982) and Fieldhouse (1984), and, indeed, the whole journal issue on 'Perspectives on imperialism and decolonisation' of which this is a part. I also draw on Kennedy (1996) and Thornton (1966: 292–347); and for the complexity of the connection between empire and popular culture, the essays in Mackenzie (1992).
9. A coincidence pointed out by Cannadine (2002: 181).
10. There is dispute about the contribution of the Falklands War to the 1983 landslide: see Sanders et al. (1987, 1990) and Clarke et al. (1990).
11. Hirst and Thompson (2000).
12. Porter (1995) and Scott (1998).
13. See Hay and Rosamond (2002) on the modes of discursive construction; and Coates and Hay (2001: 48–9) on the efforts of the Blair government to 'export' its vision of deregulated capitalism.
14. The evidence is summarized in Mackenzie (1999).
15. Quoted in Perkin (1990: 158; 158–70; for the more general history of national efficiency) see also Semmel (1959: 13–28) and Searle (1971).

16. See Coates and Hay (2001) on the New Labour version of providentialism. The flavour of Mrs Thatcher's even more spirited missionary commitment can be sampled at the website of her foundation: www.margaretthatcher.org
17. For an American polemic with some sardonic things to say about the United Kingdom, see Frank (2002: 347–53).
18. See Braithwaite and Drahos (2000: 6–10) on varieties of globalization and the links with modes of business regulation.
19. This history is examined in Burn (1999).
20. This notion of a state driven by the imperatives of the search for competitiveness is most succinctly expressed in the idea of the 'competition state' developed by Cerny (1990).
21. Marquand (1988: 103–7).
22. Braithwaite and Drahos (2000: 48).
23. Braithwaite and Drahos (2000: 539).
24. It also corresponds to the argument of Furger (1997).
25. Braithwaite and Drahos (2000: 437).
26. Watson (2002) reviews the latest clutch of comparative studies.
27. Jayasuriya (2001: 113).
28. The history and details are summarized in Bank of England (2002): 'Framework for Monetary Policy'.
29. Bank of England (2002): 'Monetary Policy Committee'.
30. McBarnet and Whelan (1991, 1999) are two classic accounts.
31. See Wiener (1999: 1–19) on the debates about these problems.
32. Picciotto (1989, 1992).
33. The Secretary of State's announcement in HC Debates, 25 July 2002.
34. S. George (1998: 42–70).
35. Burch and Holliday (1996: 87–90) and Bulmer and Burch (1998, 2000) document.
36. See Dyson (2000a,b, 2002) on its ambiguities and possibilities.
37. Marks et al. (1996).
38. This particular version comes from Hix and Goetz (2000: 4).
39. Bulmer and Burch (1998, 2000).
40. The most systematic explorations of the connection and its consequences are Prosser's work (1997: 26–30, 2000).
41. A central theme of Egan (2001: 135–65).
42. Majone (1996, 1999).
43. Therborn (1995: 4).
44. Heclo and Wildavsky (1981: 76–128) and Heclo (1977: 84–112).
45. Caporaso (1996: 45). 'Heterarchy' I take from Everson (1998: 211–12).
46. This relies on the accounts in Cram (1994), Peters (1994), Richardson (2000), and Egan (2001: 260–72).
47. See Buitendjik and van Schendelen (1995), Christiansen and Kirchner (2000), and Egan (2001: 166–209) for case studies of the complexities of standards negotiations.
48. The rise of the global legal services firm, especially in financial markets, has been sketchily documented. One of the most entertaining sources for tracking their roles is the trade press, especially the *International Financial Law Review*. For a sketch of the present leaders and the scope of their operations, see Maiden (2001). The websites of the leading firms also open a window on their world: see, for instance, www.linklaters-alliance.com and www.cliffordchance.com
49. Egan (2001: 236–59).
50. See Graham (2000: 136–49) for a discussion of this.
51. Weale et al. (2000: 182).
52. Knill (2001: 175–97).
53. D. Vogel (1986: 195).
54. Wilks and Bartle (2002: 164); see also Wilks (1999: 305–22).

55. The phrase is from Wilks (1999: 300); see also Wilks and McGowan (1996).
56. Wilks and McGowan (1996: 238).
57. Wilks and Bartle (2002).
58. Wilks (1999: 322).
59. Hunt (1997: 114).
60. See Slot and Skudder (2001) on this.
61. See Armstrong and Bulmer (1998: 169–97) and O'Reilly and Stone Sweet (1998) on this industry.
62. For this paragraph, I rely on A. Smith (1997, 2000) and Skea and Smith (1998).
63. Verdun (2000: 140) is the source of the observation and the quotation.
64. Buiter (1999) offers a trenchant democratic critique of the ECB; and, for an entirely unconvincing official response, see Issing (1999).
65. Flynn (2000: 93).
66. Bovens and 'tHart (1996: 22–34).
67. On economic policy, see J. Tomlinson (1994: 70–97); on Europe, see Milward (1992: 345–433); for some particularly choice official stupidities, see p. 432.
68. See Dixon (1976: 52–148) for some classic cases.
69. See A. Wilson (1973) on Concorde.
70. I have this example originally from Scott (1998: 225–9); for studies, see Phillips (1959: 339–58) and Coulson (1977).
71. See Reid (1982) on the banking crisis; M. Clarke (1986: 53–89) on Lloyd's.
72. For a striking, detailed comparison between the UK and one of our industrial competitors, see Howarth (1991); the national policy background is sketched in R. Dale (1989: 94–124).
73. On which the classic study, contrasting the covert rationing of medical care by UK doctors with the more open American rationing system, is Aaron and Schwartz (1984).
74. Thompson (2000: 102–3).
75. The direct quotation is from Scott (1998: 5).
76. Dunleavy (1995).
77. Rhodes (1997, 2000a: 260).
78. Marsh and Rhodes (1992: 170–87) review the many implementation gaps revealed in their collection of case studies of the Thatcher era.
79. R. Rhodes (1997: 110).
80. BSE Inquiry (2000: i. paras 1178–9).
81. The word is from BSE Inquiry (2000: i. para 1179).
82. BSE Inquiry (2000: i. para 1189) is, while polite in its language, particularly devastating on the problems created by MAFF's 'dual role' as a promoter and regulator of the food production industries.
83. The policy history, and the way it both supported, and was supported by, an enclosed policy-making community is definitively told in M. Smith (1990).
84. Foot (1996); and more generally, E. George (1996).
85. Quoted in Bank of England Board of Banking Supervision (1995: para 13.10).
86. Bank of England Board of Banking Supervision (1995: paras 13.16–13.61).
87. Bank of England Board of Banking Supervision (1995: para 13.58), italics added by me.
88. J. Stewart (1986: 19–33) and D. Wilson and Game (1994: 55–9).
89. Butler et al. (1994).
90. See Butler et al. (1994: 70–76); and p. 303 for the systemic origins of the disaster.
91. See Heseltine (2000: 509–14) for an insider's highly partisan account.
92. National Audit Office (2000a: 17).
93. National Audit Office (2000a: 27).
94. This relies on two well informed journalistic accounts: Macintyre (2000: 398–403) and Rawnsley (2000: 54–6).
95. Scott (1998: 258–9).

96. Scott (1998).
97. An official, non-partisan version of the tangled story of the privatization process is in National Audit Office (1998: 20–33).
98. National Audit Office (1998: 45).
99. Terry (2001: 4). I also rely on Select Committee on Transport, Local Government and Regions (2002*a,b*) and Crompton and Jupe (2002).
100. On the Passport Agency, see National Audit Office (1999).
101. Described in National Audit Office (2000*b*).
102. See, for instance, the details in Margetts (1999: 125–61).
103. See Margetts (1999: xiv–xv) for examples.
104. Margetts (1999: 164–5).
105. Holliday (2001).
106. Cabinet Office (1999: part 5).
107. Bastow et al. (2000: 3).
108. See Dunleavy and Margetts (1999: 25) for this example.
109. Dunleavy and Margetts (2002).
110. Dyson (1980: 40–1); see also Prosser (1996: 474–6).
111. But the underlying reasons had to do with the crisis of constitutional understandings discussed in Chapter 6, on which see Select Committee on Public Administration (2002).
112. Midwinter and McGarvey (2001).
113. R. Rhodes (1997: 199).

REFERENCES

A Note on Citation Conventions

The rise of the web as a source of material, especially of official documents, has outpaced agreement about citation conventions. My practice is as follows. Where I have downloaded a facsimile of a published document, such as a Command Paper as a pdf, I generally give the same publication details as for a hard copy. My normal practice for official publications is to follow the same convention as for scholarly publications: to cite by page, as appropriate. Occasionally, as in the case of very recent publications of Parliamentary Select Committees, official documents that will eventually be published in hard copy form were only available on the web, without page numbering. In those cases, I use part and paragraph numbers in citation. Where web pages have been downloaded, I give the url in the conventional manner and the *last* date accessed. In a small number of cases where I downloaded a pdf version of a document published in hard copy, I give the url details where it is clear that the only practical way for the reader to consult the source is via the web. This is the case, for example, with some published consultation papers produced by agencies and departments. In citing official documents, I have also favoured ease of recognition over consistency. For example, I cite the report of the Committee on Safety and Health at Work (1972) under the name of its chairman, Lord Robens, for it is universally known as the Robens Report; but the reports of the Committee on Standards in Public Life (which to date has had three chairmen) are cited under committee title.

AARON, H. and SCHWARTZ, W. (1984). *The Painful Prescription: Rationing Hospital Care.* Washington: Brookings.

ABEL, R. L. (1988). *The Legal Profession in England and Wales.* Oxford: Blackwell.

—— (1989). 'Comparative Sociology of Legal Professions', in R. L. Abel and P. Lewis (eds.), *Lawyers in Society. Volume 3: Comparative Theories.* Berkeley: University of California Press, pp. 80–153.

ABEL-SMITH, B. and STEVENS, R. (1967). *Lawyers and the Courts: a Sociological Study of the English Legal System 1750–1965.* London: Heineman.

ABRAHAM, J. (1995). *Science, Politics and the Pharmaceutical Industry.* London: UCL Press.

ABROMEIT, H. (1988). 'British Privatization Policy'. *Parliamentary Affairs*, 31/1: 68–85.

ACCOUNTANCY FOUNDATION (2002). *Independent Regulation of the Accountancy Profession*, www.accountancyfoundation.com (accessed 10 Jun. 2002).

ACCOUNTING STANDARDS BOARD (2001). 'About the ASB', www.asb.org.uk (accessed 28 Jan. 2001).

ADAM, B., BECK U., and VAN LOON, J. (eds.) (2000). *Risk Society and Beyond: Critical Issues for Social Theory.* London: Sage.

ALDERMAN, G. (1973). *The Railway Interest.* Leicester: Leicester University Press.

ALDERS, M. and WILTHAGEN, T. (1997). 'Moving Beyond Command-and-Control: Reflexivity in the Regulation of Occupational Safety and Health and the Environment'. *Law and Policy*, 19/4: 415–43.

ALLISON, L. and MONNINGTON, T. (2002). 'Sport, Prestige and International Relations'. *Government and Opposition*, 37/1: 106–34.

ALMOND, G. and VERBA, S. (1965). *The Civic Culture: Political Attitudes and Democracy in Five Nations*. Boston: Little Brown.

ARMSTRONG, K. and BULMER, S. (1998). *The Governance of the Single European Market*. Manchester: Manchester University Press.

ARMSTRONG, P. (1987). 'The Rise of Accounting Controls in British Capitalist Enterprises'. *Accounting, Organizations and Society*, 12/5: 415–36.

ARTHURS, H. W. (1985). *'Without the Law': Administrative Justice and Legal Pluralism in Nineteenth-Century England*. Toronto: University of Toronto Press.

ARTS COUNCIL (2001). *Breaking New Ground: a Review of the Year*, www.artscouncil.org.uk (accessed 11 Jul. 2002).

—— (2002). 'Championing the Arts', www.artscouncil.org.uk (accessed 7 Feb. 2002).

ASHBY, E. and ANDERSON, M. (1981). *The Politics of Clean Air*. Oxford: Clarendon Press.

ASSOCIATION OF MASTERS OF HARRIERS AND BEAGLES (2000). *The Hunting of the Hare with Hounds*, www.huntinginquiry.gov.uk/evidence (accessed 21 Aug. 2002).

ATIYAH, P. S. (1979). *The Rise and Fall of Freedom of Contract*. Oxford: Clarendon Press.

AUDIT COMMISSION (2002). *Annual Report 2001*. London: Audit Commission.

AYRES, I. and BRAITHWAITE, J. (1992). *Responsive Regulation: Transcending the Deregulation Debate*. Oxford: Oxford University Press.

BAGEHOT, W. (1873/1910). *Lombard Street: a Description of the Money Market*, new edition. London: Smith Elder.

BAGGOTT, R. (1989). 'Regulatory Reform in Britain: the Changing Face of Self-Regulation'. *Public Administration*, 67/4: 435–54.

BAKER, G. and MAY, T. (2002). 'Auditing as the Eternal Present: Organisational Transformation in British Higher Education'. *European Political Science*, 1/3: 12–22.

BALDWIN, R. and CAVE, M. (1999). *Understanding Regulation: Theory, Strategy and Practice*. Oxford: Oxford University Press.

BALTIC EXCHANGE (2002). *The Baltic Exchange: the World's Premier Maritime Market*, www.balticexchange.com (accessed 18 Aug. 2002).

BANK OF ENGLAND (2002). 'Monetary Policy', www.bankofengland.co.uk (accessed 27 Mar. 2002).

BANNISTER, N. (2000). 'Railtrack Raises Dividend: Anger as Company Rewards Shareholders Amid Passenger Chaos'. *Guardian*, 14/11/00.

BAR COUNCIL (2001). 'The Bar Council', www.barcouncil.org.uk (accessed 31 Jan. 2001).

BARTRIP, P. W. J. (1980). 'The State and the Steam-Boiler in Britain'. *International Review of Social History*, XXV/1: 77–105.

—— and BURMAN, S. B. (1983). *The Wounded Soldiers of Industry: Industrial Compensation Policy 1833–1897*. Oxford: Clarendon Press.

—— and FENN, P. T. (1980). 'The Administration of Safety: the Enforcement Policy of the Early Factory Inspectorate, 1844–1864'. *Public Administration*, 58/1: 87–102.

—— (1983). 'The Evolution of Regulatory Style in the Nineteenth Century British Factory Inspectorate'. *Journal of Law and Society*, 10/2: 201–22.

BARZELAY, M. (1997). 'Central Audit Institutions and Performance Auditing: a Comparative Analysis of Organizational Strategies in the OECD'. *Governance*, 10/3: 235–60.

BASTOW, S., DUNLEAVY, P., MARGETTS, H., and TINKLER, J. (2000). 'The Advent of a "Digital State" and Government–Business Relations', mimeo. Paper to the Political Studies Association Annual Conference, London School of Economics and Political Science, 10–13 April. Downloadable at www.governmentontheweb.org

BECK, M., FOSTER, J., RYGGVIK, H., and WOOLFSON, C. (1998). *Piper Alpha Ten Years After*, 2nd edn. Glasgow: University of Glasgow Centre for Regulatory Studies.

BECK, U. (1992). *Risk Society: Towards a New Modernity*. Trans. M. Ritter. London: Sage.

—— (2000). 'Risk Society Revisited: Theory, Politics and Research Programmes', in B. Adam, U. Beck, and J. Van Loon (eds.), *The Risk Society and Beyond: Critical Issues in Social Theory*. London: Sage, pp. 211–29.

BEER, S. (1982). *Britain Against Itself*. London: Faber.

BERDAHL, R. (1959). *British Universities and the State*. Cambridge: Cambridge University Press.

BERLANT, J. (1975). *Profession and Monopoly: a Study of Medicine in the United States and Great Britain*. Berkeley: University of California Press.

BERLE, A. and MEANS, G. (1932/1991). *The Modern Corporation and Private Property*. New Brunswick: Transaction Publishers.

BIOTECHNOLOGY AND BIOLOGICAL SCIENCES RESEARCH COUNCIL (2002). *Annual Report and Accounts*, www.bbsrc.ac.uk (accessed 22 Aug. 2002).

BIRLEY, D. (1995a). *Land of Sport and Glory: Sport and British Society 1887–1910*. Manchester: Manchester University Press.

—— (1995b). *Playing the Game: Sport and British Society 1910–45*. Manchester: Manchester University Press.

—— (1999). *A Social History of English Cricket*. London: Aurum.

BLACK, J. (1996). 'Constitutionalising Self-Regulation'. *Modern Law Review*, 59/1: 24–55.

BLUNDEN, G. (1975). 'The Supervision of the UK Banking System'. *Bank of England Quarterly Bulletin*, 15/2: 188–94.

BLUNKETT, D. (2001). 'The Challenge of Improving Schools: Lessons for Public Sector Reform'. Speech to IPPR seminar, 1 May, www.dfee.gov.uk/dfee_speeches (accessed 18 Aug. 2001).

BOARD OF BANKING SUPERVISION (1995). *Report of the Board of Banking Supervision Inquiry into the Circumstances of the Collapse of Barings 18 July 1995: 'Conclusions'*, www.numa.com/ref/barings (accessed 27 Apr. 2001).

BORN, A. and GOLDSCHMIDT, L. (1997). 'Legal Regulation and Communicative Couplings'. *Law and Policy*, 19/1: 23–49.

BORN, G. and PROSSER, T. (2001). 'Culture and Consumerism: Citizenship, Public Service Broadcasting and the BBC's Fair Trading Obligations'. *Modern Law Review*, 64/5: 657–87.

BOSWELL, J. and PETERS, J. (1997). *Capitalism in Contention: Business Leaders and Political Economy in Modern Britain*. Cambridge: Cambridge University Press.

BOTCHWAY, F. (2001). 'Contemporary Energy Regime in Europe'. *European Law Review*, 26/1: 3–19.

BOVENS, M. and 'tHART, P. (1996). *Understanding Policy Fiascos*. New Brunswick: Transaction Publishers.

BRAITHWAITE, J. (2000). 'The New Regulatory State and the Transformation of Criminology'. *British Journal of Criminology*, 40/2: 222–38.

BRAITHWAITE, J. and DRAHOS, P. (2000). *Global Business Regulation*. Cambridge: Cambridge University Press.

BRAZIER, M., LOVECY, J., MORAN, M., and POTTON, M. (1993). 'Falling from a Tightrope: Doctors and Lawyers between the Market and the State'. *Political Studies*, XLI/2: 197–213.

BREBNER, J. (1948). 'Laissez Faire and State Intervention in Nineteenth-Century Britain'. *Journal of Economic History*, VIII/supplement: 59–73.

BRIGGS, A. (1961). *The History of Broadcasting in the United Kingdom. Volume I: The Birth of Broadcasting*. Oxford: Oxford University Press.

—— (1965). *The History of Broadcasting in the United Kingdom. Volume II: The Golden Age of Wireless*. Oxford: Oxford University Press.

BSE INQUIRY (2000). *The Inquiry into BSE and Variant CJD in the United Kingdom. Volume 1: Findings and Conclusions*, www.bseinquiry.gov.uk (accessed 24 Apr. 2001).

BUITENDJIK, G. and VAN SCHENDELEN, M. (1995). 'Brussels Advisory Committees: a Channel for Influence?' *European Law Review*, 20/1: 37–56.

BUITER, W. (1999). 'Alice in Euroland'. *Journal of Common Market Studies*, 37/1: 181–210.

BULMER, S. and BURCH, M. (1998). 'Organising for Europe—Whitehall, the British State and the European Union'. *Public Administration*, 76/4: 601–28.

—— (2000). 'The Europeanisation of British Central Government', in R. Rhodes (ed.), *Transforming British Government. Volume 1: Changing Institutions*. Basingstoke: Macmillan, pp. 25–62.

BULPITT, J. (1983). *Territory and Power in the United Kingdom: an Interpretation*. Manchester: Manchester University Press.

BURCH, M. and HOLLIDAY, I. (1996). *The British Cabinet System*. London: Prentice-Hall.

BURN, G. (1999). 'The State, the City and the Euromarkets'. *Review of International Political Economy*, 6/2: 225–61.

BUTLER, D. (1953). *The Electoral System in Britain 1918–1951*. Oxford: Oxford University Press.

——, ADONIS, A., and TRAVERS, T. (1994). *Failure in British Government: the Politics of the Poll Tax*. Oxford: Oxford University Press.

—— and KAVANAGH, D. (2002). *The British General Election of 2001*. Basingstoke: Palgrave.

CABINET OFFICE (1999). *Modernising Government*. Cm4310, www.archive.official-documents.co.uk (accessed 18/03/02).

—— (2000). *Better Regulation Task Force: Principles of Good Regulation* www.cabinetoffice.gov.uk.regulation.TaskForce/2000 (accessed 31/01/01).

CADBURY, A. (1992a). *Report of the Committee on the Financial Aspects of Corporate Governance*. London: Gee.

—— (1992b). *The Code of Best Practice, Report of the Committee on the Financial Aspects of Corporate Governance*. London: Gee.

CAIRNEY, P. (2002). 'New Public Management and the Thatcher Healthcare Legacy: Enough of the Theory, What About the Implementation?' *British Journal of Politics and International Relations*, 4/3: 375–98.

CAMPBELL, C. and WILSON, G. (1995). *The End of Whitehall: a Comparative Perspective*. Oxford: Blackwell.

CANNADINE, D. (2002). *Ornamentalism: How the British Saw their Empire*. London: Penguin.

CAPORASO, J. (1996). 'The European Union and Forms of State: Westphalian, Regulatory or Post-Modern?' *Journal of Common Market Studies*, 34/1: 29–52.

CARR-SAUNDERS, A. M. and WILSON, P. A. (1933). *The Professions*. Oxford: Oxford University Press.

CARSON, W. G. (1970*a*). 'Some Sociological Aspects of Strict Liability and the Enforcement of Factory Legislation'. *Modern Law Review*, 33/4: 396–412.

—— (1970*b*). 'White-Collar Crime and the Enforcement of Factory Legislation'. *British Journal of Criminology*, 10/4: 383–98.

—— (1974). 'Symbolic and Instrumental Dimensions of Early Factory Legislation: a Case Study in the Social Origins of Criminal Law', in R. Hood (ed.), *Crime, Criminology and Public Policy: Essays in Honour of Sir Leon Radzinowicz*. London: Heinemann, pp. 107–38.

—— (1979). 'The Conventionalization of Early Factory Crime'. *International Journal for the Sociology of Law*, 7/1: 37–60.

—— (1980). 'The Institutionalization of Ambiguity: Early British Factory Acts', in G. Geis and E. Stotland (eds.), *White-Collar Crime: Theory and Research*. London: Sage, pp. 142–73.

—— (1982). *The Other Price of Britain's Oil: Safety and Control in the North Sea*. Oxford: Martin Robertson.

CATHOLIC BISHOPS' CONFERENCE (2001). *A Programme for Action: Final Report of the Independent Review on Child Protection in the Catholic Church in England and Wales*. London: Catholic Bishops' Conference of England and Wales.

CERNY, P. (1990). *The Changing Architecture of Politics: Structure, Agency and the Future of the State*. London: Sage.

CHAPMAN, P. and TEMPLE, P. (1998). 'Overview: the Performance of the UK Labour Market', in T. Buxton, P. Chapman, and P. Temple (eds.), *Britain's Economic Performance*, 2nd edition. London: Routledge, pp. 299–339.

CHEFFINS, B. (1997). *Company Law: Theory, Structure and Operation*. Oxford: Clarendon Press.

CHRISTIANSEN, T. (1997). 'Tensions of European Governance: Politicized Bureaucracy and Multiple Accountability in the European Commission'. *Journal of European Public Policy*, 4/1: 73–90.

—— and KIRCHNER, E. (2000). 'Introduction', in T. Christiansen and E. Kirchner (eds.), *Europe in Change: Committee Governance in the European Union*. Manchester: Manchester University Press, pp. 1–22.

CLAPHAM, J. (1970). *The Bank of England, a History. Volume II: 1797–1914*. Cambridge: Cambridge University Press.

CLARKE, H., MISHLER, W., and WHITELEY, P. (1990). 'Recapturing the Falklands: Models of Conservative Popularity, 1979–83'. *British Journal of Political Science*, 20/1: 83–90.

CLARKE, M. (1981). *Fallen Idols: Elites and the Search for the Acceptable Face of Capitalism*. London: Junction Books.

—— (1986). *Regulating the City*. Milton Keynes: Open University Press.

—— (1990). *Business Crime: its Nature and Control*. Cambridge: Polity.

—— (2000). *Regulation: the Social Control of Business between Law and Politics*. Basingstoke: Macmillan.

CLAY, H. (1957). *Lord Norman*. London: Macmillan.

COATES, D. (2000). *Models of Capitalism: Growth and Stagnation in the Modern Era*. Cambridge: Polity.

COATES, D. and HAY, C. (2001). 'The Internal and External Face of New Labour's Political Economy'. *Government and Opposition*, 36/4: 447–71.

COEN, D. and THATCHER, MARK (2000). 'Introduction: the Reform of Utilities Regulation in the EU'. *Current Politics and Economics in Europe*, 9/4: 377–85.

COGHLAN, J. and WEBB, I. (1990). *Sport and British Politics Since 1960*. Basingstoke: Falmer Press.

COLEMAN, W. D. (1996). *Financial Services Globalization and Domestic Policy Change: a Comparison of North America and the European Union*. London: Macmillan.

COLLEY, L. (1996). *Britons: Forging the Nation 1707–1837*. London: Vintage.

COLLINS, H. (1999). *Regulating Contracts*. Oxford: Oxford University Press.

COMMITTEE ON FINANCE AND INDUSTRY (1931a). *Report*, Cmnd 3897. London: HMSO, 1969 reprint.

—— (1931b). *Minutes of Evidence Taken Before the Committee on Finance and Industry. Volume 1*. London: His Majesty's Stationery Office.

—— (1931c). *Minutes of Evidence Taken Before the Committee on Finance and Industry. Volume 2*. London: His Majesty's Stationery Office.

COMMITTEE ON THE CIVIL SERVICE (1968). *Volume 1: Report of the Committee 1966–68*. Cmnd. 3638.

COMMITTEE ON STANDARDS IN PUBLIC LIFE (1995). *Standards in Public Life. Volume 1: Report*. Cm 2850-1.

—— (1996). *Local Public Spending Bodies. Volume 1: Report*. Cm 3270-1.

—— (1997a). *Standards of Conduct in Local Government. Volume 1: Report*. Cm 3702-1.

—— (1997b). *Review of the Standards of Conduct in Executive NDPBs, NHS Trusts and Local Public Spending Bodies*. Cm 3270-1.

—— (1998). *The Funding of Political Parties in the United Kingdom. Volume 1: Report*. Cm 4057-1.

—— (2000a). *Reinforcing Standards: Review of the First Report of the Committee on Standards in Public Life. Volume 1: Report*. Cm 4557.

—— (2000b). *Standards of Conduct in the House of Lords. Volume 1: Report*. Cm 4903-1.

—— (2001). 'Sir Nigel Wicks Responds to Speaker and Announces Review of Parliamentary Self-Regulation'. Press notice, 13 December, www.public-standards. gov.uk (accessed 18 Mar. 2002).

—— (2002). 'Defining the Boundaries Within the Executive'. Press notice, 4 March 2002, www.public-standards.gov.uk (accessed 18 Mar. 2002).

COMMITTEE ON THE WORKING OF THE MONETARY SYSTEM (1959). *Report*. Cmnd. 827.

—— (1960). *Committee on the Working of the Monetary System: Principal Memoranda of Evidence*. Volume 1. London: HMSO.

COMMITTEE TO REVIEW THE FUNCTIONING OF FINANCIAL INSTITUTIONS (1980a). *Report*. Cmnd. 7937.

—— (1980b). *Appendices*. Cmnd. 7937.

CONSERVATIVE PARTY (1979). 'The Conservative Manifesto', in Craig, F. (1990) *British General Election Manifestos*, 3rd edn. Aldershot: Dartmouth, pp. 267–83.

COOPER, J. (2000). 'A New approach to Regulation? The Utilities Bill and the New Regulatory Duties'. *Utilities Law Review*, 11/1: 23–8.

CORPORATE GOVERNANCE (1996). 'Case Study: the Case of British Gas'. *Corporate Governance*, 4/1: 21–3.

CORZINE, R. (1998). 'Utilities Green Paper: Cautious Approach but Consumers go to the Top of the Agenda'. *Financial Times*, 26 March.

COULSON, A. (1977). 'Agricultural Policies in Mainland Tanzania'. *Review of African Political Economy*, 10/September–December: 74–100.

COURPASSON, D. (2000). 'Managerial Strategies of Domination: Power in Soft Bureaucracies'. *Organization Studies*, 21/1: 141–61.

COWLING, M. (1971). *The Impact of Labour 1920–1924: the Beginning of Modern British Politics*. Cambridge: Cambridge University Press.

CRAIG, P. (1991). 'Constitutions, Property and Regulation'. *Public Law*, 538–54.

CRAM, L. (1994). 'The European Commission as a Multi-Organization: Social Policy and IT Policy in the EU'. *Journal of European Public Policy*, 1/2: 195–217.

CROMPTON, G. and JUPE, R. (2002). 'Delivering Better Transport? An Evaluation of the Ten-Year Plan for the Railway Industry'. *Public Money and Management*, 22/3: 4–8.

CROMWELL, V. (1966). 'Interpretatios of Nineteenth Century Administration'. *Victorian Studies*, 9/1: 245–55.

CUSHMAN, R. (1941). *The Independent Regulatory Commissions*. New York: Oxford University Press.

DAINTITH, T. and PAGE, A. (1999). *The Executive in the Constitution: Structure, Autonomy, and Internal Control*. Oxford: Oxford University Press.

DAHL, R. (1956/1963). *A Preface to Democratic Theory*. Chicago: Phoenix Books.

DALE, H. E. (1941). *The Higher Civil Service in Britain*. Oxford: Oxford University Press.

DALE, R. (1989). *The State and Education Policy*. Milton Keynes: Open University Press.

DAVIES, H. (2000). 'A Radical New Approach to Regulation'. Proceedings of Financial Services Authority Conference, 11 December, www.fsa.gov.uk/pubs/speeches (accessed 28 Jan. 2001).

DAVIES, P. (1997). *Gower's Principles of Modern Company Law*, 6th edn. London: Sweet and Maxwell.

DENHAM, A. and GARNETT, M. (2001). *Keith Joseph*. Chesham: Acumen Publishing.

DEPARTMENT FOR CULTURE, MEDIA AND SPORT (2000). *A Sporting Future for All*. London: DCMS.

—— (2001*a*). *The Government's Plan for Sport*. London: DCMS.

—— (2001*b*). *Creative Industries Mapping Document 2001*, www.culture.gov.uk/creative (accessed 7 Feb. 2002).

—— (2002). 'World Class Sports: World Class Performance Programme'. www.culture. gov.uk/sport/performance (accessed 7 Feb. 2002).

DEPARTMENT FOR EDUCATION AND SKILLS (2002). *Education and Skills: Delivering Results. A Strategy for 2006*. London: Department for Education and Skills.

DEPARTMENT FOR TRANSPORT (2002*a*). *Statements on Railtrack*, www.dft/gov.uk/railtrack (accessed 18 Jun. 2002).

—— (2002*b*). *Secretary of State. Statement to House of Commons on Network Rail, 27/06/02*, www.gov.uk.ministers/speeches/darling (accessed 18 Aug. 2002).

DEPARTMENT OF ENERGY (1986). *Regulation of the Gas Industry*. Cmnd 9759.

—— (1990). *The Public Inquiry into the Piper Alpha Disaster: the Hon Lord Cullen*, two volumes. Cm 1310.

DEPARTMENT OF HEALTH (1989). *Working for Patients*. Cm 555. London.

—— (1999). *Saving Lives: Our Healthier Nation*. Cm 4386.

DEPARTMENT OF NATIONAL HERITAGE (1995). *Sport: Raising the Game*. London: Department of National Heritage.

—— (1996). *Sport: Raising the Game: the First Year Report*. London: Department of National Heritage.

DEPARTMENT OF TRADE AND INDUSTRY (1998*a*). *A Framework of Independent Regulation for the Accountancy Profession: Consultation Document*, www.dti.gov.uk/cld/framework (accessed 28 Jan. 2001).

—— (1998*b*). *A Fair Deal for Consumers: Modernising the Framework of Utility Regulation*, www.dti.gov.uk/urt (accessed 2 Sept. 2002).

—— (2000). *Modern Company Law for a Competitive Economy: a Consultative Document from the Company Law Review Steering Group, November 2000*, www.dti.gov.uk/cld/reviews (accessed 9 Feb. 2001).

—— (2001). *Modern Company Law for a Competitive Economy. Volume 1: Final Report of the Company Law Steering Group*, www.dti.gov.uk./cld/final_report (accessed 18 Aug. 2002).

—— (2002). *Modernising Company Law*. Cm 5553.

DEPARTMENT OF TRADE AND INDUSTRY/DEPARTMENT FOR CULTURE, MEDIA AND SPORT (2002). *A New future for Communications*. London: DTI/DCMS.

DIXON, N. (1976). *On the Psychology of Military Incompetence*. London: Macdonald.

DOBBIN, F. (1994). *Forging Industrial Policy: the United States, Britain and France in the Railway Age*. Cambridge: Cambridge University Press.

DOUGLAS, M. (1966). *Purity and Danger: an Analysis of Conceptions of Pollution and Taboo*. London: Routledge & Kegan Paul.

—— (1990). 'Risk as a Forensic Resource'. *Daedalus*, 119/4: 1–16.

—— (1994). *Risk and Blame: Essays in Cultural Theory*. London: Routledge.

DOW, S. (2000). 'Taking Stock: Reflections on Energy Liberalisation'. *Utilities Law Review*, 11/1: 1–2.

DREWRY, G. (2000). 'The New Public Management', in J. Jowell and D. Oliver (eds.), *The Changing Constitution*, 4th edn. Oxford: Oxford University Press, pp. 167–89.

DUNCAN, C. (2001). 'The Impact of Two Decades of Reform of British Public Sector Industrial Relations'. *Public Money and Management*, 21/1: 27–34.

DUNLEAVY, P. (1995). 'Policy Disasters: Explaining the UK's Record'. *Public Policy and Administration*, 10/2: 52–70.

—— and MARGETTS, H. (1999). *Government on the Web: a Report for the National Audit Office*. HC 87, 1999–00.

—— (2002). *Government on the Web II: a Report for the National Audit Office*. HC 764, 2001–2.

DURKHEIM, E. (1933/1964). *The Division of Labor in Society*, trans. G. Simpson. New York: Free Press.

DUXBURY, N. (1995). *Patterns of American Jurisprudence*. Oxford: Clarendon Press.

DYSON, K. (1980). *The State Tradition in Western Europe*. Oxford: Martin Robertson.

—— (1992). 'Theories of Regulatory Change and the Case of Germany: a Model of Regulatory Change', in K. Dyson (ed.), *The Politics of German Regulation*. Aldershot: Dartmouth, pp. 1–28.

—— (2000*a*). 'EMU as Europeanization: Convergence, Diversity, and Contingency'. *Journal of Common Market Studies*, 38/4: 645–66.

—— (2000*b*). 'Europeanization, Whitehall Culture and the Treasury as Institutional Veto Player: a Constructivist Approach to Economic and Monetary Union'. *Public Administration*, 78/4: 897–914.

—— (2002). 'EMU as Integration, Europeanization, and Convergence', in K. Dyson (ed.), *European States and the Euro: Europeanization, Variation and Convergence*. Oxford: Oxford University Press, pp. 1–27.

ECONOMIC AND SOCIAL RESEARCH COUNCIL (2002). *Annual Report and Accounts 2001–2*, www.esrc.ac.uk/annualreport (accessed 22 Sept. 2002).

EDWARDS, J. R. (1989). *A History of Financial Accounting*. London: Routledge.

EGAN, M. (2001). *Constructing a European Market: Standards, Regulation and Governance*. Oxford: Oxford University Press.

ELECTORAL COMMISSION (2001). *Corporate Plan*, www.electoralcommission.org.uk/corplan (accessed 26 Mar. 2002).

ELTON, G. (1969). *The Tudor Revolution in Government: Administrative Changes in the Reign of Henry VIII*. Cambridge: Cambridge University Press.

ENGINEERING AND PHYSICAL SCIENCES RESEARCH COUNCIL (2002). *Annual Report and Accounts 2001–2*, www.epsrc.ac.uk (accessed 22 Sept. 2002).

ERICSON, R. and HAGGERTY, K. (1997). *Policing the Risk Society*. Oxford: Clarendon Press.

ERNST, J. (1994). *Whose Utility? The Social Impact of Public Utility Privatization and Regulation in Britain*. Buckingham: Open University Press.

ESPING-ANDERSEN, G. (1990). *The Three Worlds of Welfare Capitalism*. Cambridge: Polity.

EVERSON, M. (1998). 'Administering Europe'. *Journal of Common Market Studies*, 36/2: 195–216.

FARNHAM, D. and HORTON, S. (eds.) (1996). *Managing the New Public Services*, 2nd edn. Basingstoke: Macmillan.

FEIGENBAUM, H., HENIG, J., and HAMNETT, C. (1999). *Shrinking the State: the Political Underpinnings of Privatization*. Cambridge: Cambridge University Press.

FIELDHOUSE, D. K. (1984). 'Can Humpty-Dumpty be Put Together Again? Imperial History in the 1980s'. *Journal of Imperial and Commonwealth History*, XII/2: 9–23.

FINANCIAL REPORTING COUNCIL (2001). 'How the Council Works', www.frc.org.uk (accessed 28 Jan. 2001).

—— (2002). *Annual Review*. London: Financial Reporting Council.

FINANCIAL SERVICES AUTHORITY (2001*a*). *Introduction to the Financial Services Authority*. London: Financial Services Authority.

—— (2001*b*). 'Accountability', www.fsa.gov.uk/accountability (accessed 28 Jan. 2001).

—— (2002). *Annual Report 2001/02*. London: Financial Services Authority.

FLETCHER, G. A. (1976). *The Discount Houses in London: Principles, Operations and Change*. London: Macmillan.

FLYNN, B. (2000). 'Postcards from the Edge of Integration? The Role of Committees in EU Environment Policy-Making', in T. Christiansen and E. Kirchner (eds.), *Europe in Change: Committee Governance in the European Union*. Manchester: Manchester University Press, pp. 79–97.

FLYNN, A., MARSDEN, T., and HARRISON, M. (1999). 'Regulating the Environment: the Regulation of Food in Britain in the 1990s'. *Policy and Politics*, 27/4: 435–46.

FOLEY, M. (1989). *The Silence of Constitutions*. London: Routledge.

FOOD STANDARDS AGENCY (2000*a*). 'The origins of the Food Standards Agency', www.food.gov.uk (accessed 18 Jul. 2000).

—— (2000*b*). 'Aims and Values', www.food.gov.uk (accessed 18 Jul. 2000).

—— (2002*a*). 'Update on the Work of Other Advisory Committees and the Food Standards Agency Board', www.food.gov.uk/foodadvisory committee/papers (accessed 26 Mar. 2002).

—— (2002*b*). *Annual Report and Accounts 2000–2001*, www.food.gov.uk (accessed 26 Mar. 2002).

FOOT, M. (1996). 'International Regulatory Co-operation Post-Barings', *Bank of England Quarterly Bulletin*, 36/2: 221.

FOSTER, C. D. (1992). *Privatization, Public Ownership and the Regulation of Natural Monopoly*. Oxford: Blackwell.

—— and PLOWDEN, F. (1996). *The State Under Stress: Can the Hollow State be Good Government?* Buckingham: Open University Press.

FRANK, T. (2002). *One Market Under God: Extreme Capitalism, Market Populism and the End of Economic Democracy*. London: Vintage.

FRY, G. (1969). *Statesmen in Disguise: the Changing Role of the Administrative Class of the British Home Civil Service 1853–1966*. London: Macmillan.

FURGER, F. (1997). 'Accountability and Systems of Self-Governance: the Case of the Maritime Industry'. *Law and Policy*, 19/4: 445–76.

GAINS, F. (2001). 'Modernization and Accountability: the Experience of the UK's "Next Steps" Agencies'. Paper to the PAC Conference, 3–5 September 2001. Sunningdale: Civil Service College.

GAMBLE, A. (1994*a*). *Britain in Decline: Economic Policy, Political Strategy and the British State*, 4th edn, Basingstoke: Macmillan.

—— (1994*b*). *The Free Economy and the Strong State*, 2nd edn. London: Macmillan.

—— and KELLY, G. (2001). 'Labour's New Economics', in S. Ludlam and M. Smith (eds.), *New Labour in Government*. Basingstoke: Macmillan, pp. 167–83.

GEORGE, E. (1996). 'Some Thoughts on Financial Regulation'. *Bank of England Quarterly Bulletin*, 36/2: 213–15.

GEORGE, S. (1998). *An Awkward Partner: Britain in the European Community*, 3rd edn. Oxford: Oxford University Press.

GIBBONS, T. (1998). *Regulating the Media*, 2nd edn. London: Sweet and Maxwell.

GIDDENS, A. (1990). *Towards a New Modernity*. Cambridge: Polity.

—— (1999). 'Risk and Responsibility'. *Modern Law Review*, 62/1: 1–10.

GOODIN, R. (1990). 'Property Rights and Preservationist Duties'. *Inquiry*, 33: 401–32.

GOURVISH, T. (1980). *Railways and the British Economy 1830–1914*. London: Macmillan.

GOWER, L. C. B. (1984). *Review of Investor Protection, Report*. Cmnd 9125.

GRABOSKY, P. and BRAITHWAITE, J. (eds.) (1993). *Business Regulation and Australia's Future*. Canberra: Australian Institute of Criminology.

GRAHAM, C. (1994). 'Self-regulation', in G. Richardson, and H. Genn (eds.), *Administrative Law and Government Action: the Courts and Alternative Mechanisms of Review*, Oxford: Clarendon Press, pp. 189–209.

—— (1998*a*). 'Independent Regulation and Political Change'. *Utilities Law Review*, 9/1: 1–2.

—— (1998*b*). 'A Fairer Deal for Consumers: the Government's Green Paper on Utility Regulation'. *Utilities Law Review*, 9/4: 149–56.

—— (1999). 'Taking Politics Out of Regulation and Competition'. *Utilities Law Review*, 10/3: 87–8.

—— (2000). *Regulating Public Utilities: a Constitutional Approach*. Oxford: Hart.

—— and VASS P. (2000). 'Ownership and the Water Industry'. *Utilities Law Review*, 11/5: 148–61.

GRAY, J. and WILCOX, B. (1995). '*Good School, Bad School*': *Evaluating Performance and Encouraging Improvement*. Buckingham: Open University Press.

GREENBURY, R. (1995). *Directors' Remuneration: Report of a Study Group Chaired by Sir Richard Greenbury*. London: Gee.

GRIFFITHS, B. (1973). 'The Development of Restrictive Practices in the U.K. Monetary System'. *The Manchester School*, 41/1: 3–18.

GUNNINGHAM, N. and REES, J. (1997). 'Industry Self-Regulation: an Institutional Perspective'. *Law and Policy*, 19/4: 363–414.

——, GRABOSKY, P., and SINCLAIR, D. (1998). *Smart Regulation: Designing Environmental Policy*. Oxford: Clarendon Press.

——, and JOHNSTONE, R. (1999). *Regulating Workplace Safety: Systems and Sanctions*. Oxford: Oxford University Press.

HAAS, J. M. (1970). 'The Royal Dockyards: the Earliest Visitations and Reform 1749–1778'. *The Historical Journal*, xiii/2: 191–215.

HADDEN, T. (1977). *Company Law and Capitalism*. London: Weidenfeld and Nicolson.

HAGUE, D., MACKENZIE, W. J. M., and BARKER, A. (eds.) (1975). *Public Policy and Private Interests: the Institutions of Compromise*. London: Macmillan.

HALL, C., SCOTT, C., and HOOD, C. (2000). *Telecommunications Regulation: Culture, Chaos and Interdependence Inside the Regulatory Process*. London: Routledge.

HALSEY, A. H. and TROW, M. (1971). *The British Academics*. London: Faber.

HAMPEL, R. (1998). *Final Report, Committee on Corporate Governance*. London: Gee.

HANCHER, L. (1990). *Regulating for Competition: Government, Law, and the Pharmaceutical Industry in the United Kingdom and France*. Oxford: Clarendon Press.

HANLON, G. (1997). 'A Profession in Transition? Lawyers, the Market and Significant Others'. *Modern Law Review*, 60/6: 798–822.

HANSARD SOCIETY (1996). *The Report of the Commission on the Regulation of Privatised Utilities*. London: Hansard Society/European Policy Forum.

HARRISON, S., HUNTER, D., and POLLITT, C. (1990). *The Dynamics of British Health Policy*. London: Routledge.

HAWKINS, K. (1984). *Environment and Enforcement: Regulation and the Social Definition of Pollution*. Oxford: Clarendon Press.

HAY, C. (1999). *The Political Economy of New Labour: Labouring Under False Pretences*. Manchester: Manchester University Press.

—— and ROSAMOND, B. (2002). 'Globalization, European Integration and the Discursive Construction of Economic Imperatives'. *Journal of European Public Policy*, 9/2: 147–67.

HEALTH DEVELOPMENT AGENCY (2002). *Annual Report 2001*. London: Health Development Agency.

HECLO, H. (1977). *A Government of Strangers: Executive Politics in Washington*. Washington: Brookings Institution.

—— and WILDAVSKY, H. (1981). *The Private Government of Public Money: Community and Policy Inside British Politics*, 2nd edn. London: Macmillan.

HEIN, L. (1978). *The British Companies Acts and the Practice of Accounting*. New York: Arno Press.

HER MAJESTY'S GOVERNMENT (1990). *The Citizen's Charter*. Cm 1599.

HESELTINE, M. (2000). *Life in the Jungle: My Autobiography*. London: Hodder and Stoughton.

HEWITT, P. (2002). 'Company Law: Speech to Cambridge Law Faculty, 5 July 2002', www.dti.gov.uk/ministers/speeches (accessed 19 Aug. 2002).

HIGHER EDUCATION FUNDING COUNCIL FOR ENGLAND (1995). *Report on Quality Assessment 1992–5*. Bristol: HEFCE.

—— (2002). 'HEFCE Announces Major Review of Research Assessment'. www.hefce.rae.ac.uk/news (accessed 10 Aug. 2002).

HINSLIFF, G. (2002). '£12 Million Ceiling on Election Cash Planned'. *Observer*, 18 August.

HIRSCH, F. (1977). 'The Bagehot Problem'. *The Manchester School*, 45/3: 41–57.

HIRST, P. and THOMPSON, G. (2000). 'Globalization in One Country: the Peculiarities of the British'. *Economy and Society*, 29/3: 335–56.

HIX, S. and GOETZ, K. (2000). 'Introduction: European Integration and National Political Systems'. *West European Politics*, 23/4: 1–26.

HOBSBAWM, E. (1962/1997). *The Age of Revolution*. London: Abacus.

HOEY, K. (2001). 'A Noble Art that is Ethically Cleansed from Tyson'. *Guardian*, 22 October.

HOFSTADTER, R. (1962). *The Age of Reform: from Bryan to FDR*. London: Jonathan Cape.

HOGWOOD, B., JUDGE. D., and MCVICAR, M. (2000). 'Agencies and Accountability', in R. Rhodes (ed.), *Transforming British Government*, Volume 1. Basingstoke: Macmillan, pp. 195–222.

HOLLIDAY, I. (2001). 'Steering the British State in the Information Age'. *Government and Opposition*, 36/3: 314–29.

HOLMES, M. (1985). *The First Thatcher Government 1979–83*. Brighton: Wheatsheaf.

HOLT, R. (1989). *Sport and the British: a Modern History*. Oxford: Clarendon Press.

—— and MASON, T. (2000). *Sport in Britain 1945–2000*. Oxford: Blackwell.

HOME OFFICE (1995). *Review of Prison Service Security in England and Wales and the Escape from Parkhurst Prison on Tuesday 3rd January 1995*. Cm 3020

—— (2000a). *Raising Standards and Upholding Integrity*. Cm 4759.

—— (2000b). *Final Report of the Committee of Inquiry into Hunting with Dogs in England and Wales*. Cm 4763.

HOOD, C. (1976). *The Limits of Administration*. London: Wiley.

—— (1982). 'Governmental Bodies and Government Growth', in A. Barker (ed.), *Quangos in Britain*. London: Macmillan, pp. 44–68.

—— (1991). 'A Public Management for all Seasons?' *Public Administration*, 69/1: 3–19.

—— (1994). *Explaining Economic Policy Reversals*. Buckingham: Open University Press.

—— (1998). *The Art of the State: Culture, Rhetoric and Public Management*. Oxford: Clarendon Press.

——, ROTHSTEIN, H., and BALDWIN, R. (2001). *The Government of Risk: Understanding Risk Regulation Regimes*. Oxford: Oxford University Press.

—— and JAMES, O. (2000). 'Regulation of Government: Has it Increased, Is it Increasing, Should it be Diminished?' *Public Administration*, 78/2: 283–304.

——, SCOTT, C., JAMES, O., JONES, G., and TRAVERS, T. (1999). *Regulation Inside Government: Waste-Watchers, Quality Police, and Sleaze-Busters*. Oxford: Oxford University Press.

HOPWOOD, A. G. (1987). 'The Archeology of Accounting Systems'. *Accounting, Organizations and Society*, 13/3: 207–34.

HOSKYNS, J. (2000). *Just in Time: Inside the Thatcher Revolution*. London: Aurum Press.

HOWARTH, M. (1991). *Britain's Educational Reform: a Comparison with Japan*. London: Routledge.

HOWELL, D. (1986). *A Lost Left: Three Studies in Socialism and Nationalism*. Manchester: Manchester University Press.

HUGHES, R., MEARS, R., and WINCH, C. (1997). 'An Inspector Calls? Regulation and Accountability in Three Public Services'. *Policy and Politics*, 25/3: 299–313.

HUMAN FERTILISATION AND EMBRYOLOGY AUTHORITY (2000). *Annual Report 2000*, /www.hfea .gov.uk/annrep2000 (accessed 26 Mar. 2002).

—— (2001*a*). *Code of Practice*, 5th edn, www.hfea.gov.uk/downloads (accessed 22 Oct. 2002).

—— (2001*b*). *Summary of Minutes of the One Hundred and Sixth Meeting of the Human Fertilisation and Embryology Authority*, 22 February 2001, www.hfea.gov.uk/archived_minutes (accessed 22 Oct. 2002).

HUMPHREYS, P. (1996). *Mass Media and Media Policy in Western Europe*. Manchester: Manchester University Press.

HUNT, A. (1997). 'Regulation of Telecommunications: the Developing EU Regulatory Framework and its Impact on the United Kingdom'. *European Public Law*, 3/1: 93–115.

HUTTER, B. (1997). *Compliance: Regulation and Environment*. Oxford: Clarendon Press.

—— (2001). *Regulation and Risk: Occupational Health and Safety on the Railways*. Oxford: Oxford University Press.

HUTTON, W. (1996). *The State We're In*. London: Vintage.

INGHAM, G. (1984). *Capitalism Divided? The City and Industry in British Social Development*. Basingstoke: Macmillan.

INSTITUTE OF CHARTERED ACCOUNTANTS OF ENGLAND AND WALES (2001). 'Working in the Regulated Areas', www.icaew.co.uk/institute/governance (accessed 20 Jan. 2001).

ISSING, W. (1999). 'The Eurosystem: Transparent and Accountable or "Willem in Euroland" '. *Journal of Common Market Studies*, 37/3: 503–19.

JAMES, P. (1992). 'Reforming British Health and Safety Law: a Framework for Discussion'. *Industrial Law Journal*, 21/2: 83–105.

—— and WALTERS, D. (1997). 'Non-Union Rights of Involvement: the Case of Health and Safety at Work'. *Industrial Law Journal*, 26/1: 35–50.

JAYASURIYA, K. (2001). 'Globalization and the Changing Architecture of the State: the Regulatory State and the Politics of Negative Coordination'. *Journal of European Public Policy*, 8/1: 101–23.

JENKINS, K., CAINES, K., and JACKSON, A. (1988). *Improving Management in Government: the Next Steps*. London: Her Majesty's Stationery Office.

JESSOP, R. D. (1971). 'Civility and Traditionalism in English Political Culture'. *British Journal of Political Science*, 1/1: 1–24.

JOHNSON, T. (1972). *Professions and Power*. London: Macmillan.

JONES, S. G. (1988). *Sport, Politics and the Working Class*. Manchester: Manchester University Press.

JORDAN, A. (1993). 'IPC and the Evolving Style and Structure of Environmental Regulation in the UK'. *Environmental Politics*, 2/3: 406–27.

KAVANAGH, D. (1980). 'Political Culture in Great Britain: the Decline of the Civic Culture', in G. Almond and S. Verba (eds.), *The Civic Culture Revisited*. Boston: Little Brown, pp. 124–76.

KEIR, D. (1966). *The Constitutional History of Modern Britain Since 1485*, 8th edn. London: Adam and Charles Black.

KELMAN, S. (1980). 'Occupational Safety and Health Administration', in J. Q. Wilson (ed.), *The Politics of Regulation*. New York: Basic Books, pp. 236–66.

—— (1981). *Regulating America, Regulating Sweden: a Comparative Study of Occupational Safety and Health Policy*. Cambridge, MA: MIT Press.

KENNEDY, D. (1996). 'Imperial History and Post-Colonial Theory?' *Journal of Imperial and Commonwealth History*, XXIV/3: 345–63.

KLEIDMAN, S. (1990). 'How Well the Media Report Health Risk'. *Daedalus*, 119/4: 119–32.

KLEIN, R. (1990). 'The State and the Profession: the Politics of the Double Bed'. *British Medical Journal*, 301: 700–2.

—— (1995). *The New Politics of the National Health Service*, 3rd edn. London: Longman.

KNIGHT, F. (1933). *Risk, Uncertainty and Profit*. London: London School of Economics and Political Science. (Reprints of scarce tracts in economic and political science.)

KNILL, C. (2001). *The Europeanisation of National Administrations: Patterns of Institutional Change and Persistence*. Cambridge: Cambridge University Press.

—— and LEHMKUHL, D. (2000). 'An Alternative Route of European Integration: the Community's Railways Policy'. *West European Politics*, 23/1: 65–88.

KOOIMAN, J. (1993). 'Socio-Political Governance—an Introduction', in J. Kooiman (ed.), *Modern Governance: New Government–Society Interactions*. London: Sage, pp. 1–6.

KYNASTON, D. (1994). *The City of London. Volume I: a World on its Own 1815–90*. London: Chatto & Windus.

—— (1995). *The City of London. Volume II: Golden Years 1890–1914*. London: Chatto & Windus.

—— (1999). *The City of London. Volume III: Illusions of Gold 1914–1945*. London: Chatto & Windus.

LANDIS, J. (1938). *The Administrative Process*. New Haven: Yale University Press.

LARKIN, P. (1988). *Collected Poems*, A. Thwaite (ed.). London: Faber.

LARSON, M. (1977). *The Rise of Professionalism: a Sociological Analysis*. Berkeley: University of California Press.

LAUGHLIN, R. and BROADBENT, J. (1997). 'Contracts and Competition: a Reflection on the Nature and Effects of Recent Legislation on Modes of Control in Schools'. *Cambridge Journal of Economics*, 21/2: 277–90.

LAW SOCIETY (2000). 'The Law Society: Roles', www.lawsociety.org.uk (accessed 28 Jan. 2001).

LAWSON, N. (1992). *The View from No. 11: Memoirs of a Tory Radical*. London: Bantam Press.

LEHMBRUCH, G. and SCHMITTER, P. (eds.) (1982). *Patterns of Corporatist Policy-Making*. London: Sage.

LE MAY, G. (1979). *The Victorian Constitution: Conventions, Usages, Contingencies*. London: Duckworth.

LETWIN, O. (1988). 'International Experience in the Politics of Privatization', in M. Walker (ed.), *Privatization: Tactics and Techniques*. Vancouver, BC: The Fraser Institute, pp. 49–60.

LEWIS, D. (1997). *Hidden Agendas: Politics, Law and Disorder*. London: Hamish Hamilton.

LISLE-WILLIAMS, M. (1984). 'Merchant Banking Dynasties in the English Class Structure: Ownership, Solidarity and Kinship in the City of London, 1850–90'. *British Journal of Sociology*, XXXV/3: 333–62.

LITTLECHILD, S. (1983). *Regulation of British Telecommunications' Profitability: a Report by Stephen C. Littlechild*. London: Department of Industry.

—— (1986). *Economic Regulation of Privatised Water Authorities: a Report Submitted to the Department of the Environment*. London: Her Majesty's Stationery Office.

LLOYD'S (2000). 'Lloyd's Regulatory Plan 2000', www.lloydsoflondon.co.uk (accessed 9 Feb. 2001).

—— (2002). *The Chairman's Strategy Group: Consultation Documents*, www.lloydsoflondon.co.uk (accessed 30 Sept. 2002).

LOFT, A. (1986). 'Towards a Critical Understanding of Accounting: the Case of Cost Accounting in the U.K., 1914–25'. *Accounting, Organisations and Society*, 11/2: 137–69.

LUHMANN, N. (1990). *Essays on Self-Reference*. New York: Columbia University Press.

—— (1995). *Social Systems*, trans. J. Bednarz and D. Baecker. Stanford: Stanford University Press.

MCBARNET, D. and WHELAN, C. (1991). 'The Elusive Spirit of the Law: Formalism and the Struggle for Legal Control'. *Modern Law Review*, 54/6: 848–73.

—— (1999). 'Challenging the Regulators: Strategies for Resisting Control', in C. McCrudden (ed.), *Regulation and Deregulation: Policy and Practice in the Utilities and Financial Services Industries*. Oxford: Oxford University Press, pp. 67–77.

MCCRAW, T. (1984). *Prophets of Regulation*. Cambridge, MA: Belknap Press.

MCCRUDDEN, C. (1999). 'Social Policy and Economic Regulators: Some Issues in the Reform of Utility Regulation', in C. McCrudden (ed.), *Regulation and Deregulation: Policy and Practice in the Utilities and the Financial Services Industries*. Oxford: Oxford University Press, pp. 275–91.

MACDONAGH, O. (1958). 'The Nineteenth-Century Revolution in Government: a Reappraisial'. *Historical Journal*, I/1: 152–67.

—— (1961). *A Pattern of Government Growth 1800–1860: the Passenger Acts and their Enforcement*. London: Macgibbon and Kee.

—— (1977). *Early Victorian Government 1830–1870*. London: Weidenfeld and Nicolson.

MCHARG, A. (1998). 'Government Intervention in Privatised Industries: the Potential and Limits of the Golden Share'. *Utilities Law Review*, 9/4: 198–201.

MCHUGH, M., O'Brien, G., and Ramondt, J. (2001). 'Finding an Alternative to Bureaucratic Models of Organization in the Public Sector'. *Public Money and Management*, 21/1: 35–42.

MACINTYRE, D. (2000). *Mandelson and the Making of New Labour*. London: Harper Collins.

MACKENZIE, J. (ed.) (1992). *Imperialism and Popular Culture*. Manchester: Manchester University Press.

—— (1999). 'The Popular Culture of Empire in Britain', in J. Brown and W. R. Louis (eds.), *The Oxford History of the British Empire. Volume IV: the Twentieth Century*. Oxford: Oxford University Press, pp. 212–31.

MCKIBBIN, R. (1974). *The Evolution of the Labour Party 1910–1924*. Oxford: Oxford University Press.

MCKINNON, J. (1993). 'Conference on Regulatory Reform: Friction Between Regulator and Regulatee'. *Utilities Law Review*, 4/3: 119–22.

MACHLUP, F. (1952). *The Political Economy of Monopoly: Business, Labor and Government*. Baltimore: Johns Hopkins Press.

MAIDEN, B. (2001). 'Linklaters Top as Equities Market Hits the Brakes'. *International Financial Law Review*, XX/9: 15–21.

MAJONE, G. (1991). 'Cross-National Sources of Regulatory Policymaking in Europe and the United States'. *Journal of Public Policy*, 11/1: 79–109.

MAJONE, G. (1996). *Regulating Europe*. London: Routledge.

—— (1999). 'The Regulatory State and its Legitimacy Problems'. *West European Politics*, 22/1: 1–24.

MALONEY, W. (2001). 'Regulation in an Episodic Policy-Making Environment: the Water Industry in England and Wales'. *Public Administration*, 79/3: 625–42.

MARCUS, A. (1980). 'Environmental Protection Agency', in J. Q. Wilson (ed.), *The Politics of Regulation*. New York: Basic Books, pp. 267–303.

MARGETTS, H. (1999). *Information Technology in Government: Britain and America*. London: Routledge.

MARKS, G., HOOGE, L., and BLANK, K. (1996). 'European Integration from the 1980s: State-Centric V. Multi-Level Governance'. *Journal of Common Market Studies*, 34/3: 341–78.

MARQUAND, D. (1988). *The Unprincipled Society: New Demands and Old Politics*. London: Jonathan Cape.

MARSH, D. (1992). *The New Politics of British Trade Unionism: Union Power and the Thatcher Legacy*. Basingstoke: Macmillan.

—— and RHODES, R. (eds.) (1992). *Implementing Thatcherite Policies: Audit of an Era*. Buckingham: Open University Press.

MARTIN, R. (1997). 'The British Tradition of Industrial Relations Research: the Contribution of W. E. J. (Lord) McCarthy'. *British Journal of Industrial Relations*, 36/1: 83–97.

MATTHEWS, D., ANDERSON, M., and EDWARDS, J. R. (1998). *The Priesthood of Industry: the Rise of Professional Accountants in British Management*. Oxford: Oxford University Press.

MEDICAL RESEARCH COUNCIL (2002). 'About the Medical Research Council', www.mrc.ac.uk/index (accessed 26 Mar. 2002).

MELVILLE, A. (1994). 'Power, Strategy and Games: Economic Regulation of a Privatized Utility'. *Public Administration*, 72/3: 385–408.

MERRISON, A. W. (1975). *Report of the Committee of Inquiry into the regulation of the medical profession*. Cmnd 6018.

MIDWINTER, A. and MCGARVEY, N. (2001). 'In Search of the Regulatory State: Evidence from Scotland'. *Public Administration*, 79/4: 825–49.

MIERS, D. (1996). 'Regulation and the Public Interest: Commercial Gambling and the National Lottery'. *Modern Law Review*, 59/4: 489–516.

MILLER, P. and POWER, M. (1995). 'Calculating Corporate Failure', in Y. Dezalay and D. Sugarman (eds.), *Professional Competition and Professional Power*. London: Routledge, pp. 51–76.

MILLERSON, G. (1964). *The Qualifying Associations: a Study in Professionalization*, London: Routledge and Kegan Paul.

MILWARD, A. (1992). *The European Rescue of the Nation-State*. London: Routledge.

MINISTRY OF RECONSTRUCTION (1918). *Report of the Machinery of Government Committee*. Cd 9230.

MOHAN, J. (1995). *A National Health Service?* Basingstoke: Macmillan.

MORAN, M. (2001). 'Property, Business Power and the Constitution.' *Public Administration*, 79/2: 277–96.

MORONE, J. (1990). *The Democratic Wish: Popular Participation and the Limits of American Government*. New York: Basic Books.

MORGAN, E. V. and THOMAS, W. A. (1962). *The Stock Exchange: its History and Functions.* London: Elek.

MORROW, S. (1999). *The New Business of Football: Accountability and Finance in Football.* Basingstoke: Macmillan.

MURPHY, R. (1988). *Social Closure: the Theory of Monopolization and Exclusion.* Oxford: Clarendon Press.

NATIONAL AUDIT OFFICE (1998). *The Flotation of Railtrack.* HC 25, 1998–9.

—— (1999). *The United Kingdom Passport Agency: the Passport Delays of Summer 1999.* HC 812, 1998–9.

—— (2000*a*). *The Millennium Dome: Report of the Comptroller and Auditor General.* HC 936, 1999–2000.

—— (2000*b*). *The Cancellation of the Benefits Payment Card Project: Report by the Comptroller and Auditor General.* HC 857, 1999–2000.

—— (2002). *Helping the Nation Spend Wisely: Annual Report 2001.* London: National Audit Office.

NATIONAL ECONOMIC DEVELOPMENT OFFICE (1976). *A Study of the UK Nationalised Industries: their Role in the Economy and Control in the Future.* London: Her Majesty's Stationery Office.

NATIONAL ICE SKATING ASSOCIATION (2002). *NISA Mission Statement,* www.jtngroup.co.uk/nisa (accessed 7 Feb. 2002).

NATIONAL LOTTERY COMMISSION (2002). *Annual Report and Accounts 2001/2002.* HC 977, 2001–2.

NEAVE, G. (1988). 'On the Cultivation of Quality, Efficiency, and Enterprise: an Overview of Recent Trends in Higher Education in Western Europe, 1986–88'. *European Journal of Education,* 23/1–2: 7–23.

NOBLE, C. (1986). *Liberalism at Work: the Rise and Fall of OSHA.* Philadelphia: Temple University Press.

NOLAN, B. (ed.) (2001). *Public Sector Reform: an International Perspective.* Basingstoke: Palgrave.

NONET, P. and SELZNICK, P. (2001). *Towards Responsive Law: Law and Society in Transition.* London: Transaction Publishers.

NORMANTON, E. L. (1966). *The Accountability and Audit of Government: a Comparative Study.* Mancester: Manchester University Press.

NORTON, P. (1984). *The Constitution in Flux.* Oxford: Martin Robertson.

NUGENT, N. (2001). *The European Commission.* Basingstoke: Palgrave.

OAKESHOTT, M. (1962). *Rationalism in Politics and Other Essays.* London: Methuen.

O'BRIEN, D. and EPP, J. A. (2000). 'Salaried Defenders and the Access to Justice Act 1999'. *Modern Law Review,* 63/3: 394–412.

OFFICE OF FAIR TRADING (2000). 'The Likely Competitive Effects of Amendments to the Consolidated Regulation of the Inns of Court'. OFT304, www.oft.gov.uk/research/reports/ (accessed 28 Jan. 2001).

—— (2001*a*). 'The Work and Duties of the OFT', www.oft.gov.uk/ (accessed 8 Feb. 2001).

—— (2001*b*). 'The OFT's New Approach to Consumer Codes of Practice: a Consultation Paper'. OFT 331, www.oft.gov.uk/business/codes of practice/ (accessed 13 Jun. 2002).

—— (2001*c*). *Competition in Professions.* OFT 328, www.oft.gov.uk (accessed 10 Jun. 2002).

OFFICE OF FAIR TRADING (2002*a*). 'Core Criteria for Consumer Codes of Practice: Guidance for those Drawing up Codes of Practice'. OFT 390, www.oft.gov.uk/business/codes of practice/ (accessed 13 Jun. 2002).

—— (2002*b*). *Competition in Professions: Progress Statement.* OFT 385, www.oft.gov.uk (accessed 10 Jun. 2002).

OFFICE OF GAS AND ELECTRICITY MARKETS (OFGEM) (2002*a*). 'Statement by CAA, Water Industry Commissioner for Scotland, Oftel, Ofgem, Ofwat, ORR, Ofreg NI and Postcomm on Joint Working July 2002', www.ofgem.gov.uk/docs (accessed 18 Aug. 2002).

—— (2002*b*). *Corporate Strategic Plan 2002–5,* www.ofgem.gov.uk/docs (accessed 18 Aug. 2002).

OFFICE OF SCIENCE AND TECHNOLOGY (1998). 'The DR and the Research Councils: Review of the First Five Years', www.ost.gov.uk/research (accessed 12 May 2001).

OGUS, A. (1992). 'Regulatory Law: Lessons from the Past'. *Legal Studies,* 12/1: 1–19.

—— (1995). 'Rethinking Self-Regulation'. *Oxford Journal of Legal Studies,* 15/1: 97–108.

O'LEARY, C. (1962). *The Elimination of Corrupt Practices in British Elections.* Oxford: Oxford University Press.

OLIVER, D. and DREWRY, G. (1996). *Public Service Reforms: Issues of Accountability and Public Law.* London: Pinter.

O'REILLY, D. and STONE SWEET, A. (1998). 'The Liberalization and Reregulation of Air Transport'. *Journal of European Public Policy,* 5/3: 447–66.

O'RIORDAN, T. and WEALE, A. (1989). 'Administrative Reorganisation and Policy Change: the Case of Her Majesty's Inspectorate of Pollution'. *Public Administration,* 67/3: 277–94.

OSBORNE, D. and GAEBLER, T. (1992). *Reinventing Government: How the Entreprenurial Spirit is Transforming the Public Sector.* Reading, MA: Addison Wesley.

PANEL ON TAKE-OVERS AND MERGERS (1979). *Written Evidence to the Committee to Review the Functioning of Financial Institutions, Second Stage Evidence,* Volume 1. London: HMSO, pp. 1–39.

—— (2002). *The Code,* www.thetakeoverpanel.org.uk (accessed 19 Aug. 2002).

PARKINSON, J. E. (1993). *Corporate Power and Responsibility: Issues in the Theory of Company Law.* Oxford: Clarendon Press.

PARRIS, H. (1960). 'The Nineteenth-Century Revolution in Government: a Reappraisal Reappraised'. *Historical Journal,* III/1: 17–37.

—— (1965). *Government and the Railways in Nineteenth-Century Britain.* London: Routledge & Kegan Paul.

—— (1969). *Constitutional Bureaucracy.* London: Allen and Unwin.

PARRISH, R. (2001). 'The Path to a European Union Sports Policy'. PhD thesis, Faculty of Economic and Social Studies, University of Manchester.

PAULUS, I. (1974). *The Search for Pure Food: A Sociology of Legislation in Britain.* London: Martin Robertson.

PERKIN, H. (1969). *The Origins of Modern English Society 1780–1980.* London: Routledge & Kegan Paul.

—— (1990). *The Rise of Professional Society: England Since 1880.* London: Routledge.

PETERS, B. G. (1994). 'Agenda-Setting in the European Community'. *Journal of European Public Policy,* 1/1: 9–26.

PHILLIPS, J. (1959). *Agriculture and Ecology in Africa*. London: Faber.

PHILPOT, J. (1998). 'The Performance of the UK Labour Market: is "Anglo-Saxon" Economics the Answer to Structural Unemployment?', in T. Buxton, P. Chapman, and P. Temple (eds.), *Britain's Economic Performance*, 2nd edn. London: Routledge, pp. 340–66.

PICCIOTTO, S. (1989). 'Slicing a Shadow: Business Taxation in an International Environment', in L. Hancher and M. Moran (eds.), *Capitalism, Culture and Economic Regulation*. Oxford: Oxford University Press, pp. 11–47.

—— (1992). *International Business Taxation: a Study in the Internationalization of Business Regulation*. London: Butterworths.

PIERRE, J. (ed.) (2000). *Debating Governance*. Oxford: Oxford University Press.

PINTO-DUSCHINSKY, M. (1981). *British Political Finance: 1830–1980*. Washington: American Enterprise Institute.

POLLITT, C., GIRRE, X., LONSDALE, J., MUL, R., SUMMA, H., and WAERNESS, M. (1999). *Performance or Compliance? Performance Audit and Public Management in Five Countries*. Oxford: Oxford University Press.

PORTER, T. (1995). *Trust in Numbers: the Pursuit of Objectivity in Science and Public Life*. Princeton, NJ: Princeton University Press.

POSTAL SERVICES COMMISSION (2001). *Annual Report 2000–2001*. HC 188, 2000–2001.

POWER, M. (1997). *The Audit Society: Rituals of Verification*. Oxford: Oxford University Press.

PRESNELL, L. (1956). *Country Banking in the Industrial Revolution*. Oxford: Clarendon Press.

PRESSMAN, J. and WILDAVSKY, A. (1973). *Implementation: How Great Expectations in Washington are Dashed in Oakland*. Berkeley: University of California Press.

PRING, R. (2001). 'Managing the Professions: the Case of Teachers'. *Political Quarterly*, 72/3: 278–90.

PROSSER, T. (1986). *Nationalised Industries and Public Control*. Oxford: Blackwell.

—— (1990). 'Constitutions and Political Economy: the Privatisation of Public Enterprises in Britain and France'. *Modern Law Review*, 53/3: 304–20.

—— (1996). 'Understanding the British Constitution'. *Political Studies*, XLIV/3: 473–87.

—— (1997). *Law and the Regulators*. Oxford: Clarendon Press.

—— (1999). 'Theorising Utility Regulation'. *Modern Law Review*, 62/2: 196–217.

—— (2000). 'Public Service Law: Privatization's Unexpected Offspring'. *Law and Contemporary Problems*, 63/4: 63–82.

—— (2001). 'Regulating Public Enterprises'. *Public Law*, Autumn: 505–25.

PUBLIC RELATIONS CONSULTANTS ASSOCIATION (2001). 'PRCA Professional Charter', www.martex.co.uk/taf (accessed 31 Jan. 2001).

QUALITY ASSURANCE AGENCY FOR HIGHER EDUCATION (2002). *Handbook for Institutional Audit*. Gloucester: QAA.

RADICE, H. (2000). 'Globalization and National Capitalisms: Theorizing Convergence and Differentiation'. *Review of International Political Economy*, 7/4: 719–42.

RAWNSLEY, A. (2000). *Servants of the People: the Inside Story of New Labour*. London: Hamish Hamilton.

READER, W. J. (1966). *Professional Men: the Rise of the Professional Classes in Nineteenth Century England*. London: Weidenfeld and Nicolson.

REDLICH, J. and HIRST, F. (1970). *The History of Local Government in England*, 2nd edn. London: Macmillan.

REES, J. (1997). 'Development of Communitarian Regulation in the Chemical Industry'. *Law and Policy*, 19/4: 477–528.

REICH, C. (1964). 'The New Property'. *The Yale Law Journal*, 73/5: 733–87.

REID, M. (1982). *The Secondary Banking Crisis 1973–5*. London: Macmillan.

—— (1988). *All Change in the City: the Revolution in Britain's Financial Sector.* Basingstoke: Macmillan.

RENTOUL, J. (2001). *Tony Blair: Prime Minister*. London: Little Brown.

RHODES, G. (1981). *Inspectorates in British Government: Law Enforcement and Standards of Efficiency*. London: Allen and Unwin.

RHODES, R. A. W. (1997). *Understanding Governance: Policy Networks, Governance, Reflexivity and Accountability*. Buckingham: Open University Press.

—— (ed.) (2000*a*). *Transforming British Government. Volume 1: Changing Institutions.* Basingstoke: Macmillan.

—— (ed.) (2000*b*). *Transforming British Government. Volume 2: Changing Roles and Relationships*. Basingstoke: Macmillan.

RICHARDS, D. (1997). *The Civil Service Under the Conservatives: Whitehall's Political Poodles?* Brighton: Sussex Academic Press.

RICHARDSON, J. (2000). 'Government, Interest Groups and Policy Change'. *Political Studies*, 48/5: 1006–25.

RIDLEY, N. (1991). *My Style of Government*. London: Hutchinson.

RILEY, A. (2000). 'A Unique Antitrust Regulatory Problem: Co-ordinating Concurrent Competition Powers'. *Utilities Law Review*, 11/2: 36–40.

ROBENS, A. (1972). *Safety and Health at Work: Report of the Committee, 1970–72, Chairman Lord Robens*. Cmnd 5034.

ROBERTS, D. (1969). *Victorian Origins of the British Welfare State*. Yale: Archon Books.

ROBINSON, E. (1968). *The New Polytechnics*. Harmondsworth: Penguin.

ROYAL COLLEGE OF GENERAL PRACTITIONERS (1992). *The European Study of Referrals: Report to the Concerted Action Committee of Health Services for the European Community*. London: Royal College of General Practitioners.

ROYAL COMMISSION ON ENVIRONMENTAL POLLUTION (1976). *Fifth Report: Air Pollution Control: an Integrated Approach*. London: HMSO.

ROYAL COMMISSION ON TRADE UNIONS AND EMPLOYERS' ASSOCIATIONS (1968). *Report.* Cmnd 3623.

ROYAL SOCIETY (1992). *Risk: Analysis, Perception, Management*. London: Royal Society.

RUGBY FOOTBALL LEAGUE (1999). *Minimum Standards Guidelines 1999*, www.rfl.com (accessed 7 Feb. 2002).

SALTER, B. (2001). 'Who Rules? The New Politics of Medical Regulation'. *Social Science and Medicine*, 52: 871–83.

SANDERS, D., WARD, H., MARSH, D., and FLETCHER, T. (1987). 'Government Popularity and the Falklands War: a Reassessment'. *British Journal of Political Science*, 17/3: 281–313.

——, ——, and MARSH, D. (1990). 'A reply to Clarke, Mishler and Whiteley'. *British Journal of Political Science*, 20/1: 83–90.

SAPOLSKY, H. (1990). 'The Politics of Risk'. *Daedalus*, 119/4: 83–96.

SAUTER, W. (1996). 'The Evolution of Universal Service Obligations in the Liberalisation of the European Telecommunications Sector'. *Utilities Law Review*, 7/3: 104–10.

SAYERS, R. S. (1976). *The Bank of England 1891–1944*, 2 volumes. Cambridge: Cambridge University Press.

SCANNELL, P. and CARDIFF, A. (1991). *A Social History of British Broadcasting. Volume 1: 1922–1939. Serving the Nation*. Oxford: Blackwell.

SCHLESINGER, A. (1960). *The Coming of the New Deal*. London: Heinemann.

—— (1961). *The Politics of Upheaval*. London: Heinemann.

SCHMITTER, P. and LEHMBRUCH, G. (eds.) (1979). *Trends Towards Corporatism Intermediation*. London: Sage.

SCOTT, J. (1998). *Seeing Like a State: How Certain Schemes to Improve the Human Condition Have Failed*. New Haven: Yale University Press.

SEARLE, G. R. (1971). *The Quest for National Efficiency: a Study in British Political and Social Thought, 1899–1914*. Oxford: Blackwell.

SELECT COMMITTEE ON EMPLOYMENT (1995). *The Remuneration of Directors and Chief Executives of Privatised Utilities*. HC 159, 1994–5.

SELECT COMMITTEE ON ENERGY (1986). *Regulation of the Gas Industry: First Report*. HC 15, 1985–6.

SELECT COMMITTEE ON ENVIRONMENT, TRANSPORT AND REGIONAL AFFAIRS (2000). *Recent Events on the Railways*. HC 17, 2000–01.

SELECT COMMITTEE ON NATIONALISED INDUSTRIES (1968). *Ministerial Control of the Nationalised Industries. Volume 1: Report*. HC 371-I, 1967–8.

SELECT COMMITTEE ON PUBLIC ADMINISTRATION (2002). *'These Unfortunate Events': Lessons of Recent Events at the Former DTLR*. HC303, 2001–2.

SELECT COMMITTEE ON SCIENCE AND TECHNOLOGY (2002a). *The Research Assessment Exercise*. HC 507, 2001–2.

—— (2002b). *Developments in Human Genetics and Embryology*. HC 791, 2001–2.

SELECT COMMITTEE ON TRANSPORT, LOCAL GOVERNMENT AND THE REGIONS (2002a). *Passenger Rail Franchising and the Future of Railway Infrastructure: First Report*. HC 239-1, 2001–2.

—— (2002b). *Passenger Rail Franchising and the Future of Railway Infrastructure: Minutes of Evidence*, www.parliament.uk/pa/cm200102 (accessed 20 Aug. 2002).

SELF, P. and STORING, H. (1962). *The State and the Farmer: British Agricultural Policies and Politics*. London: Allen and Unwin.

SELIGMAN, J. (1982). *The Transformation of Wall Street: a History of the Securities and Exchange Commission and Modern Corporate Finance*. Boston: Houghton Mifflin.

SEMMEL, B. (1959). *Imperialism and Social Reform: English Social-Imperial Thought 1895–1914*. London: Allen and Unwin.

SHAOUL, J. (2000). 'Water Mutualisation: the Financial Reality of the New Form of Ownership'. *Utilities Law Review*, 11/5: 135–47.

SHARPE, L. J. (1982). 'The Labour Party and the Geography of Inequality: a Puzzle', in D. Kavanagh (ed.), *The Politics of the Labour Party*. London: Allen and Unwin, pp. 135–70.

SHONFIELD, A. (1965). *Modern Capitalism: Changing Balance of Public and Private Power*. Oxford: Oxford University Press.

SINCLAIR, D. (1997). 'Self-Regulation Versus Command and Control? Beyond False Dichotomies'. *Law and Policy*, 19/4: 529–59.

SISSON, C. H. (1959). *The Spirit of British Administration*. London: Faber.

SKEA, J. and SMITH, A. (1998). 'Integrating Pollution Control', in P. Lowe and S. Ward (eds.), *British Environmental Policy and Europe*. London: Routledge, pp. 265–81.

SLOT, P. J. and SKUDDER, A. (2001). 'Common Features of Community Law Regulation in the Network-Bound Agencies'. *Common Market Law Review*, 38/1: 887–929.

SMITH, A. (1997). *Integrated Pollution Control: Change and Continuity in the UK Industrial Pollution Policy Network*. Aldershot: Ashgate.

—— (2000). 'Policy Networks and Advocacy Coalitions: Explaining Policy Change and Stability in UK Industrial Pollution Policy'. *Environment and Planning C: Government and Policy*, 18: 95–114.

SMITH, D. (1995). 'Beyond Self-Regulation: Towards a Critique of Self-Regulation as a Control Strategy for Hazardous Activities'. *Journal of Management Studies*, 32/5: 619–36.

SMITH, M. (1990). *The Politics of Agricultural Support in Britain: the Development of the Agricultural Policy Community*. Aldershot: Dartmouth.

—— (1991). 'From Policy Community to Issue Network: Salmonella in Eggs and the New Politics of Food'. *Public Administration*, 69/2: 235–55.

SMITH, R. (1989). 'Discipline 1: the Hordes at the Gate'. *British Medical Journal*, 298: 1502–5.

SPORT ENGLAND (2002). 'Sport England's Aims', www.sportengland.org (accessed 7 Feb. 2002).

STACEY, M. (1989a). 'The General Medical Council and Professional Accountability'. *Public Policy and Administration*, 4/1: 12–27.

—— (1989b). 'A Sociologist Looks at the GMC'. *The Lancet*, 1 April: 713–14.

—— (1992). *Regulating British Medicine: the General Medical Council*. Chichester: Wiley.

STACEY, N. (1954). *English Accountancy: a Study in Social and Economic History, 1800–1954*. London: Gee.

STEWART, J. (1986). *The New Management of Local Government*. London: Allen and Unwin.

STEWART, R. (1988). 'Regulation and the Crisis of Legalisation in the United States', in T. Daintith (ed.), *Law as an Instrument of Economic Policy: Comparative and Critical Approaches*. Berlin: de Gruyter, pp. 97–133.

STIRLING, A. (1997). 'Multi-Criteria Mapping: Mitigating the Problems of Environmental Evaluation', in J. Foster (ed.), *Valuing Nature: Economics, Ethics and the Environment*. London: Routledge, pp. 186–210.

—— (1998). 'Risk at a Turning Point?' *Journal of Risk Research*, 1/2: 97–109.

—— (1999). 'The Appraisal of Sustainability: Some Problems and Possible Responses'. *Local Environment*, 4/2: 111–35.

STOCK EXCHANGE (1979). *Written Evidence by the Stock Exchange*, in Committee to Review the Functioning of Financial Institutions, Second Stage evidence, Volume 4. London: HMSO, pp. 1–64.

STOKES, M. (1986). 'Company Law and Legal Theory', in W. Twining (ed.), *Legal Theory and Common Law*. Oxford: Blackwell, pp. 155–83.

STRANGE, S. (1994). *States and Markets*, 2nd edn. London: Pinter.

SUGARMAN, D. (1995). 'Who Colonized Whom? Historical Reflections on the Intersection Between Law, Lawyers and Accountants in England', in Y. Dezalay and D. Sugarman (eds.), *Professional Competition and Professional Power*. London: Routledge, pp. 226–37.

SUN, J.-M. and PELKMANS, J. (1995). 'Regulatory Competition in the Single Market'. *Journal of Common Market Studies*, 33/1: 67–89.

SUNSTEIN, C. (1990). *After the Rights Revolution: Reconceiving the Regulatory State*. Cambridge, MA: Harvard University Press.

SWANN, D. (1988). *The Retreat of the State: Deregulation and Privatisation in the UK and US*. London: Harvester Wheatsheaf.

SWIFT, J. (1999). 'Transparency, Consistency and Predictability as Regulatory Objectives', in C. McCrudden (ed.), *Regulation and Deregulation: Policy and Practice in the Utilities and Financial Services Markets*. Oxford: Clarendon Press, pp. 171–83.

SYKES, J. (1926). *The Amalgamation Movement in English Banking 1825–1924*. London: P.S. King.

TALBOT, C. (1996). 'The Prison Service: a Framework of Irresponsibility'. *Public Money and Management*, 16/1: 6–8.

—— (2000). 'Performing "Performance": a Comedy in Five Acts'. *Public Money and Management*, 20/4: 63–68.

TAYLOR, F. W. (1911/1985). *The Principles of Scientific Management*. Easton: Hive Publishing.

TAYLOR, R. (1993). *The Trade Union Question in British Politics: Government and the Unions Since 1945*. Oxford: Blackwell.

TEMPEST, M. (2002). 'State Funding of Political Parties Inevitable'. *Guardian*, 16 April.

TERRY, F. (2001). 'The Nemesis of Privatization: Railway Policy in Retrospect'. *Public Money and Management*, 21/1: 4–6.

TEUBNER, G. (1987). 'Juridication—Concepts, Aspects, Limits Solutions', in G. Teubner (ed.), *Juridification of Social Spheres: a Comparative Analysis of the Areas of Labor, Antitrust and Social Welfare Law*. Berlin: de Gruyter, pp. 3–48.

—— (1993). *Law as an Autopoietic System*. Oxford: Blackwell (trans. by A. Bankowska and R. Adler, ed. by Z. Bankowski).

THATCHER, MARGARET (1993). *The Downing Street Years*. London: Harper Collins.

THATCHER, MARK (1997). 'Institutions, Regulation and Change: New Regulatory Agencies in the British Privatised Utilities'. *West European Politics*, 21/1: 120–47.

—— (1999). *The Politics of Telecommunications: National Institutions, Convergence, and Change*. Oxford: Oxford University Press.

—— (2000). 'The National Politics of European Regulation: Institutional Reform in Telecommunications'. *Current Politics and Economics in Europe*, 9/4: 387–405.

—— (2002). 'Delegation to Independent Regulatory Agencies: Pressures, Functions and Contextual Mediation', in Mark Thatcher and A. Stone Sweet (eds.), pp. 125–47.

—— and STONE SWEET, A. (eds.) (2002). *The Politics of Delegation: Non-Majoritarian Institutions in Europe*. West European Politics 25/1.

THERBORN, G. (1995). *European Modernity and Beyond: the Trajectory of European Societies 1945–2000*. London: Sage.

THOMAS, M. (1948). *The Early Factory Legislation: a Study in Legislative and Administrative Evolution*. Leigh-on-Sea: Thames Bank Publishing.

THOMAS, R. (1989). *The British Philosophy of Administration*, 2nd edn. Cambridge: Centre for Business and Public Sector Ethics.

THOMPSON, J. (2000). *Political Scandal: Power and Visibility in the Media Age*. Cambridge: Polity.

THORNTON, A. P. (1959). *The Imperial Ideal and its Enemies: a Study in British Power*. London: Macmillan.

—— (1966). *The Habit of Authority: Paternalism in British History*. London: Allen and Unwin.

TOMLINSON, B. (1982). 'The Contraction of England: National Decline and the Loss of Empire'. *Journal of Imperial and Commonwealth History*, X/1: 58–72.

TOMLINSON, J. (1994). *Government and the Enterprise Since 1900: the Changing Problem of Efficiency.* Oxford: Clarendon Press.

TRADE ASSOCIATION FORUM (2002). 'List of Members', www.taforum.org (accessed 13 Jun. 2002).

TREASURY, H. M. (1997). *Memorandum of Understanding Between HM Treasury, the Bank of England and the Financial Services Authority,* www.hm-treasury.gov.uk/documents/ Financial_Services/Regulation (accessed 30 Sept. 2002).

TROPP, A. (1957). *The School Teachers: the Growth of the Teaching Profession in England and Wales from 1800 to the Present Day.* London: Heinemann.

TRUPTIL, R. J. (1936). *British Banks and the Money Market.* London: Jonathan Cape.

UK SPORT (2002*a*). *Sport in the UK—History of UK Sport,* www.uksport.gov.uk (accessed 7 Feb. 2002).

—— (2002*b*). 'Exchequer and Lottery Funding 1999/2000', www.uksport.gov (accessed 7 Feb. 2002).

UTILITIES LAW REVIEW (2000). 'Joint Working on Utility Regulation'. *Utilities Law Review,* 11/1: 3–5.

VAN ZWANENBERG, P. (1998). 'Public Engagement and UK Agricultural Biotechnology Policy', in A. Jamison (ed.), *Technology Policy Meets the Public.* Aalborg: Aalborg University Press, pp. 189–206.

—— and MILLSTONE, E. (2000). 'Beyond Skeptical Relativism: Evaluating the Social Constructions of Expert Risk Assessments'. *Science, Technology and Human Values,* 25/3: 259–82.

VELIJANOSKI, C. (1990). 'The Political Economy of Regulation', in P. Dunleavy, A. Gamble, and G. Peele (eds.), *Developments in British Politics 3.* Basingstoke: Macmillan, pp. 291–304.

VERDUN, A. (2000). 'Governing by Committee: the Case of Monetary Policy', in T. Christiansen and E. Kirchner (eds.), *Europe in Change: Committee Governance in the European Union.* Manchester: Manchester University Press, pp. 132–44.

VOGEL, D. (1981). 'The "new" Social Regulation in Historical and Comparative Perspective', in T. McCraw (ed.), *Regulation in Perspective: Historical Essays.* Cambridge, MA: Harvard University Press, pp. 155–85.

—— (1983). 'The Political Power of Business in America: a Reappraisal'. *British Journal of Political Science,* 13/1: 19–43.

—— (1986). *National Styles of Regulation: Environmental Policy in Great Britain and the United States.* Ithaca: Cornell University Press.

—— (1996). *Kindred Strangers: the Uneasy Relationship Between Politics and Business in America.* Princeton: Princeton University Press.

VOGEL, S. (1996). *Freer Markets, More Rules: Regulatory Reform in Advanced Industrial Countries.* Ithaca: Cornell University Press.

WADDINGTON, I. (1984). *The Medical Profession in the Industrial Revolution.* Dublin: Gill and Macmillan.

—— (1990). 'The Movement Towards the Professionalisation of Medicine'. *British Medical Journal,* 301: 688–90.

WALKER, P. (1991). *Staying Power: an Autobiography.* London: Bloomsbury.

WARREN, R. (1999). 'Company Legitimacy in the New Millennium'. *Business Ethics,* 8/4: 214–24.

WATSON, M. (2002). 'The Institutional Paradoxes of Monetary Orthodoxy: Reflections on the Political Economy of Central Bank Independence'. *Review of International Political Economy*, 9/1: 183–96.

WEALE, A. (2001). 'Can we Democratize Decisions on Risk and the Environment?' *Government and Opposition*, 36/3: 355–78.

——, PRIDHAM, G., CINI, M., KONSTADAKOPULOS, D., PORTER, M., and FLYNN, B. (2000). *Environmental Governance in Europe: an Ever Closer Ecological Union*. Oxford: Oxford University Press.

WEBSTER, C. (1988). *The Health Services Since the War. Volume 1: Problems of Health Care: the National Health Service Before 1959*. London: HMSO.

—— (1996). *The Health Services Since the War. Volume II: Government and Health Care. The National Health Service 1958–1979*. London: The Stationery Office.

WIENER, J. (1999). *Globalization and the Harmonization of Law*. London: Pinter.

WILCOX, B. and GRAY, J. (1996). *Inspecting Schools*. Buckingham: Open University Press.

WILDAVSKY, A. (1989). *Searching for Safety*. New Brunswick: Transaction Publishers.

—— and DAKE, K. (1990). 'Theories of Risk Perception: Who Fears What and Why?' *Daedalus*, 119/4: 41–60.

WILDING, P. (1982). *Professional Power and Social Welfare*. London: Routledge.

WILKS, S. (1999). *In the Public Interest: Competition Policy and the Monopolies and Mergers Commission*. Manchester: Manchester University Press.

—— and BARTLE, I. (2002). 'The Unanticipated Consequences of Creating Independent Competitive Agencies'. *West European Politics*, 25/2: 148–72.

—— and McGOWAN, L. (1996). 'Competitition Policy in the European Union: Creating a Federal Agency', in G. Doern and S. Wilks (eds.), *Comparative Competitition Policy*. Oxford: Clarendon, pp. 225–67.

WILLMOTT, H. (1985). 'Setting Accounting Standards in the UK: the Emergence of Private Accounting Bodies and their Role in the Regulation of Public Accounting Practice', in W. Streeck and P. Schmitter (eds.), *Private Interest Government: Beyond Market and State*. London: Sage, pp. 44–71.

WILSON, A. (1973). *The Concorde Fiasco*. Harmondsworth: Penguin.

WILSON, D. and GAME, C. (1994). *Local Government in the United Kingdom*. Basingstoke: Macmillan.

WILSON, G. (1984). 'Social Regulation and Explanations of Regulatory Failure'. *Political Studies*, XXXII/2: 203–25.

WILSON, J. (1980). 'The Politics of Regulation', in J. Wilson (ed.), *The Politics of Regulation*. New York: Basic Books, pp. 357–94.

WILSON, R. (1999). 'The Civil Service in the New Millennium', www.cabinet-office.gov.uk/1999/senior/rw (accessed 18 Mar. 2002).

WOOD, B. (2000). 'New Labour and Health', in D. Coates and P. Lawler (eds.), *New Labour in Power*. Manchester: Manchester University Press, pp. 195–206.

WRIGHT, M. (1991). 'The Comparative Analysis of Industrial Policies: Policy Networks and Sectoral Governance Structures in Britain and France'. *Staatswissenschaft and Staatspraxis*, 2/4: 503–33.

YOUNG, A. (2001). *The Politics of Regulation: Privatised Utilities in Britain*. Basingstoke: Palgrave.

ZEFF, S. (1972). *Forging Accounting Principles in Five Countries*. Champagne, IL: Stipes Publishing.

INDEX

Printed in the United Kingdom
 by Lightning Source UK Ltd.
117422UKS00001B/92